SPIRAL GUIDES

Travel with Someone You Trust®

S0-BIX-453

ROME

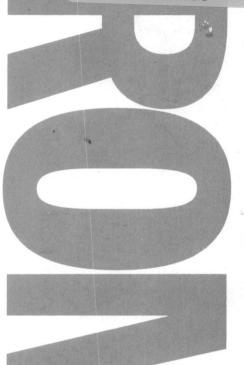

Contents

Written by Tim Jepson

Copy edited by Audrey Horne
Americanization by Georgetta Sharman
Page layout by Nautilus Design (U.K.) Limited
Illustrations by Julian Baker Illustrations
Verified by Sara Liney
Indexed by Marie Lorimer

Edited, designed and produced by AA Publishing
© Automobile Association Developments Limited 2001
Maps © Automobile Association Developments Limited 2001

Published in the United States by AAA Publishing,
1000 AAA Drive,
Heathrow, Florida 32746
Published in the United Kingdom by AA Publishing

ISBN 1-56251-404-0

Color separation by Leo Reprographics
Printed and bound in China by Leo Paper Products

10 9 8 7 6 5 4 3 2

the magazine

Rome is more than 3,000 years old: that's a lot of history and a lot of myth. Intimidating? Not really – you probably know more about both than you think. Do Spartacus, crossing the Rubicon, the rape of Lucretia, or Romulus and Remus mean anything? And what about Rome's Seven Hills, Antony and Cleopatra, the Ides of March? Chances are you know the names but can't quite place the story, so here is a checklist of myths and well-known historical incidents that Rome has given the world.

Myth & History

The Seven Hills

Nothing mythical here: Rome's celebrated hills exist to this day, although they're smaller than you might expect and have been all but obliterated by modern building. Rome probably began life as a farming village on one of the hills, the Capitolino (Capitoline), which provided a safe refuge above the marshes of the River Tiber. By the 9th century BC, there were probably villages on all the remaining hills: the Aventino, Caelio, Esquilino, Palatino, Quirinale and Viminale.

The Rape of Lucretia

Rome was probably ruled in its earliest days by Etruscan kings, as part of a civilization that prospered across much of central Italy from about the 8th century BC. According to the historian Livy (59 BC–AD 17), the event that precipitated the overthrow of the

The Colosseum seen from the Aventino, the most southerly of Rome's original Seven Hills

Etruscan dynasty and the establishment of Roman independence occurred in 507 BC, when Lucretia, a respectable Roman matron, was raped by Sextus, son of Tarquinius, the Etruscan ruler. Racked with shame, Lucretia committed public suicide, prompting a mob of outraged Romans to chase Tarquinius from the city. The Roman republic was proclaimed the same day.

Spartacus

In 82 BC, a conservative army general, Sulla, gained control of Rome during a period of political instability. He subjected the city to a brutal dictatorship that led – among other things – to an uprising of some 70,000 slaves and dispossessed farmers under the command of a gladiator, Spartacus. The revolt was put down, Spartacus died in battle

Below: Symbol of the city – the she-wolf suckling Romulus and Remus, Rome's legendary founders

Romulus and Remus

Rome probably began life as a hilltop village some 1,200 years before the birth of Christ, but for most people the myth of its origins – the story of Romulus and Remus – is far more interesting.

The way the Roman historian Livy tells it, the story begins in a place called Alba Longa, the capital of a tribe known as the Latins. Its ruler, Numitor, had been usurped by his brother, Amulius, who, to prevent any rival claimants to his throne, forced Numitor's only daughter, Rhea Silvia, to become a Vestal Virgin (► 54).

Rhea, however, became pregnant through the attentions of the god Mars and gave birth to twins, Romulus and Remus. Amulius had the twins cast adrift in a basket, only for the gods to guide them to the safety of the Velabrum, a marshy area on the banks of the Tiber. Here they were found and suckled by a she-wolf – you'll see statues recording the event across the city – before being adopted by a shepherd. In later life, Mars appeared to the twins and told them it was their destiny to found a city, which – in 753 BC, according to legend – they duly did.

Unfortunately, both Romulus and Remus wished to rule the new city. Worse, neither could agree on a name for their domain: Remus wanted Rema, Romulus preferred Roma. They

decided to invoke the gods to help settle the dispute. Remus saw six vultures over his chosen hill, but Romulus saw 12 of the same birds over his refuge, and he marked a line around it using a plough. Remus, incensed, jumped over the line and was killed by his brother – not an auspicious start.

at Lucania and 6,000 of his followers were crucified on the Via Appia Antica, the Roman road that leads south from the city to this day.

Crossing the Rubicon

Julius Caesar, then just an army general, brought his troops back to Italy from campaigns in northern Europe in 49 BC. En route he crossed the Rubicon, a river in northern Italy. In doing so, he deliberately broke a law that forbade returning armies to travel beyond the river without permission from the Senate, the body that ruled the Roman republic. Faced with Caesar's challenge to its authority, the Senate's power crumbled and its members fled on his return to Rome. A year later Caesar became the absolute ruler of Rome.

"Beware the Ides of March"

Why? Because the Ides, the 15th day of the month in the Roman calendar, was the day in March 44 BC that a jealous clique in the Roman Senate murdered Julius Caesar. The conspirators included Brutus, Caesar's adopted son.

Julius Caesar was murdered by a jealous clique in the Senate

Antony and Cleopatra

Famous names, but who were they? After Julius Caesar's murder, control of the Roman Empire was divided among three leaders: Lepidus, Mark Antony and Octavius (Caesar's grand nephew). Antony and Octavius became the dominant players, but Antony compromised his chances of total power by repeated absence from Rome in the arms of Cleopatra, the queen of Egypt. Octavius concentrated on building up his military strength, and defeated Antony in 31 BC. Antony and Cleopatra both committed suicide; Octavius changed his named to Augustus Caesar and became the first true Roman emperor.

Antony and Cleopatra's love affair was infamously played out by Richard Burton and Elizabeth Taylor

What's in a word

Rome has given the English-speaking world a host of words and phrases which are still in common use.

Asylum The word comes from an area of sanctuary in the early days of Rome, between the twin peaks of the Capitoline Hill.

Bread and circuses Coined by the Roman satirist Juvenal (CAD 55–140) to mock the indolence of a Roman populace that had sold its freedoms for the trivial entertainments of the Colosseum.

Caesarean Legend claims Julius Caesar was the first person to be born by "caesarean" section, hence the present-day name for this operation.

Capitol Capitol Hill and the Capitol Building derive from the Capitolino, one of Rome's Seven Hills and the site of the city's earliest citadel.

Forum The Roman Forum gave us forum, but also – directly or indirectly – words such as censor, census, civic, committee, dictator, forensic, plebiscite, pontiff, pontificate, suffrage and many more.

Money Comes from the Latin *moneta*, which in turn comes from the Temple of Juno Moneta on the Capitolino Hill, where some of the first Roman coins were minted.

Nepotism From the Italian *nipote*, meaning nephew, because medieval popes often gave favored positions to their "nephews" (many of whom were actually their sons).

Palace Derives from "Palatino," after the large houses built by Roman emperors and others on the Roman hill of the same name.

Republic Comes from *res publica,* used after the fifth century BC to describe Rome, where in theory the state was literally the thing *(res)* or concern of the "public" *(publica)*.

Rostrum From the bronze prows of ships *(rostra)* captured by the Romans and used to adorn the platforms of orators in the Roman Forum.

Rome's streets are its curse and its salvation. Many were built for horses and carts, and prove horribly ill suited to the demands of a modern city. Some are grand papal thoroughfares, others – such as Via dei Fori Imperiali – the result of Fascist megalomania.

The 64 Bus

One of the best ways to explore Rome's tight labyrinth of central streets is to walk (▶ 180–182). Another is to take a bus, and one bus in particular – the infamous number 64. Rome's bus numbers change all the time: one year the number 27 takes you to the Colosseum, the next it's the 81. But the 64 – for now at least – seems immune to bureaucratic meddling; the 64 is a way of life.

Jump on board and you'll be following in the footsteps of millions before you. Why? Because the 64 plies one of Rome's seminal routes, starting in the sprawl of buses outside Termini, Rome's central train station, and then struggling through the heart of the city before arriving at the most majestic destination any bus could hope for – St. Peter's basilica.

The route is a battle for bus and passenger alike. The confrontation starts at Termini, where the arrival of each new bus is the cue for an assault by Romans on three fronts – the bus's trio of doors. No quarter is given, and no such thing as a line has ever been known to form. Give as good as you get – shove, push and jostle with elbows if you want to get aboard, never mind find a seat. Hold back and allow good manners to prevail and you'll be left standing – probably on the sidewalk.

Once on board, you become part of a close-knit band. Often too close-knit, for the 64 is notorious for the occasional

Rome's policemen (left) often fight a losing battle against the city's traffic (right)

Crossing a Roman Street

Crossing the street in Rome is no easy matter unless you know one salient fact: cars are supposed to stop or slow down to let you cross. The secrets of success are never to dither – stride purposefully through gaps in the traffic – and never to look as if you might blink first or back down in that decisive encounter between you and the leading car. If in doubt, walk in the slipstream of a Roman crossing ahead of you.

Bus Tours

If the 64 seems too daunting (see text), then Rome's ATAC bus company offers a more sedate sightseeing excursion by bus. The number 110 City Tour lasts 2 hours and 30 minutes, currently with five departures daily (at 10:30, 2, 3, 5 and 6) from outside Stazione Termini. It visits more than 80 sites of historic and artistic interest and stops at important sights such as the Colosseum and St. Peter's. Tickets are available from the ATAC office (Bay C) in Piazza dei Cinquecento in front of Termini. Further information, tel: 06 4695 2252 or 06 4695 2256 (daily 9–7).

Five Specialist Streets

Via dei Cestari Stores here specialize in ecclesiastical dress.

Via Condotti Rome's smartest shopping street.

Via dei Coronari One of Rome's best streets for antiques.

Via Margutta Contains some of Rome's best art galleries.

Via della Croce Noted for its fine food and wine stores.

should look out for the police officer directing traffic with almost balletic poise. Then it's a stop-start shunt down Corso Vittorio Emanuele II, with hordes of passengers trying to board what is invariably an already full bus at Torre di Largo Argentina and points west. When you cross the river you know that St. Peter's – and relief – is almost at hand.

groping hand; Roman women won't stand for this, turning round to hurl a well-aimed insult at the presumed perpetrator. Stray hands also find their way elsewhere – the 64 is a favored haunt of pickpockets, so keep an eye on your valuables.

Forewarned, you can then enjoy the fray. Look at the bus windows. Are they open or shut? If they are shut, that means it's not yet summer – whatever you might think and whatever the weather. The Roman matrons who guard the windows seem to have some mysterious and unspoken sense of when the season turns: one day the windows are shut, the next they are open. And they will stay that way – summer showers aside – until the elderly collective decides fall has come. Don't dare open or close them on your own account.

Stay on board to the bitter end and you will rumble down Via Nazionale and into Piazza Venezia, where you

...and Five Special Streets

Via Appia Antica Paved with large cobbles and lined with tombs, this old Roman road survives close to the Christian catacombs southeast of the city center.

Via del Corso One of central Rome's key streets, full of stores and invariably full of people. The fact that it's largely pedestrianized is a bonus.

Via Giulia One of Rome's most elegant streets; addresses here are some of the most coveted in the whole of the city.

Via Rasella Infamous for being the location of an ambush of Nazi troops by partisans in 1944 that led to reprisals that caused the death of 335 innocent Romans.

Via Veneto Famous for being Rome's most fashionable street during the 1950s and 1960s. Now living slightly on its past reputation.

Below: A good trick in a tight squeeze – parking in Rome is legendary

Bottom: Via Appia Antica, an old Roman highway

BAROQUE *Pearls*

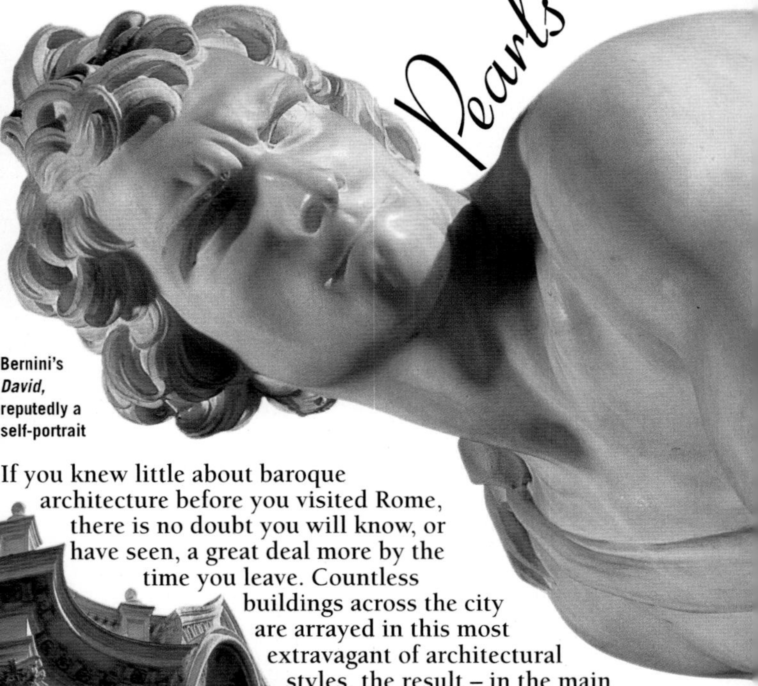

Bernini's
David,
reputedly a
self-portrait

If you knew little about baroque architecture before you visited Rome, there is no doubt you will know, or have seen, a great deal more by the time you leave. Countless buildings across the city are arrayed in this most extravagant of architectural styles, the result – in the main – of papal munificence and the work of two larger-than-life architects.

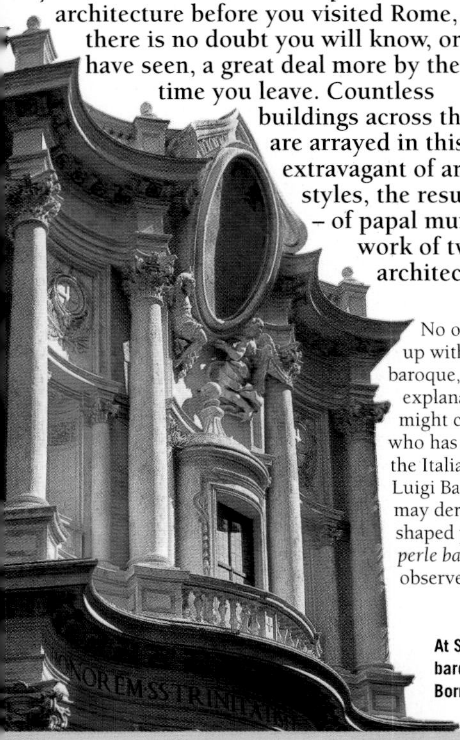

No one has been able to come up with a decent definition of baroque, or a totally convincing explanation of where the word might come from. The person who has perhaps come closest was the Italian writer and journalist Luigi Barzini. Noting that the word may derive from large, irregularly shaped pearls – still known as *perle baroche* in Italian – Barzini observed that the word came to be

At San Carlo alle Quattro Fontane baroque master Francesco Borromini showed his disdain for convention

used metaphorically to describe "anything pointlessly complicated, otiose, capricious and eccentric."

This goes some way to describing the architectural style that succeeded the Romanesque (simple lines and rounded arches) and Gothic (soaring spaces and pointed arches). So fully did the style sweep all before it in Rome that there is barely a building that escaped its transforming touch.

One reason for the transformation was money, for the popes were rich and keen to spend lavishly; another was the buoyant spirit of the times and the air of self-confidence engendered by the success of the Counter-Reformation, the Roman Catholic response to the rise of Protestantism across northern Europe.

Two architects of contrasting outlook dominated Rome's baroque heyday – Gian Lorenzo Bernini and Francesco Borromini – and both owe their fame and success to the largesse of three prominent popes: Urban VIII (pope from 1623 to 1644), Innocent X (1644–55) and Alexander VII (1655–67).

Bernini and Borromini

Bernini (1598–1680) was born in Naples but settled with his family in Rome at the age of seven. He would live and work in the city for the rest of life. A youthful prodigy and near universal genius, he was an accomplished painter and poet as well as an architect and sculptor. His fame as a sculptor was already secure by his early twenties, thanks to virtuoso works such as *David* and *Apollo and*

Daphne (➤ 129), the first major sculptures executed in Italy since the days of Michelangelo almost a century earlier. He went on to take charge of work on St. Peter's and designed countless major Roman monuments, notably Piazza Navona's Fontana dei Fiumi, and Piazza San Pietro; smaller masterpieces such as the church of Sant'Andrea al Quirinale are also scattered across the city.

Borromini (1599–1667) was born near Lake Lugano in northern Italy. He came to

Five Great Baroque Buildings

Gesù A great Jesuit church whose facade and ornate interior were the models for Counter-Reformation churches across Europe.
Sant'Andrea della Valle Apparently Bernini's personal favorite among the churches on which he worked; brims with ideas and almost aristocratic elegance.
San Carlo alle Quattro Fontane A tiny church in which Borromini shows the disdain of genius for convention to create a masterpiece of design and spatial composition.
Sant' Ivo alla Sapienza There's no church spire quite like it anywhere in Italy; the twisting cupola was based on a bee's sting. ➤ 102.
St. Peter's Building by committee: numerous baroque architects were involved in the building of the church, including Bernini and Borromini.

Rome in 1619, where he obtained work as a stone-carver on the new St. Peter's. In time, he became Bernini's chief assistant at St. Peter's, but the two shared an uneasy relationship. Borromini – who was a consummate craftsman – despised what he saw as Bernini's technical shortcomings.

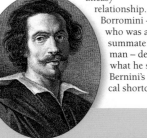

Detail from Sant'Andrea della Valle

Left: Gian Lorenzo Bernini

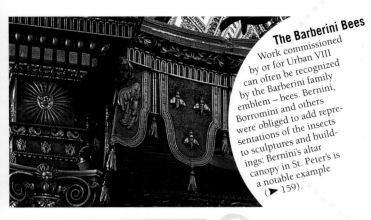

The Barberini Bees

Work commissioned by or for Urban VIII can often be recognized by the Barberini family emblem – bees. Bernini, Borromini and others were obliged to add representations of the insects to sculptures and buildings: Bernini's altar canopy in St. Peter's is a notable example (➤ 159).

Five Great Works of Art

Apollo and Daphne One of several Bernini statues in which marble is almost made flesh; this is arguably the artist's masterpiece ➤ 113 and 129.

Baldacchino You may not like Bernini's altar canopy in St. Peter's basilica, but you can't help but be impressed by its colossal scale ➤ 159 and 160.

Cappella Cornaro Bernini's chapel in Santa Maria della Vittoria is a triumph of color, illusion, lighting, perspective and sublime sculpture.

Fontana dei Quattro Fiumi Bernini's grandiose fountain occupies pride of place in Piazza Navona, one of the grandest stages in the city ➤ 83.

Fontana di Trevi No one is sure who dreamed up Rome's loveliest fountain – Bernini may have been involved – but the result is a triumph ➤ 124–125.

The two parted company for good in 1634.

Where Bernini was joyous, outgoing and self-confident, his chief and most jealous rival was a lonely, neurotic and tortured individual who may have suffered from schizophrenia. Introspective and frustrated, Borromini was eventually driven to suicide – possibly by what he saw as his failure to secure the commissions he deserved. At the same time, he was the more innovative and iconoclastic architect. In churches such as Sant'Ivo alla Sapienza and San Carlo alle Quattro Fontane he produced buildings in which strangeness and skill combine to dazzle architects to this day.

QUOD NON FECERUNT BARBARI, FECERUNT BARBERINI

Builders and Barbarians

Pope Urban VIII, one of the baroque's chief patrons, belonged to the Barberini, an important Roman family that razed or altered so many of the city's buildings to make way for their own creations that the Romans coined a famous pun: *Quod non fecerunt barbari, fecerunt Barberini* – "what was not done by the barbarians was done by the Barberini."

Secrets and Oddities

Rome is a city fuller than most of the weird and wonderful. Many of its more unusual sights are connected with death – notably the catacombs – or are the sometimes strange consequences of religion. Others are not so much bizarre as secret, unusual places seen by few visitors: here are some of the best to whet your appetite.

Macabre decoration in Santa Maria della Concezione

A Way With Bones

One of the city's most bizarre sights lurks inside the 17th-century church of Santa Maria della Concezione. In its crypt lie the skeletons and loose bones of some 4,000 Capuchin monks – strange enough on their own; stranger still is the way many of the bones have been used to create chandeliers and beautifully crafted decorative patterns. Monks were originally buried here in soil brought from Jerusalem. When this ran out, they were left in the open, a practice that continued until as recently as 1870. *Santa Maria della Concezione, Via Vittorio Veneto 27 (tel: 06 487 1185). Crypt open Fri.–Wed. 9:30–noon, 3–6*

Secret Keyhole

Rome's most charming view can be enjoyed from Piazza dei Cavalieri di Malta – a square designed by Giovanni Piranesi – on the Aventine Hill southwest of the Colosseum. To find it, walk to the left of the church of Santa Sabina as you face it (the church and the gardens to its right are lovely places in their

own right). Continue to the end of the piazza and look through the keyhole of the huge door of the Priory of the Knights of Malta (No. 3). Through the tiny hole you see a secret garden and an avenue of trees cleverly framing…but let's not spoil the surprise: see for yourself.

Wall of Horrors

Here's a departure from the mosaics and refined paintings of many of Rome's churches.

Above: The frescoes decorating the circular walls of the fifth-century church of Santo Stefano Rotondo portray many grisly martyrdoms

Frescoes in the church of Santo Stefano Rotondo portray all manner of grisly martyrdoms, their subjects described by an enthralled Charles Dickens during a visit in the 19th century: "Gray-bearded men being boiled, fried, grilled, crimped, singed, eaten by wild beasts, worried by dogs, buried alive, torn asunder by horses, chopped up with small hatchets; women having their breasts torn off with iron pincers, their tongues cut out, their ears screwed off, their jaws broken, their bodies stretched on the rack, or skinned on the stake, or crackled up and melted in the fire – these are among the mildest subjects."

Santo Stefano Rotondo, Via di Santo Stefano Rotondo 7 (tel: 06 421199 for information). Tue.–Sat. 9–1, 3:30–6, Mon. 3:30–6

Going Underground

Burial within the city limits was forbidden to all but emperors in ancient Rome. As a result the city boasts some 184 miles of catacombs, the burial place of pagans, Jews and – above all – early Christians. Most date from between the fourth century BC and first century AD, and most consist of long passages and chambers filled with niches used to inter the linen-wrapped bodies. Some have larger chambers, often the resting places of saints or martyrs. Many were cleared when the catacombs – long forgotten – were rediscovered in the ninth century. Many relics were removed to St. Peter's and other churches, although it was not until the 16th century that the catacombs' full extent was realized.

The most visited catacombs lie close together near the Via Appia Antica in the south of the city. These are the catacombs of Domitilla, San Sebastiano and San Callisto, of which San Callisto is the largest and the busiest. Other catacombs are less well known but often even more atmospheric: try the Catacombe di Priscilla on the city's northern fringes, or the smaller catacombs below the church of Sant'Agnese fuori le Mura, a short way southeast of the Catacombe di Priscilla. The church and its near neighbor, Santa Costanza, are worth a visit in their own right for their superb early mosaics. Note that a moderate admission fee is charged to all the catacombs below.

Catacombe di Domitilla, Via delle Sette Chiese 282 (tel: 06 511 0342). Mon., Wed.–Sun. 8:30–noon, 2:30–5:30

Catacombe di San Sebastian, Via Appia Antica 136 (tel: 06 788 7035). Fri.–Wed. 9–noon, 2:30–5:30

Catacombe di San Callisto, Via Appia Antica 110 (tel: 06 5130 6725). Thu.–Tue. 9:30–noon, 2:30–5:30

Catacombe di Priscilla, Via Salaria 430 (tel: 06 8620 6272). Tue.–Sun. 9–noon, 2:30–5

Catacombe di Sant'Agnese, Via Nomentana 349 (tel: 06 861 0840). Tue.–Sat. 9–noon, 4–6, Mon. 9–noon

Below: The catacombs at San Callisto are the largest in the city with some 12 miles of galleries and 170,000 burial places

Right: Ancient decoration in the Catacombe di Domitilla

The image is a familiar one: trattoria tables scatter the sidewalks, children run riot between courses, and heaped plates of spaghetti arrive to appreciative exclamations. Trams rumble in the background and Pappa talks women and football, while Mamma keeps a steady eye on proceedings.

At least, this is how we think it is done, and it's the image Federico Fellini gave us in movies such as *Roma*. Yet these days the old image is not always the reality of eating in Rome. True, you can still find the odd humble trattoria of popular imagination, and on a summer Sunday Campo dei Fiori and similar delightful outdoor locations around the city still play host to families tucking into their ritual lunchtime feasts.

The old Felliniesque vignettes are increasingly a fading memory, however – restaurants and eating out in Rome have moved on as they have in many European and other culinary capitals. But if the traditional atmosphere of eating out has changed, then the quality and variety of the food available, not to mention

the types of places to dine out, have improved beyond recognition.

Once, eating out in Rome almost cost less than cooking for yourself at home. A rickety chair, a rough wooden table and a plate of fresh pasta – plus a flask of Frascati – was all a Roman wanted and all a visitor could get. Then came the 1980s and rampant expense accounts, resulting in a rash of luxurious and ludicrously overpriced restaurants.

Between the extremes of traditional trattoria and top-price restaurant, Rome has recently seen the emergence of predominantly young, stylish eating places where the food – often lighter and more innovative than in the past – takes center stage. Furthermore, restaurant

Dining alfresco is one of the greatest pleasures of summer in Rome

Snails are eaten on the Festival of San Giovanni

interiors now increasingly eschew the unsophisticated paintings and wicker-wrapped wine bottles of traditional

Awful Offal

The most traditional Roman specialities include tripe (*trippa*), oxtail braised in celery broth (*coda alla vaccinara*), strips of cartilage (*nervetti*), brain (*cervello*) – delicious with peas – the pancreas and thyroid glands (*animelle*), and *pajata*: baby veal's intestines with the mother's milk still inside (cooked in lard for added effect). And how about *lingua* (tongue), *guanciale* (pig's cheek) and *insalata di zampa* (hoof jelly salad)? You'll need a strong stomach!

trattoria decor in favor of light, airy dining rooms and decorative grace notes of stone, glass and steel.

If the notion of modernization fills you with dread, if you want to eat in Rome as you imagine the Romans eat, all is not lost. There are still old places, still pizzerias and authentic bars for stand-up

snacks. And eating in Rome will always have an atmosphere that is all its own, if only because the surroundings, especially outdoors on a balmy summer's evening, are so magical.

As with almost any Italian city or region, Rome has a plethora of culinary specialties that set it apart from the gastronomic mainstream. Among these are the widely available *saltimbocca alla Romana* (veal with ham and sage) and *bucatini all'Amatriciana* (pasta with a hot tomato and pancetta sauce). Other culinary influences include those introduced over the centuries by the city's Jewish population – restaurants in the old Ghetto and elsewhere serve wonderful and otherwise little known dishes such as deep-fried artichokes, pasta and chickpea broth, and *minestra d'arzilla* (ray fish soup).

Rome has other specialties (that you will not necessarily want to try). Traditional Roman cooking is based on the *quinto quarto* – the so-called "fifth quarter," or what is left of an animal when everything that would normally be considered edible has been stripped from the carcass. This penchant for the obscure originally had little to do with taste and everything to do with the huge old slaughterhouse in the Testaccio district – where off-cuts went to workers and led to recipes that made use of the "perk" – and to poverty, long the culinary mother of invention in what for centuries was a mostly impoverished city. In practice this meant – and still means – menus filled with items that might startle even the most adventurous diner.

Buon Appetito!

A SNAPSHOT OF ROME

One of the greatest pleasures of exploring Rome is the number of times you stumble across hidden corners, wonderful viewpoints, evocative street scenes and telling vignettes of daily life.

Finding Your Feet

First Two Hours

Arriving at Fiumicino Airport

Scheduled international and internal Italian flights land at Rome's main airport, officially called Leonardo da Vinci (tel: 06 65951 or 06 659 53640) but more usually known as Fiumicino after its nearest village. The airport lies just over 22 miles southwest of the city center.

- The airport (open 24 hours daily) has two main **terminal complexes**: international departures (*Partenze Internazionali*) and international arrivals (*Arrivi Internazionali*), and linked domestic departures (*Partenze Nazionali*) and domestic arrivals (*Arrivi Nazionali*). The international terminal is divided into two: arrivals is on the lower floor, departures on the floor above: stairs, elevators and escalators link the two.
- Facilities in arrivals include foreign exchange desks (*cambio*), automated exchange and cash machines, a small bar and a branch of the EPT, or Rome tourist board (tel: 06 6595 4471; daily 8:15 a.m.–7 p.m.).
- Avoid all taxi and hotel touts who approach you in the airport, even those who appear simply to be offering general help. Keep a close watch on your luggage at all times.

Getting to Central Rome by Public Transportation

- The best way to get from Fiumicino Airport to the city center is the **express rail service** to Stazione Termini, Rome's main central train station and the focus of the city's bus and subway systems. For information on onward travel from Termini (➤ 31–33). Trains depart from a dedicated rail terminal situated close to the main international terminal – look for the raised covered walkway from the main terminal building, reached by escalator or steps from outside the departures terminal. It can also be reached via an underpass from the arrivals hall (turn left when you exit customs) or by walking across the road and bus parking area from outside the arrivals terminal.
- **Tickets** ($$$) for the express rail service can be bought from automatic machines in the arrivals terminal and on the station concourse, or from a small ticket office on the right of the station as you face the platforms. Consider buying a second ticket for your return trip, as there can be long lines at Stazione Termini.
- Tickets are **validated** at Fiumicino by passing through the ticket barrier. On your return from Rome you must stamp your ticket immediately before traveling in the small yellow or gold machines on each platform. Failure to do so results in a heavy fine.
- **Express trains depart hourly** between about 7:30 a.m. and 10 p.m. and take just over 30 minutes to reach Termini. Be sure to board the right train, as departures from the airport station also link (roughly every 20 minutes) to four other Rome stations: Ostiense, Tuscolana, Tiburtina and Trastevere. It is possible that your hotel may be close to the last of these (Trastevere), in which case this other train service is a convenient approach. It takes longer to get there, around 50 minutes, but costs about half the price of the express train. Tickets ($$) can be bought from the same sources as tickets for the express trains (see above).
- Outside express train hours, a **bus service** ($$) runs approximately hourly from outside the arrivals hall to Tiburtina station. This is an unpleasant place at night, so aim to take a taxi either from the station or directly from the airport.

Public transportation and taxi fares
The following categories have been used to denote prices for transportation.
$ up to €1.30 $$ €1.30–€3.90 $$$ over €3.90

Getting to Central Rome by Taxi
Taxis from the airport to the city center are expensive, costing in the region of €41.3 to €51.65. The ride to the center is around 40 minutes, but often takes considerably longer because of heavy traffic.

- Make sure the **meter** is set and running before you depart, and note that special supplements are payable for taxis between Fiumicino and Rome (higher from Rome to the airport), as well as for items of luggage placed in the trunk, trips on Sunday, and trips at night. All surcharges must be clearly displayed by law inside the taxi.
- Only take rides in **licensed cabs** (generally white or yellow), which wait in a line immediately outside the arrivals hall. Under no circumstances accept the offer of a taxi from touts, even those who seem to have an "official" badge and uniform.
- **Prepaid taxis** and limousine services can be booked at dedicated desks in the arrivals hall. These cost about the same or a little more than taxis, and have the advantage that you know exactly how much you're paying before setting off.

Car Rental
Driving into the city center is not advised as traffic and parking present enormous problems.The car rental desks at Fiumicino are not in the main arrivals hall, but are located in the same complex as the airport train station (► 28).

Arriving at Ciampino Airport
Many charter flights and a few European low-cost scheduled flights use Ciampino, Rome's second airport (tel: 06 794 941), which lies about 9 miles southeast of the city center. There are few facilities at the airport, so it is a good idea to have some Italian currency before you arrive.

Getting to the City Center
- Links between Ciampino and the center by public transportation are more complicated than those from Fiumicino. The easiest approach is by **taxi**, which costs from about €36.40.
- By public transportation, you need to take a COTRAL **bus** (► 32) from in front of the airport building to the Anagnina *Metropolitana* (Metro) station on the Metro system's Line A (► 32). The trip takes approximately 25 minutes. From here, subway trains link to Termini in about 20 minutes. COTRAL buses leave from outside the arrivals hall every 30–60 minutes from about 7 a.m. to 11 p.m. Tickets ($$) can be bought from an automated machine in arrivals or the newspaper stand (*edicola*) in departures.
- The no-frills airline GO operates its own **shuttle service** from the airport to Termini. Passengers can buy return tickets for this chartered nus service on the plane.

Arriving by Train
- Most national and international train services arrive at **Termini** train station (5 a.m.–midnight. Information tel: 147 888 088).
- Some long-distance services, and services arriving at night, terminate at **Ostiense** or **Tiburtina** stations, from which the best way into the city center at night is by taxi (► 33). During the day, you can take a Metro train from Piramide station close to Ostiense station.

From Termini to Your Hotel

The station lies on the eastern side of central Rome and it is too far to walk with luggage from here to the heart of the old city or to most central hotels. Money lavished on a taxi at this point is money well spent.

Termini is a haven for pickpockets, so it is vital to keep a close watch your luggage and valuables at all times. Never accept offers from any hotel, taxi or other touts who approach you.

- **Taxis** depart from immediately outside the front of the station building – do not exit using the side entrances off the central concourse and walkway. Be aware that lines for taxis are often long.
- The huge open area that serves as central Rome's main **bus terminal** spreads out beyond the taxis. Finding your bus in the big and busy area can be an intimidating prospect on a first visit. If you do decide to take a bus, however, note that you must buy tickets before boarding (➤ 32). You will also have to pay a supplement for pieces of luggage over a certain (small) size; taking cumbersome luggage on buses is frowned upon and difficult as they get very crowded.
- Depending on where in the city your hotel is located, you may be able to take advantage of the two **Metro** lines from Termini (➤ 32). These present a less intimidating prospect than the buses. Follow signs from the main station concourse for the relevant platforms. The Metro is especially useful for hotels north of the Vatican or in the area around Piazza di Spagna.

Tourist Information

- Rome's **main visitor center** is close to Piazza della Repubblica at Via Parigi 5 (tel: 06 4889 9253 or 06 4889 9255; web: www.informaroma.it; e-mail: mail@informaroma.it). It is open Monday to Friday 8:15–7:15, and Saturday 7:15 a.m.–1:45 p.m.
- There are also nine **Tourist Information Points** (PIT) at key tourist locations around the city. All are open daily 9–6 (except Termini, which opens daily 8 a.m.–9 p.m.). The locations are as follows:

Piazza di Spagna, Largo Goldoni (tel: 06 6813 6061)
Castel Sant'Angelo, Piazza Pia (tel: 06 6880 9707)
Fori Imperiali, Piazza Tempio della Pace (tel: 06 6992 4307)
Piazza Navona, Piazza delle Cinque Lune (tel: 06 6880 9240)
Via Nazionale, Palazzo delle Esposizioni (tel: 06 4782 4525)
Trastevere, Piazza S Sonnino (tel: 06 5833 3457)
San Giovanni in Laterano, Piazza San Giovanni (tel: 06 7720 3535)
Santa Maria Maggiore, Via dell'Olmata (tel: 06 4788 0294)
Termini (main hall), Piazza dei Cinquecento (tel: 06 4782 5194)

- For information on **gay and lesbian matters** contact Arci-Gay Caravaggio on Via Lariana (tel: 06 855 5522), Arci-Lesbica Roma on Via dei Monti di Pietralata 16 (tel: 06 418 0369) or Circolo Mario Mieli on Via Corinto 5 (tel: 06 541 3985).

Websites

The following websites are useful sources of general information:
- **www.informaroma.it**
- **www.vatican.va** is the official site of the Vatican
- **www.romeguide.it** provides a general guide to the city's principal monuments and most famous sights
- **www.catacombe.roma.it** is devoted to Rome's catacombs
- **www.capitolium.org** is the official site of the Forums

Getting Around

Much of central Rome is small enough to explore on foot, but you will probably need to use taxis or public transportation at some point during your visit, especially to reach the more outlying sights and for excursions from the city.

The city's transportation system has three basic components: **ATAC**, which runs Rome's distinctive orange buses and trams; **COTRAL**, which operates longer distance (regional) blue buses and the city's two *Metropolitana* subway lines; and the **FS**, or Ferrovie dello Stato, which runs the state railroads. Note that COTRAL's old acronym, ACOTRAL, is still shown on some signs.

The network is generally safe, reliable and inexpensive, although Rome's heavy traffic can make travel by bus frustratingly slow. Buses and Metro trains are often crowded, especially at **peak times** – roughly 7:30–9 a.m, 12:30–1:45 p.m. and 7:30–8:30 p.m. Trains and buses are also uncomfortably hot in high summer.

It is essential to be on your guard against pickpockets on crowded buses. The popular 64 bus between Termini and St. Peter's is notorious in this regard.

Public transportation and taxi fares
The following categories have been used in this section to denote approximate prices for transportation:
  $** up to €1.30   **$$** €1.30– €3.90   **$$$ over €3.90

Buses and Trams
ATAC's orange buses and trams run on a web of routes across the city. The main terminus is outside Termini train station, which is where you'll find the main **ATAC information kiosk** (tel: 06 4695 4444 or toll-free 800-431784; open daily 7:30 a.m.–7 p.m.). Kiosk staffers speak English, but the phone line (Mon.–Sat. 8 a.m.–8 p.m.) is Italian-speaking only.

Bus Routes
Relevant bus and tram **route numbers** are given alongside individual sights throughout the book but these may be subject to change. The free *Charta Roma: The Official City-Map* contains an up-to-date bus-tram-Metro map. It is available from visitor centers and tourist information points throughout the city (▶ 30). Otherwise, buy a *Lozzi* transportation map, available from most newspaper stands.

Useful bus services in the city include:

  23 San Paolo–Ostiense–Piazza Risorgimento (for the Vatican Museums)
  64 Termini–Piazza Venezia–Corso Vittorio Emanuele II–St. Peter's
  75 Termini–Piazza Venezia–Trastevere
  81 Colosseum–St. Peter's–Piazza Risorgimento (for the Vatican Museums)
  116 Via Veneto–Campo dei Fiori–Piazza Navona
  117 San Giovanni in Laterano–Colosseum–Piazza di Spagna–Piazza del Popolo
  119 Circular minibus service in the historic centre: Piazza Augusto Imperatore–Piazza della Rotonda (Pantheon–Via del Corso–Piazza di Spagna
  714 Termini–Santa Maria Maggiore–Terme di Caracalla

Bus Essentials

- Tickets must be bought before boarding a bus or tram (➤ Tickets, below).
- You should always **board a bus** by the rear doors (*Salita*) and exit by the central doors (*Uscita*). If you have a validated ticket (➤ below), then you may enter at the front doors by the driver. Often buses are too crowded for you to reach the central doors, in which case it is acceptable – if sometimes difficult – to leave by front or rear doors.
- Route numbers, headstops (*capolinea*) and main intermediate stops are listed at each bus stop (*una fermata*) for the direction of travel. Note that the city's one-way system means that buses' outward and return routes may be different.
- **Night buses** operate after the main bus, metro and tram services cease after about midnight. Most have conductors, and here you *are* permitted to buy tickets on board.

Tickets

- A ticket (*un biglietto*) for buses and trams must always be bought in advance of your ride. Inspectors board buses frequently to carry out random checks: traveling without a valid ticket means a heavy automatic fine. Tickets are sold from automated ATAC machines around the city, and from stores, newsstands, tobacco shops (*tabacchi*) and bars displaying an ATAC sticker.
- Tickets must be **validated** immediately you enter the bus by stamping them in the small orange or yellow boxes at the rear of buses.
- The basic ticket ($) is a timed ticket known as the **Biglietto Integrato a Tempo** (BIT). Ask for "*un biglietto per l'autobus per favore*" (a ticket for the bus please) and this is what you will be given. It is valid for 75 minutes from the time of validation for any number of bus journeys and one Metro journey.
- The integrated ticket ($$), the **Biglietto Integrato Giornaliero** (BIG), is valid for a day across the ATAC and COTRAL network and FS suburban services, excluding the Fiumicino airport express train.
- Also available are integrated weekly (**Carta Integrata Settimanale**, or CIS) and monthly (**Abbonamento Mensile**) tickets (both $$$), but these are unlikely to be useful for most casual visitors.

Metro

Rome's simple subway system, known as *la Metropolitana*, or Metro for short, consists of just two lines, A and B, which intersect at Stazione Termini. Primarily a commuter service, it serves several key sites in the city center and provides fast trans-city journeys. Extensions to the system are under construction – though the wealth of archeological treasures that lie beneath the city's streets inevitably make the process slow.

- Station entrances are marked by a red M on a white background.
- Services run daily from 5:30 a.m. to 11:30 p.m., except Saturday when they stop at 12:30 a.m.
- Buy standard **BIT tickets** from the usual sources (see above) for use on the Metro. Tickets valid for a single Metro journey are also available from machines at Metro stations.
- **Line A** is the most useful for the majority of visitors, linking Termini with stations near Piazza Barberini (Barberini), Piazza di Spagna (Spagna), Piazza del Popolo (Flaminio), the Vatican Museums (Ottaviano-San Pietro) and San Giovanni in Laterano (San Giovanni).
- **Line B**, which also runs through Termini, has a useful station (Colosseo) directly across from the Colosseum.

Taxis

Licensed Roman taxis are either white or yellow and are identified by a name and number, usually on the outside of the rear door and/or a plaque inside the car.

- Cabs are generally difficult to hail on the street. Instead you should go to a **taxi stand**, indicated by blue signs with "TAXI" written in white: key central stands can be found at Termini, Piazza Venezia, Largo di Torre Argentina, Piazza San Silvestro, Piazza di Spagna and Piazza Sonnino (in Trastevere).
- When you pick up a cab, make sure that the **meter** is set at zero. As you set off it will jump to the current minimum fare ($$) for the first 200 yards and then rise quickly.
- **Supplements** are charged on Sundays, public holidays, for trips between 10 p.m. and 7 a.m., for trips to and from Fiumicino, and for each individual item of luggage placed in the trunk. All current supplements should be clearly posted on a list inside the cab.
- If you suspect the driver has been dishonest, take the cab's name and number – making it clear to the driver that you are doing this is often enough to set matters right. Register any complaint with the drivers' co-operative – the number is displayed in cabs – or, in serious cases, with the police (▶ 189).
- The best way to be sure of a taxi is to call a **phone cab**. Most operators speak a little English; or you can ask your hotel to call for you. When you call, give the address where you wish to be picked up. The operator will then give you a taxi-code number (always a geographical location followed by a number), plus the time you will have to wait: for example, *"Londra dodici in cinque minuti"* (London 12 in five minutes). Meters run from the moment a taxi sets off to pick you up.

Phone cab numbers include:
Samarcanda 06 5551
Cosmos Radio Taxis 06 88 177
Autoradio Taxi Roma 06 3570
Capitale Radio 06 4994

Bicycles and Scooters

Several outlets rent bicycles and scooters, but it is vital to realize that Rome's traffic is busy and potentially extremely dangerous if you are not used to such conditions. However, bicycles are good for exploring the quieter city center streets and the open spaces of the Villa Borghese park.

- To rent a **moped** (*motorino*) you must be over 21. Rental requires a credit card, ID and/or a cash deposit. Helmets are mandatory.
- When you rent a **bicycle** it is usual to leave your passport or other ID such as driver's license as a deposit.

Admission Charges

The cost of admission for museums and places of interest mentioned in the text is indicated by the following price categories. Note, from January 2002, euro bills and coins will be introduced (▶ 187).

inexpensive under €3
moderate €3–€6
expensive over €6

Accommodations

Rome has hundreds of hotels in all price categories. Prices are often rather high for the facilities available, however, and good hotels in the mid-range bracket are in short supply. Rooms may be small, even in the most exclusive hotels, and noise is a problem just about everywhere. Central options are best, but you need to make a reservation early to be sure of securing a room.

Grading

Lodgings range from simple hotels to luxurious resorts. An en suite bathroom, telephone and TV are standard in most mid- to high-end properties, and private bathrooms can be expected in all but the most basic establishment. Even in the smartest hotels, however, bathrooms may have only a shower (*una doccia*) and no bath (*una vasca*).

Always ask to see a selection of rooms – you may be shown the worst first. All-day room service and air-conditioning are rare in all but the most upscale hotels.

Location

In Rome it pays to be in the center, despite the fact that traffic and other street noise may be worse here. The areas around Piazza Navona or Piazza di Spagna are best. Trastevere is pleasant, but has relatively few hotels. Via Vittorio Veneto (Via Veneto) is also a good, if slightly peripheral, place to stay but has mostly larger and grander hotels. The area around Stazione Termini has the biggest selection of inexpensive hotels, but this is not a pleasant area, especially at night, and is some distance from most of the key sights. Hotels north of St. Peter's are also inconvenient, but this area is quieter and generally more pleasant than Termini. To reduce noise problems, try to choose a hotel away from main streets, or request a room at the rear or overlooking an internal courtyard.

Reservations

It is advisable to reserve all hotels in advance, especially in high season (Easter and May–Sep.). Reservations should be made by phone and followed by a faxed confirmation. It is also a good idea to reconfirm reservations a couple of days before arrival. Hoteliers are obliged to register every guest, so when checking in you have to hand in your passport. Usually it is returned within a few hours, or on the day of departure. Check-out times range from around 10 a.m. to noon, but you should be able to leave luggage at reception for collection later in the day.

Prices

All prices are officially set, and room rates must by law be displayed in the reception area and in each room. Prices for different rooms can vary within a hotel, but all taxes and services should be included in the rate. Hotels often levy additional charges for air-conditioning and garage facilities, while laundry, drinks from mini-bars and phone calls made from rooms invariably carry surcharges.

Room rates usually include breakfast (*colazione*), but where breakfast is optional (see rate cards in rooms), it always costs less to eat at the nearest bar. Breakfasts in better hotels are improving – buffets are now more common – but for the most part *colazione* just means a "continental" breakfast: coffee, roll and jam.

Reservation Agencies

If you haven't made a reservation, then *on no account* accept offers of rooms from touts at Fiumicino airport or Termini train station. Instead, contact **Enjoy Rome**, Via Varese 39 (tel: 06 445 1843), which operates a free room-finding service. Or try the free **Hotel Reservation Service** (06 699 1000), which has desks at Fiumicino and Termini – the latter desk is often extremely busy.

Budget Accommodations

Youth Hostel: Ostello del Foro Olimpico (Viale delle Olimpiadi 61, tel: 06 324 2571)
YWCA (Via C Balbo 4, tel: 06 488 0460, fax: 06 487 1028). Women and married couples only.
Sandy (Via Cavour 136, tel: 06 488 4585) Dormitory hostel-type rooms.
Suore Pie Operaie (Via di Torre Argentina 76, tel: 06 686 1254). Centrally located, women only.

Price Categories

Price categories below are for double (*una matrimoniale*) or twin (*una camera doppia*) rooms, and are given for guidance only. Seasonal variations may apply, with more reasonable low season (winter) rates.

$ under €103 $$ €103–€180 $$$ over €180

Campo de' Fiori $$

This inexpensive hotel could not have a better location, housed as it is in an ocher-colored palazzo close to the central Campo dei Fiori, one of Rome's most colorful and pleasant squares (▶ 80–81). The 27 rooms vary considerably in size and in decoration – most are rather small – but all are clean and appealing. Only 12 have bathrooms. The hotel has a bar but no restaurant, and no elevator or air-conditioning. From the roof terrace there are fine views of the city center.

🔲 198 C2 ✉ Via del Biscione 6
☎ 06 6880 6865; fax: 06 687 6003

Celio $$

The mid-range Celio appeals on several counts; its intimacy (it has just 10 rooms); its location, which is in a reasonably quiet street close to the Colosseum; and its comfort and aesthetics. All the rooms are taste-fully appointed and frescoed with scenes inspired by Renaissance painters.

🔲 206 A4 ✉ Via SS Quattro 35c
☎ 06 7049 5333; fax: 06 7096 6377

Cesari $$–$$$

Opened in 1787, the mid-range Cesari has been in the hotel business long enough to get things right, and has maintained its standards through the pleasant efficiency of its staff and regular renovation – the last major overhaul was in 1999. It also has the bonus of a quiet and central position in a hard-to-find little street between the Pantheon and Via del Corso. The 48 rooms are comfortable and have modern decorative touches, as well as TVs and air-conditioning. Prices are mostly at the lowest end of the $$$ category.

🔲 199 E4 ✉ Via di Pietra 98a
☎ 06 679 2386; fax: 06 679 0882

Crowne Plaza Minerva $$$

The Minerva does not yet have the cachet of Rome's other luxury hotels, but none of its upscale rivals can claim such a central and enticing position – immediately behind the Pantheon and church of Santa Maria sopra Minerva. The hotel was first converted by the Holiday Inn group in the 1980s, but has since left the chain and benefited from another makeover that has improved still further the already first-rate rooms and common areas. Service is excellent, the facilities are the equal of – and often superior to – hotels in a similar category, and little can beat the view as you step from the hotel's front door.

➕ 199 D3 ✉ Piazza della Minerva 69
☎ 06 6994 1888; fax: 06 679 4165; e-mail: minerva@pronet.it

Eden $$$

The luxury Eden ranks among Rome's three or so top hotels for its style, old-fashioned luxury, and a more relaxed atmosphere than many of its stuffier rivals on nearby Via Veneto. It's been an exclusive favorite among celebrities for more than a century, attracting European royalty, and stars of screen and stage. Renovation of the 101 rooms and 11 suites in 1994 reinforced its position as one of the world's great hotels. At the same time it retained its distinctive and sumptuous decoration, enormous rooms (most of them different), antique furniture and marble bathrooms. The Terrazza (► 137) restaurant is superb, and there are spectacular views from the roof terrace.

➕ 202 C3 ✉ Via Ludovisi 49
☎ 06 478 121, toll free in Italy 800 820 088; fax: 06 482 1584; e-mail: reservations@hotel-eden.it

Hotel d'Inghilterra $$$

A 19th-century gentleman on the Grand Tour would feel more than at home in the upscale Inghilterra, which has remained the best of Rome's traditional old-world hotels since it opened in 1850. The hotel's aristocratic air comes in part from the building itself, the 15th-century former Palazzo Torlonia, but also from the opulent common areas, period furniture and oriental carpets, precious Neapolitan paintings and fine collection of prints and pictures. Past guests have included composer Franz Liszt and writer Ernest Hemingway. The atmosphere at the Inghilterra may be too decorous and

dignified for some, and not all 105 rooms are as spacious as they could be – those on floors four and five tend to be larger. The location is good, however, in a quiet side street close to the shopping district around Via Condotti.

➕ 199 E5 ✉ Via Bocca di Leone 14
☎ 06 69 981 or 800 505050; fax: 06 6992 2243; web: www.charminghotels.it; e-mail: reservations-hir@ charminghotels.it

Navona $

Never mind that this is a budget hotel: its location is unbeatable – just a minute from Piazza Navona, in a quiet side street away from the hustle and bustle. The vast majority of its 21 rooms have been renovated to a standard that make a nonsense of its lowly rating, and the owners are a friendly Italo-Australian couple who make light of any communica-tion problems.

The poor breakfast is the only drawback (take it in a nearby bar instead) and air-conditioning, if you want it, requires a hefty supplement. Parts of the building, which was built over the ancient Baths of Agrippa, date back to the first century AD. English poets Keats and Shelley once occupied the top floor.

Credit cards are not accepted here. If the hotel is full, the owners may suggest you stay in the more upscale, co-owned and slightly more expensive Zanardelli hotel just north of Piazza Navona.

➕ 198 C3 ✉ Via dei Sediari 8
☎ 06 686 4203; fax: 06 6880 3802

Piazza di Spagna $$

The mid-range Piazza di Spagna is not on the piazza from which it take its name – it is actually located in a side street nearby, a better place than the square itself because it is considerably less noisy. The attrac-tive old building is covered in creeper and though its 17 rooms are not enormous, their facilities are good: all rooms have air-conditioning, TV and telephones, as well as a private bathroom. The location, especially if you intend to do a lot of shopping, could not be better.

🔛 199 E5 ✉ Via Mario de' Fiori 61
☎ 06 679 6412; fax: 06 679 0654

Piccolo $

The Piccolo (meaning "Small") is one of a number of simple and inexpensive hotels, like the Campo dei Fiori (► 35), whose modest demeanor is more than compensated for by a perfect location close to Campo dei Fiori and the heart of the old city. All 16 rooms are immaculately maintained by the charming Italian couple who own the hotel, and most have private bathrooms or shower rooms. There is a small bar in the hotel, but no restaurant. All major credit cards are accepted.

🔛 198 C2 ✉ Via dei Chiavari 32
☎ 06 6880 2560

Rinascimento $

This mid-range hotel occupies an historic building in an excellent central location just to the west of Campo dei Fiori: it also lies close to appealing streets such as Via dei Branchi Vecchi, Via Giulia and Via del Governo Vecchio. Although its 18 well-equipped rooms do not number among the largest available in Rome, they have all been attractively refurbished.

🔛 198 B3 ✉ Via del Pellegrino 122
☎ 06 687 4813; fax: 06 683 3518

Scalinata di Spagna $$$

What you pay for this mid-range hotel might buy you a bigger room elsewhere, but it would take a considerable sum to purchase a setting quite as romantic as this – the hotel sits at the top of the famous Spanish Steps looking down over Keats' House and the Piazza di Spagna. Some of the 16 traditionally furnished rooms are small, but all are charming, as are the old twisting staircases and secret little roof garden.

🔛 199 F5 ✉ Piazza Trinità dei Monti 17 ☎ 06 694 0848; fax: 06 6994 0598

Smeraldo $

Renovation means that this budget hotel has added a modern and comfortable aspect to what was already a good location just a couple of minutes walk from the Campo dei Fiori. Bathrooms are all new, most of the 35 rooms have TV and air-conditioning, and the public spaces are well presented. Though breakfast is available, it offers relatively poor value for money – try one of the local bars instead.

🔛 198 C2 ✉ Vicolo Chiodaroli 9
☎ 06 687 5929; fax: 06 6880 5495

Teatro di Pompeo $$–$$$

In Rome you walk through history, but in this mid-range hotel you can sleep in it as well. Situated on a quiet square north of Campo dei Fiori, the hotel occupies the site of the ancient Teatro di Pompeo (Theatre of Pompey), which dates from the first century BC. Parts of the original building can still be seen in the remarkable rough-stone vaulted dining room and elsewhere. History aside, this is a pleasant hotel thanks to a welcoming owner, modest size – just 13 rooms – and the charm of many of the rooms: the attic rooms with their beamed ceilings and terracotta floors are some of the nicest. Rooms are equipped with TVs and air-conditioning.

🔛 198 C2 ✉ Largo del Pallaro 8
☎ 06 6830 0170; fax: 06 6880 5531

Trastevere $

The friendly Trastevere is the best of only a handful of hotels, inexpensive or otherwise, in the lively, old-fashioned district of Trastevere (► 95–98). Though the nine rooms are quite small, they were renovated in 1999 and boast bright, modern bathrooms, terra-cotta floors and wood paneling. Four private apartments with kitchens are good value if there are more than two of you or if you are spending a longer period of time in the city. It can be noisy here at night.

🔛 201 E1 ✉ Via Luciano Manara 24
☎ 06 581 4713; fax: 06 588 1016

Food and Drink

Eating out is one of Rome's great pleasures. The city has a huge range of restaurants, from humble trattorias to chic hotel dining rooms. Prices are generally reasonable, and there are plenty of places where you can get inexpensive snacks and sandwiches. In summer – as an extra bonus – it's often possible to eat outside.

Don't be put off by Rome's specialties, many of which require a strong stomach (➤ 18–19), because most restaurants offer a broad range of familiar Italian dishes.

■ Differences between types of restaurants in Italy are becoming increasingly blurred. An *osteria* was once the humblest type of eating place, but now tends to describe new and unstuffy restaurants serving simple, often innovative, food in relaxed surroundings. Anywhere described as a *pizzeria* is likely to be even simpler; it will often serve a few pastas, salads and other dishes as well as pizzas. A *trattoria* is the general name for a traditional and unpretentious restaurant, while *un ristorante* is usually more upscale and more expensive. A chic and expensive restaurant in Rome, more than most cities, does not guarantee good food; often you can eat well in the humblest places.
■ For most of the eating places listed in the guide it is well worth trying to **make reservations**, the exception being pizzerias, which rarely take them. For the more popular restaurants you may even need to reserve a few days in advance.
■ Menus begin with *antipasti* (hors d'oeuvres), followed by *il primo* (pasta, gnocchi, risotto or soup) and *il secondo* (meat or fish). Vegetables (*il contorno*) or salad (*insalata*) are usually served separately from the *secondo*. For dessert you can choose between *il dolce*, *formaggio* (cheese) and *frutta* (fruit). Puddings are often disappointing; buying an ice cream from a *gelateria* can be a better choice (see panel).
You're not obliged to wade through all the courses on the menu, and none but the top-ranking restaurants should mind if you just have a salad and a plate of pasta, especially at lunch.

Ice Cream Etiquette

Choose whether you want your ice cream in a cone (*un cono*) or a cardboard cup (*una coppa*). Both come in different sizes, costing from about €1 for the smallest portion to €2.50 or more for the largest. You name your price and then choose flavors from the tubs laid out in front of you – usually you can choose a mixture of one, two or three flavors, even in the lowest price range. You will usually be offered a topping of optional – and usually free – whipped cream (*panna*).

■ Romans take **lunch** (*il pranzo*) after about 12:30 p.m. and **dinner** (*la cena*) from 8 p.m. The famous long Roman lunch followed by a lengthy siesta is largely a thing of the past, except on Sunday, which is still an excuse for a big traditional lunchtime meal.
■ **Service** (*servizio*) and *pane e coperto* (bread and cover charge) may bump prices up in all restaurants. Both should be itemized on the bill. If a service charge is not included, then you should **tip** at your discretion, up to about

10 percent: in less expensive places it's enough to round up to the nearest €2.50 or €5.

■ The **check** (*il conto*) should be a properly printed receipt. If all you receive is prices scrawled on a scrap of paper then the restaurant is breaking the law and you are entitled to request a proper check (*una ricevuta*).

Eating on a budget

■ Many restaurants, especially around Termini train station, offer a set-price tourist menu (*un menù turistico*), but the quality and quantity of food are often poor.

■ Keep costs down by drinking **house wine** (*vino della casa*), usually a good white Frascati or similar, available in a carafe (*un quartino*), which holds about a half pint, or a jug (*un mezzo litro),* which holds about a pint.

■ Most bars offer **sandwiches** (*tramezzini*), which are invariably made from the blandest white bread with crusts removed. Far better are *panini*, or filled rolls, which you can often have heated (*riscaldato*).

■ **Pizza** by the slice (*pizza al taglio*) is often sold from tiny hole-in-the-wall bakeries, but check the quality of the topping; in the worst places it amounts to no more than a smear of tomato.

■ A *pasticceria* specializes in cakes and pastries. A *torrefazione* is a bar that also roasts coffee for retail sale.

Best For

To sample the best that Rome has to offer, try the following places

… **Tazza d'Oro** (➤ 94) for coffee

… **La Rosetta** (➤ 108) for fish

… **Gelateria di San Crispino** (➤ 138) for ice cream

… **Pizzeria Leonina** (➤ 72) for pizza by the slice

… **Agata e Romeo** (➤ 136), **Il Convivio** (➤ 107) or **La Terrazza** (➤ 137) for a romantic meal

… **Bar della Pace** (➤ 108) for people-watching

What to Drink

■ The first drink of the day is generally **coffee** (see panel below), usually as a cappuccino accompanied by a sweet croissant (*un cornetto*). After lunch or dinner, Italians always drink an espresso, *never* cappuccino.

Coffee Essentials

• *un espresso* (or, more colloquially, *un caffè)* – an espresso coffee (short and black)

• *una doppia* – double espresso

• *un lungo* – espresso with a little more water than usual

• *un macchiato* – espresso with a dash of milk (literally "stained" with milk)

• *un caffè corretto* – espresso with a dash of whisky or other liqueur

• *un cappuccino* – espresso with added frothed milk

• *un caffè latte* – cappuccino with more milk and no froth.

• *un Americano* – espresso with lots of hot water added to make a long drink.

• *un caffè Hag* – decaffeinated coffee

• *un caffè freddo* – iced coffee. It is usually served with sugar already added. Ask for "*amaro*" if you want it without sugar.

• *un cappaccino freddo* – iced milky coffee.

- **Tea** (*un tè*) is common, but the Romans take it with lemon (*un tè al limone*) and without milk. If you want tea with milk, ask specifically for *un tè con latte* – sometimes you may have to insist on *latte freddo* (cold milk), otherwise it'll be the warm milk used for cappuccinos.
- **Mineral water** (*acqua minerale*) is widely drunk with meals, either fizzy (*acqua gassata*) or still (*acqua non gassata*). If you want a glass of water in a bar ask for *un bicchiere d'acqua*. If you're happy with tap water – and Rome's water is generally very good – ask for a free *bicchiere d'acqua dal rubinetto* or *acqua normale*.
- Bottled **fruit juice** (*un succo di frutta*) is often drunk at breakfast, and comes in a wide variety of flavors. Freshly squeezed juice is a *una spremuta* of either orange (*un spremuta d'arancia*), grapefruit (*...di pompelmo*) or lemon (*...di limone*). Lemon Soda (the brand name), a bitter lemon drink, is another good soft drink.
- **Beer** (*birra*) is generally light lager, and darker British-style beer (*birra scura, nera* or *rossa*) is sometimes available. The least expensive way to buy beer is from the keg: ask for *un birra alla spina* and specify the size – *piccola* (small; about 8 ounces), *media* (medium; about 16 ounces) or *grande* (large; nearly 2 pints). Bottled beers are usually more expensive; the exceptions are Italian bottled beers such as Peroni or Nastro Azzurro.
- **Aperitifs** include fortified wines such as Martini, Cinzano and Campari. Note that if you ask for a Campari Soda it comes ready mixed in a bottle; for the real thing ask for *un bitter Campari*. You'll often see people drinking a lurid orange-colored aperitif – this is the non-alcoholic Crodino. Prosecco, a good white sparkling wine from northeast Italy, is another good *aperitivo*. Gin and tonic is simply *gin e tonica*.

  After dinner, most (male) Romans drink brandy (Vecchia Romagna is the best brand), *limoncello* (lemon-flavored alcoholic drink), or *amaro*, literally "bitter." The last is the most Italian thing to drink, the best-known brand being the very bitter Fernet Branca: a good and less demanding brand is Averna. Romans may also have *grappa* after a meal, a strong clear *eau de vie*, or sweeter drinks such as the almond-flavored Amaretto or aniseed-flavored Sambuca (sometimes drunk with added coffee bean).

Bar Etiquette

Waiter service at a table costs twice or three times as much as ordering and standing at the bar. Prices for bar service and sitting (*tavola* or *terrazza*) should be listed by law somewhere in the bar. If you do sit down, remember you can occupy your table almost as long as you wish. Ordering at the bar means paying first, which you do by stating your order at the separate cash desk (*la cassa*). After you've paid, the cashier will give you a receipt (*lo scontrino*) which you then take to the bar and present to the bar person (*barista*). If service seems slow, a coin placed on the bar as a tip with your *scontrino* often works wonders. Never try to pay at the bar, and never pay the standing rate and then to try to sit at a table.

Web Guide

For the latest information on restaurants, the following websites may be useful:

www.gamberorosse.it – a site devoted to restaurants and eating out in Rome
www.enjoyrome.com – with information, listings and good web links
www.informaroma.it – good for general visitor information

Shopping

Rome might not be in the same shopping league as London, Paris or New York, and even in Italy takes second place to Milan. Yet it has plenty of top designer stores, as well as countless specialty shops and many interesting markets.

- The largest concentration of **designer, accessory and luxury goods** stores are concentrated in the grid of streets surrounding **Via Condotti**, or Via dei Condotti (➤ 139).
- **Less expensive clothing and shoe stores** line several key streets, notably Via del Corso – which you'll find packed with shoppers on Saturdays – Via del Tritone and Via Nazionale. Shoes and clothing generally are good buys, as are food, wine, accessories such as gloves, leather goods, luxury items and fine antiques.
- Other smaller streets have their own specialties: **antiques and art galleries,** for example, on Via dei Coronari, Via Giulia, Via del Babuino, Via del Monserrato and Via Margutta; paper and wickerwork on Via Monterone; religious ephemera and clothing on Via dei Cestari. Via del Governo Vecchio or Via dei Banchi Nuovi, for example, are dotted with second-hand stores, jewelry stores and small artisans' workshops.
- Rome does not offer much in the way of one-stop shopping: there are only one or two **department stores** in the center (the best is **Rinascente** ➤ 140) and no shopping malls.
- The city has several fine **markets**, notably the picturesque **Campo dei Fiori** (➤ 80–81), the bigger and more prosaic **Piazza Vittorio Emanuele** southeast of Termini (this is central Rome's main market, open Monday to Saturday 10 a.m. to 6 p.m.), and the famous Sunday flea market at **Porta Portese** southwest of the center near Porta Sublicio in Trastevere. Porta Portese is reputedly the largest flea market in Europe, with around 4,000 booths selling anything and everything, from antiques to organic food. It becomes extremely crowded by mid-morning, so try to arrive early (it finishes at 2 p.m.). The market is particularly popular with pickpockets, so keep a close eye on your belongings at all times.
- Most **shopping for food** is still done in tiny neighborhood stores known as *alimentari*. These general stores sell everything from olive oil and pasta to basic toiletries. They usually have a delicatessen counter, where you can have a sandwich (*panino*) made up from the meats and cheeses that are on display.
- Rome sales staff have a reputation for aloofness, especially in more upscale boutiques. If they pretend you don't exist, ignore them or politely ask for help: the phrase is *mi può aiutare, per favore?*
- Don't be tempted to bargain – **prices are fixed**. Prices may drop in sales: look for the word "*saldi.*"

Opening Times

- In the **city center**, opening times are fast becoming closer to those of northern Europe – that is, Monday to Saturday 9 a.m. to 7 or 8 p.m. Even those stores that still close for lunch often close for only an hour or so from 1 p.m. rather than observing the 1–4 p.m. break of times past.
- The vast majority of stores are **closed on Monday morning**. Many food stores close on Thursday afternoon in winter and Saturday afternoon in summer.
- **In August many stores close** completely for weeks at a time (*chiuso per ferie* is the tell-tale sign – closed for holidays).

Entertainment

You won't find a great deal of world-class classical music, opera, ballet and other cultural entertainment in Rome, but the city does offer fine jazz and church music, and has a sprinkling of good clubs and live music venues.

Information

- Information on most cultural activities and performing arts can be obtained from the main visitor center and information kiosks around the city (➤ 30).
- The main **listings** magazine is *roma c'è*, an invaluable weekly publication with details of classical and other musical events, theater, dance, opera, nightclubs, current museum and gallery opening times, shopping, restaurants and much more: it also has a short summary of key events and galleries in English at the back. It can be obtained from most newspaper stands and bookstores. The English-language *Wanted in Rome* is published every other Wednesday.
- If you read some Italian, listings can also be found in *Time Out Roma* (issued on Thursday); *Trova Roma*, a "what's on" insert in the Thursday editon of *La Repubblica* newspaper; or the daily editions of newspapers such as *Il Messaggero*.
- Otherwise, contact box offices listed in individual chapters – although sales staff may not speak much English – or keep your eyes peeled for posters advertising events such as small church recitals or occasional concerts.

Tickets

Rome does not yet have one-stop ticket agencies and nor do all individual venues accept reservations and pre-payment with credit cards over the phone. Often you are obliged to visit individual box offices before a performance. The alternative is to visit one of two ticket agencies: **Orbis** (Piazza dell'Esquilino 37; tel: 06 474 4776; open Mon.–Sat. 9:30–1, 4–7:30), or **Box Office** (Viale Giulio Cesare 88 (tel: 06 372 0216; open Mon. 3:30–7; Tue.–Sat. 10–1:30, 2:30–7). Note information only is available over the phone from these agencies; if you want to buy tickets you must visit them in person.

Nightclubs

- Where nightclubs are concerned, be aware that a popular club one year can lose its following or reappear with a facelift and new name by the next.
- Discobars are popular across the city – smaller than clubs but with room to dance as well as drink and talk.
- Long-established **gay bars and clubs** include L'Alibi (➤ 112) and L'Hangar (Via in Selci 29, tel: 06 488 1379). Other clubs such as Piper (➤ 142) often have gay nights.
- For most clubs **admission prices** are high, but entry often includes the price of your first drink. For tax and other reasons, some clubs or bars define themselves as private clubs, which in practice means you have to fill out a (usually free) membership card. Remember, too, that many clubs close during summer or move to outdoor or seafront locations beyond the city.

Classical Music

The key classical music and opera venues and companies remain fairly fixed, but one area of classical music which is subject to change is the location of the city's various outdoor summer concert cycles. These can be one of the city's best cultural attractions, if only because of the lovely settings. Contact visitor centers for current information.

The Ancient City

Getting Your Bearings

What remains of ancient Rome is not confined to a single area of the modern city. Buildings and monuments from the era of empire and earlier are scattered far and wide, yet the heart of the old city – around the Capitoline, Palatine and Esquiline hills – still boasts the largest present-day concentration of ancient monuments.

VIA C BATTISTI

VIA D PLEBISCITO

Piazza Venezia **1**

Colonna Traiano **5**

LARGO MAGNANAPOLI

VIA PANISPERNA

VIA DI SAN MARCO

Mercati Traianei

Monumento a Vittorio Emanuele II

VIA DEI

VIA DEL SERPENTI

S Maria in Aracoeli

Capitolino **2**

Fori Imperiali **4**

PIAZZA DEL CAMPIDOGLIO

3

Palazzo Nuovo

VIA

GIOVA

CAVOUR

VIA

Palazzo dei Conservatori

Musei Capitolini

FORI IMPERIALI

PIAZZA DI SAN PIETRO IN VINCOLI

VIA DEGLI ANNIBALDI

8 **San Pietro in Vincoli**

Parco di Traiano

LUNG DI PIERLEONI

VIA PETROSELLI

Foro Romano **6**

VIA

SACRA

Monte Esquili

Domus Aurea **9**

Colle Oppio **10**

Monte Palatino

Colosseo **7**

PIAZZA DEL COLOSSEO

Cleme

Arco di Costantino

VIA DI S

V DI SAN GREGORIO

VIA CLAUDIA

Parco del Celio

As such it makes an excellent point from which to start your visit, placing into context much of what you'll see elsewhere in the city. The itinerary starts where Rome itself probably started, on the Capitoline Hill, close to the busy Piazza Venezia. This piazza is the hub of the modern city with roads leading off from it to the four points of the compass: Via del Corso to the north and Piazza del Popolo; Corso Vittorio Emanuele II to the west and St. Peter's; Via IV Novembre to the east and Stazione Termini; and Via dei Fori Imperiali to the south and the Colosseum.

Villa Celimontana

Previous page: The Colosseum
Right: Statues of Castor and Pollux, Piazza del Campidoglio

The Capitoline Hill, however, was the early focus of the ancient city. From its slopes you can look over and then explore the open spaces of the Roman Forum (Foro Romano), the social, political and mercantile heart of the old Roman Empire. From here it's only a few steps to the Colosseum, the greatest of all ancient Roman monuments, and then on to a quieter residential area and your first church, San Clemente, a fascinating historical hybrid that contains a beautiful medieval interior, the remains of an older fifth-century church, and the partially excavated ruins of a Roman temple.

Just a few minutes' walk away stands San Giovanni in Laterano, Rome's cathedral church, and among the most important churches in the city after St. Peter's. In between times you can take time out in the park of the Colle Oppio,

| 0 | 250 metres |
| 0 | 250 yards |

The huge hands in the courtyard of the Palazzo dei Conservatori are always popular with children

VIA

VIALE A MANZONI

VIA EMANUELE FILIBERTO

LABICANA

MERULANA

VANNI IN LATERANO

PIAZZA DI SAN GIOVANNI IN LATERANO

PIAZZA DI PORTA S GIOVANNI

12 **San Giovanni in Laterano**

VIA AMBA ARADAM

VIA SANNIO

PIAZZALE APPIO

NZA

just a few moments from either the Colosseum or San Clemente. And if you still have time to kill, you can retrace your steps to the Capitoline Hill and explore the Capitoline museums, which are filled with artistic masterpieces from the Roman era.

Begin your stay in Rome by exploring some of the city's greatest monuments, starting on the Capitoline Hill and moving to the Forum and Colosseum before concluding with two of Rome's most important churches.

The Ancient City in a Day

9:00 a.m.

Begin the day by walking to the southwest corner of the busy **Piazza Venezia** (➤ 66), taking time to admire the colossal Vittorio Emanuele II Monument. Then climb the shallow ramp of steps near the monument to Piazza del Campidoglio (below).

9:30 a.m.

Explore the lovely church of **Santa Maria in Aracoeli** (➤ 49) and admire the view of the Roman Forum from the lanes off the piazza's right- and left-hand corners. The latter offers a first-hand view of the Arco di Settimio Severo, a Roman triumphal arch. Then follow the steps here down to Via dei Fori Imperiali.

10:00 a.m.

Cross Via dei Fori Imperiali to look at the **Colonna Traiano** (➤ 68) and **Fori Imperiali** (➤ 67). Then recross the road to the main entrance to the **Roman Forum** (➤ right, 50–55), some of the world's most historic and romantic ruins.

12:30 p.m.

After seeing the Forum you emerge close to the **Colosseum** (► right, 56–60) and **Arco di Costantino** (► 58). You can visit them now or save them for after lunch. You could take a snack lunch in Cavour 313 wine bar (► 72), the café of the Colle Oppio park, or a fuller meal in Nerone (► 73). Or buy picnic provisions in Via Cavour and head for the Colle Oppio.

1:30 p.m.

Spend time in the **Colle Oppio** (► 71), perhaps with an after-lunch coffee in the park's café, and look at the Colosseum and Arco di Costantino if you haven't done already done so.

3:30 p.m.

Walk a short distance on Via di San Giovanni in Laterano to **San Clemente** (► 61–63), in time for when it opens in the afternoon. The church not only has a lovely medieval interior – complete with superb frescoes and early mosaics – but also two fascinating subterranean places of Christian and pagan worship from earlier eras (left).

4:30 p.m.

Make your way along one of the quieter side streets – notably Via dei Santi Quattro Coronati – towards the soaring San Giovanni in Laterano, the cathedral church of Rome and one of the most important places of worship in the city.

5:30 p.m.

Explore **San Giovanni in Laterano** (right, ► 64–65), not forgetting its ancient baptistery and cloister, the latter graced with countless superbly decorated columns. Then take a bus or Metro if you don't want to retrace your steps to the Colosseum and Piazza Venezia.

Capitolino

The Capitolino, or Capitoline Hill, is the smallest but most important of Rome's original Seven Hills. Home to Bronze Age tribes as early as the 14th century BC, it formed the city's birthplace, eventually becoming the hub of its military, religious and political life. Its history, central position and many sights make it the perfect introduction to the ancient city.

Today, much of the Capitoline has been obscured by the Vittorio Emanuele Monument, the huge white edifice that dominates **Piazza Venezia** (➤ 66). In earliest times, however, the hill had two distinct crests: one to the north, which was known as the *Arx,* or Citadel, and is now the site of the church of Santa Maria in Aracoeli; and one to the south, known as the *Capitolium,* which is now largely given over to palaces such as the Palazzo dei Conservatori.

Between the two lay the *Asylum,* an area reputedly created by Romulus as a place of sanctuary, the aim being to attract refugees to the fledgling city. Today this area is occupied by **Piazza del Campidoglio,** a square largely laid out by Michelangelo and bounded by Rome's town hall, the Palazzo Senatorio (to the rear) and the Musei Capitolini, or Capitoline Museums, to either side (➤ 66–67).

Start your visit in Piazza d'Aracoeli to the right of the Vittorio Emanuele Monument. Ignore the long flight of steps climbing to Santa Maria in Aracoeli – there's an easier entrance to the church in the piazza above – and climb the shallow stepped ramp (1536), or *cordonata,* in front of you. This was designed by

Renaissance frescoes by Pinturicchio in Santa Maria in Aracoeli

The equestrian statue of Emperor Marcus Aurelius in the Piazza del Campidoglio

The approach to Piazza del Campidoglio from Piazza Venezia

Michelangelo for the triumphal entry of Emperor Charles V into Rome, and is crowned by two huge Roman statues of Castor and Pollux placed here in 1583. At the heart of the piazza stands a copy of a famous equestrian statue of Emperor Marcus Aurelius – the original is in the Palazzo Nuovo on your left, part of the Capitoline Museums (the rest of the museum is in the Palazzo dei Conservatori on your right).

Head for the space between the Palazzo Nuovo and Palazzo Senatorio, where you'll find steps on the left that take you into **Santa Maria in Aracoeli**, a church already considered ancient when it was first recorded in AD 574. The church was rebuilt between 1285 and 1287, and is filled with chandeliers, ancient columns and a beautifully decorated ceiling. It also contains two major treasures: frescoes on the *Life of San Bernardino* (1486) by the Umbrian artist Pinturicchio (in the first chapel of the right, or south aisle), and the *Tomb of Luca Savelli* (1287), attributed to the Florentine sculptor Arnolfo di Cambio (on the left side of the south transept).

TAKING A BREAK

For a friendly, informal atmosphere, moderately priced snacks and an excellent selection of wines, try **Cavour 313** (➤ 72).

Santa Maria in Aracoeli

🕂 199 F2 ✉ Piazza d'Aracoeli ☎ 06 679 8155 🕙 Hours vary, but generally daily 8–6:30, Jun.–Sep.; 7–5:30, Oct.–May 🍴 Cafés on Via del Teatro di Marcello 🚇 Colosseo 🚌 44, 46, 60, 63, 64, 70, 75, 81, 85, 87, 175 and all other services to Piazza Venezia 💷 Free

---

CAPITOLINO: INSIDE INFO

Top tips Be sure to walk through the passages to the left and right of the Palazzo Senatorio for views over the Roman Forum (➤ 50–55).

• The Capitoline Museums contain some magnificent paintings and sculptures, but other museums have even better collections – so only see them if you have plenty of time. Many people choose to combine a visit to the museums with a visit to Piazza del Campidoglio.

Roman Forum

The Roman Forum, or Foro Romano, was the heart of the Roman Empire for almost a thousand years. Today, its once mighty ensemble of majestic buildings has been reduced almost to nothing, yet the surviving ruins provide a romantic setting in which you can still catch a glimpse of the glory that was Rome.

Exploring the Forum

When exploring the Forum, it's essential to remember the site's 3,000-year history and the degree to which monuments over this period were built, rebuilt, moved, destroyed, adapted, plundered or left to fall into wistful ruin. Be warned, therefore, that only a handful of structures such as the Arco di Settimio Severo or the Basilica di Massenzio hint at their original size or layout.

If monuments are all you seek from the site, you will probably leave disappointed, or at best bemused by the jumble of stones and columns. The trick here is to enjoy the beauty and romance of such ruins, and appreciate their historical associations: after all, you are literally walking in the footsteps of Julius Caesar, Nero, Caligula, Claudius, Hadrian and countless other resonant names from antiquity. With this in mind, allow anything up to two hours to amble around the site, more if you decide to walk up and see the Palatino.

Though little remains of the Forum's former glory (left and below), it is still one of the city's most captivating and romantic sites

Marsh to Majesty

The Forum was not Rome's original heart – that honor probably went to a fortress hamlet on the more easily defended Capitoline Hill to the northwest. The future hub of the empire actually began life as the "Velabrum," a marshy inlet of the Tiber between the Capitoline and Palatine hills. This was the area that featured in the myth of Romulus and Remus (► 7), for it was here that the twins were found and suckled by the she-wolf and here that Romulus – according to legend – founded Rome in 753 BC.

During the Iron Age, the area probably served as a cemetery for villages on neighboring hills, and later as a meeting place, common land and garbage heap for the shepherds and other inhabitants of these early settlements. It was at this point that the Forum may have acquired its name, for "*forum*" comes from a word that means "beyond" or "outside the walls" (*fuori* in modern Italian still means "outside").

As Rome prospered, so the area was drained by the first century BC Cloaca Maxima, or Great Drain, and became the obvious place to build not just stores and houses, but temples, courts, basilicas and the other great buildings of state. Successive emperors, consuls and other prominent power-brokers vied with one another to leave ever-grander memorials to their military and political achievements. This state of

Ruins on the Palatine Hill above the Roman Forum

Hill of Palaces

The Palatino, or Palatine Hill, which rises above the Forum to the south, is one of Rome's Seven Hills. Sometimes called Rome's Beverly Hills, the area contains ruins of grand palaces built after the first century BC by the city's rich and powerful (the word "palace" comes from Palatino). You come here not for monuments – the ruins are even more confusing than those of the Forum – but to enjoy the area's lovely gardens, shady walks, fountains, box hedges, orange groves and pretty views over the Forum. It's a charming, atmospheric place, but the admission charge is expensive (▶ 190).

affairs continued until about the second century AD, when a growing shortage of space meant that political power followed the emperors to their new palaces on the Palatino, or Palatine Hill. Trade and commerce, meanwhile, moved to the Mercati Traianei (➤ 68), while new building projects were diverted to the nearby Fori Imperiali, or Imperial Forums (➤ 67–68).

After the fall of Rome, the site declined swiftly; many of the monuments tumbled, and much of the stone was plundered for building Rome's medieval churches and palaces. By the 16th century the Forum was little more than an overgrown meadow. Excavations began around 1803, but remain far from complete to this day. Major excavations to explore previously untouched ground around the Curia and Argiletum began in 1996, and are now proceeding apace here and elsewhere, although much remains to be uncovered, not least under the Via dei Fori Imperiali.

Above: Most visitors to Rome are drawn to the Forum

The Forum

On entering the Forum from Via dei Fori Imperiali, the first ruin you see is the **Tempio di Antonino e Faustina**, built in AD 141 by Emperor Antoninus to honor his wife, Faustina. It makes a good introduction to the site, mainly because it is so well preserved, its survival due to its consecration as a church in the 11th century. Some of the oldest graves ever found in Rome were uncovered close by.

Turning right brings you to the **Via Sacra**, once the Forum's principal thoroughfare and the route taken by victorious generals and emperors parading the spoils of war. On your right as you walk along the surviving flagstones are the ruins of the Basilica Aemilia, built in 179 BC as a business and moneylending center. The large brick building ahead of you and to the right is the much-restored Curia, or Senate House, probably completed by Augustus in 28 BC, when it became the meeting place of Rome's 300 or so senators.

The area to the Curia's right is the **Argiletum**, the site of a now-vanished temple that once held a statue of Janus, the two-faced god. Its twin doors were kept open in times of war and closed in times of peace: in 1,000 years, it is said, they were closed on only three occasions. In front of the Curia is the **Lapis Niger**, or Black Stone (protected by railings), an ancient stone inscribed in old Latin that covers a shrine dating back to the sixth century BC or beyond. Modern scholars are unsure of the inscription's meaning, as were Romans in the first century, for whom the stone was a sacred but mysterious object. The accepted theory of the time was that it marked the grave of Romulus himself.

Many of the ruins in the Forum are more than 2,000 years old

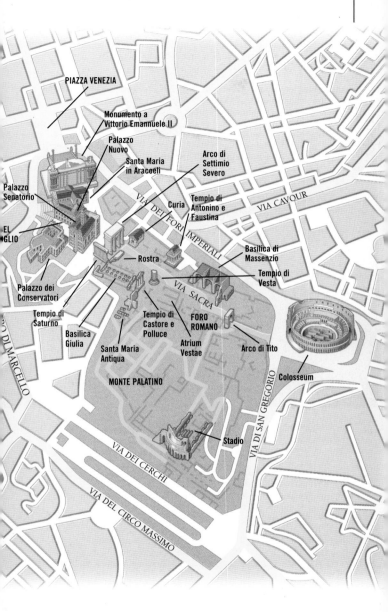

The Forum and Palatine Hill

Beyond the stone rises the **Arco di Settimio Severo**, a huge arch raised in AD 203 to mark the 10th year of the reign of Emperor Septimius Severus. It also commemorated the minor military victories of his sons, Geta and Caracalla, hence the battle scenes depicted in the large marble reliefs. To the left and a little in front of the arch a line of brick marks the remains of the **Rostra**, or orator's platform, the place at which Mark Antony reputedly made his "Friends, Romans, countrymen" speech after the assassination of Julius Caesar. The platform took its name from the bronze prows (*rosta*) from ships captured by the Romans in battle which decorated it. They have given their name to the speaker's "rostrum" ever since.

The eight-columned **Tempio di Saturno**, or Temple of Saturn, to the south is one of the Forum's oldest temples – it dates from around 497 BC – perhaps because Saturn, a god of

The Tempio di Saturno (center), with the unmistakable Arco di Settimio Severo to its left

agriculture, was one of Rome's most venerated gods from earliest times. The ancient Romans believed the city's initial prosperity and power was based on its agricultural prowess.

Walking away from the Capitoline Hill above, you pass the patchy **Basilica Giulia** on your right, begun by Julius Caesar in 54 BC to complement the Basilica Aemilia opposite. The nearby **Tempio di Castore e Polluce**, or Temple of Castor and Pollux, was supervised by the city's *equites*, or knights, and was home to the Empire's weights and measures standards. To its south is the infrequently open **Santa Maria Antiqua**, the forum's most important Christian building: it was converted from an earlier pagan monument in the sixth century.

Beyond the Temple of Castor and Pollux are the **Tempio di Vesta** and **Atrium Vestae**, respectively the Temple and House of the Vestal Virgins. It was in the temple that the Vestal Virgins tended Rome's sacred flame, a symbol of the city's continuity.

Beyond the Atrium on the left stands part of the **Basilica di Massenzio** (begun AD 306), one of the Forum's most impressive monuments: in its day it would have been still more

The impressive remains of the Forum's market

awe-inspiring, for what remains is only a single aisle of what was once a 328-foot nave. Remarkably, only one of what originally must have been dozens of columns from the basilica still survives, and now it stands in front of the church of Santa Maria Maggiore (► 118–119).

The Forum's last major monument before the Colosseum is the **Arco di Tito**, Rome's oldest triumphal arch, built in AD 81 by Emperor Domitian to honor Titus (Tito), his brother and predecessor as emperor. Titus' most famous victory was over the Jews in AD 70, and the arch's beautiful reliefs depict a series of scenes of the emperor's triumphal return to Rome with spoils from the campaign.

TAKING A BREAK

There are no places for refreshments inside the Forum: the nearest cafés are to be found on Via Cavour. For a light snack, try **Cavour 313** (► 72), an informal wine bar on the left (north) side of the street just a couple of minutes' walk from the Forum's entrance.

➕ 205 E4 ✉ Main entrance at Largo Romolo e Remo 5/6 near the intersection of Via Cavour and Via dei Fori Imperiali ☎ 06 699 0110 ⓒ Forum and Palatino: Mon.–Sat. 9–1 hour before sunset, Sun. 9–8; occasional later opening Ⓡ Colosseo 🚌 75, 85, 117, 175, 186, 810, 850 to Via dei Fori Imperiali 🎫 Forum: free. Palatino: expensive. Combined pass available (► 190)

ROMAN FORUM: INSIDE INFO

Top tips Before exploring the Roman Forum, **enjoy an overview of the site** from the steps and terraces on the rear eastern side of the Campidoglio, accessed from Piazza del Campidoglio. Steps from the balconies lead down to Via dei Fori Imperiali and the site entrance.

• Avoid visiting the Forum in the heat of the afternoon – there is little shade on the site and sightseeing can be uncomfortable.

• If you only have **limited time** to spend exploring the Forum, the most significant among the ruins (and sites definitely not to be missed) are the Curia, Arco di Settimio Severo, Tempio di Vesta and Basilica di Massenzio.

Colosseum

Little else in Rome is likely to compare with your first sight of the Colosseum (Colosseo), once the scene of gladiatorial combat and other entertainment and now the city's most majestic and awe-inspiring ancient monument.

First Impressions

To grasp the Colosseum's scale you need to admire it from afar. The best place for an overview is the Colle Oppio, a park to the northeast of the monument, or the belvedere (Largo Agnes) immediately above the Colosseo Metro station exit (best reached from Via Cavour via Via del Colosseo or up the steps just to the right of the Metro as you face the station exit). The more usual viewpoint – the open ground to the amphitheater's west, alongside the flank of the Roman Forum – is less satisfactory. The entrance to the monument's upper levels is close by, and from here you can walk around a part of the exterior well away from the roaring traffic that blights the Colosseum's surroundings: you can also admire the Arco di Costantino from the same point (▶ panel, page 58).

The Colosseum is the largest surviving monument from Roman antiquity

Gladiatorial combats in the Colosseum involved men, women and animals

Early Days

The Colosseum was begun around AD 70 by Emperor Vespasian. Its inspiration was the Teatro di Marcello and its site one that had previously been used for an artificial lake annexed to Nero's palatial Domus Aurea, or Golden House (➤ 69). The area's marshy conditions proved problematic, and required the laying of enormous drains – many of which still survive – and the creation of immense foundations. The costs of building the monument were met by the spoils of war, in this case the Romans' triumph over the Jews in AD 70, which realized more than 50 tons of gold and silver from the temple of Jerusalem alone. Jewish slaves captured in the campaign provided the labor force.

By the time of Vespasian's death in AD 79, the monument had been completed to its third tier. Additions were made by Vespasian's son, Titus, who inaugurated the Colosseum in AD 80 with celebrations that saw the slaughter of 5,000 animals and 100 days of festivities.

The completed structure was an architectural triumph. Its simple design has provided a model for stadiums to this day, with tiered seating and 80 exits, or *vomitoria*, that allowed huge crowds – estimates of the Colosseum's capacity range from 50,000 to 73,000 people – to leave the stadium in minutes. Above the seating, a vast sailcloth roof, or *velarium*, could be pulled into place by sailors of the Imperial fleets to shade spectators from the elements. It was supported by 240 wooden masts, the supports and sockets for which you can still see in a ring below the structure's uppermost cornice.

The wooden floor that once covered the stage area was destroyed by fire, and today the Colosseum's complex substructure is clearly visible

Inside the Colosseum

Inside, the monument is perhaps less spectacular, if only because much of the original seating and flooring

Arco di Costantino

In any other context, the Arch of Constantine (AD 315) would be a major monument. Being overshadowed by the Colosseum, it is often ignored in favor of its neighbor. A triumphal arch like the Arco di Tito and Arco di Settimio Severo in the Roman Forum (▶ 55 and 54), it was raised to commemorate the triumph of Emperor Constantine over Maxentius, his imperial rival, at the Battle of Milvian Bridge (AD 312) just north of Rome. It is the city's largest and best-preserved arch, and one of the last major monuments built in ancient Rome.

Most of its materials were pilfered from other buildings. These included many of the sculptural reliefs, notably the eight reliefs framing the inscription, which portray scenes of an emperor at war or engaged in civic duties. They were probably removed from a monument raised to celebrate victories by Marcus Aurelius in AD 176. Wherever the face of Aurelius appeared, masons simply recarved the reliefs to portray Constantine.

The same happened in the arch's central passage, where the two main reliefs show scenes carved during the reigns of Domitian or Trajan. With a little judicious recarving and relabelling (*Fundator quietis* – "founder of calm"), the panels were altered to show Constantine riding into battle against the barbarians (on the monument's west side) and being crowned by the figure of Victory.

has disappeared. A major fire in AD 217 devastated the upper levels and wooden arena (from the *arena*, or sand, used to cover the stage area). Other fires and earthquakes over the next 400 years further damaged the structure. By the sixth century the arena was being used as workshops and a cemetery; by 1320 the entire south side of the monument had collapsed. This and other parts of the building were then ransacked for building stone, most of which found its way into churches, roads, wharves and palaces such as the Palazzo Venezia, Palazzo Farnese and Palazzo Barberini. The

desecration ceased in 1744, when Pope Benedict XIV consecrated the site in memory of the Christians who had supposedly been martyred there.

Contrary to popular myth, however, few if any Christians were killed in the Colosseum, whose primary function was to stage gladiatorial and other games. Today, you can look down on the maze of tunnels and shafts that lay under the stage, the means by which the games' animals, gladiators and other protagonists were brought to the stage from distant pens. Clever plumbing, it's said, also meant the stage area could be flooded to stage mock sea battles.

Spectators were rigidly segregated by status and sex, and they were expected to dress specially for the occasion. The emperor and Vestal Virgins faced each other at the lowest levels in special boxes. Alongside them, on wide platforms, sat the senators, all of whom were expected to dress in white togas and bring their own chairs (*bisellia*). Above them sat the knights and aristocrats, then came the ordinary Roman citizens (*plebeians*) and finally – more than 130 feet up and 144 feet from the stage – the women, slaves and poor (though few women, by all accounts, ventured to the games). Some groups had separate sections, notably soldiers, scribes and heralds, and some were banned altogether, namely gravediggers, actors and retired gladiators. A special official, or *designator*, kept everyone in their rightful place.

Emperors and spectators often had control over a protagonist's destiny. A wounded man could appeal for mercy by

Above left: A bas-relief from the Arco di Costantino

Left: Stone from the Colosseum was plundered to build many of Rome's churches and palaces

raising a finger on his left hand. The wave of a handkerchief would then indicate a reprieve; the sinister and still-familiar downturned thumb meant death. The wounded were often dispatched in any case, regardless of the crowd's verdict, and those who tried to escape by feigning death, would be poked with red-hot irons to discover whether they were still alive.

TAKING A BREAK

Avoid the expensive and touristy cafés and bars in the monument's immediate vicinity. Alternatives are available in **Via Cavour** or the streets off **Via di San Giovanni in Laterano** to the east. For a snack lunch try **Cavour 313** wine bar (➤ 72) or, if you want a more substantial meal, **Nerone** (➤ 73).

🔁 205 F4 ✉ Piazza del Colosseo, Via dei Fori Imperiali ☎ 06 700 4261
🕐 Interior: Mon.–Sat. 9–7 (last ticket 6 p.m.), Sun. and holidays 9–8 (last ticket 7 p.m.), Apr.–Sep.; daily 9–5 (last ticket 4:30), Oct.–Mar. 🚇 Colosseo
🚌 30B, 75, 85, 87, 117, 175, 186 🎟 Moderate. Combined pass ➤ 190

The floodlit Colosseum is one of Rome's unmissable sights

COLOSSEUM: INSIDE INFO

Top tips Return to the Colosseum after nightfall, to see the monument when it is spectacularly floodlit.

• Be sure to climb to the monument's **upper tiers** for a proper idea of the structure's size and to appreciate the complexity of the tunnels and corridors below the stage area.

• If the intense noise and bustle of the crowds and traffic around the Colosseum wear you down, it's just a couple of minutes' walk to the relative peace and quiet of the Colle Oppio park (➤ 71).

In more detail Before delving inside, spend time looking at some of the exterior's easily missed details, notably the half-columns framing every arch, which are Doric at ground level, Ionic on the second tier and Corinthian on the third; the arrangement was a direct copy of the Teatro di Marcello. Also note the many holes pockmarking the building, most of which originally held the 330 tons of iron clamps that helped bind the blocks of stone.

San Clemente

Little in San Clemente's deceptively plain exterior suggests you are looking at one of Rome's most remarkable churches. Not only is the building home to the city's loveliest medieval interior – complete with some sublime frescoes and mosaics – but it also contains two earlier places of worship that span 2,000 years of religious observance.

San Clemente divides into three components, stacked one on top of the other: a 12th-century church above a fourth- or fifth-century church which sits on a late second-century Mithraic temple. The church alone would be worth a special visit, but the two lower structures make the complex unmissable. Note that you enter the main church via a side door on Via di San Giovanni in Laterano. You should allow around 40 minutes here, more if you are interested in the temple and excavations on the lowest level.

The main body of the church at ground level was built between 1108 and 1184 to replace the church that now lies beneath it, which was destroyed by Norman raiders in 1084. Inside, it retains Rome's finest medieval interior. Most of the city's churches were modified in the baroque age – only Santa Maria in Cosmedin (▶ 176) rivals San Clemente.

The highlights are many. Among the paintings, pride of place goes to a Renaissance **fresco cycle** on the *Life of St. Catherine* (1428), one of only a handful of works by the influential Florentine artist Masolino da Panicale (it's in the rear left aisle chapel, to your right as you enter).

Medieval mosaics and frescoes adorn the apse of San Clemente

Among the **mosaics**, the star turn is the 12th-century *Triumph of the Cross*, which forms a majestic swathe of color across the apse. Scholars think its design was based on that of a similar mosaic that was lost when the earlier church was destroyed in the 11th century. The work is full of detail and incident: note in particular the 12 doves on the cross, symbols of the Apostles, and the four rivers of paradise that spring from the cross, their waters quenching the thirst of the faithful, represented here by stags. The imposing 14th-century tabernacle below and to the right is by the Florentine sculptor Arnolfo di Cambio.

More noticeable than either the frescoes or the mosaics, however, is the **choir screen** (fifth–ninth century), whose marble-panelled walls dominate the nave. Such screens were a typical feature of early medieval churches but are now rare. Many of the panels were salvaged from the earlier church, while various of the columns originally hailed from the Foro Traiano (Trajan's Forum) in the Fori Imperiali (➤ 67–68). Equally beautiful and almost as venerable are the pulpit, candleholder and altar canopy, or *baldacchino*.

Steps accessed from the rear right-hand (south) side of the church take you down to what remains of the earlier church, the existence of which was only discovered in 1857. The remains here are relatively scant, although traces of very early frescoes survive, some dating back to the fifth century.

Far more is to be gained by dropping down yet another level, where you encounter the remains of two Roman-era buildings, parts of which are still only partially excavated. Almost the first thing you encounter is the cast of a **Mithraic altar**. Mithraism was a popular Roman cult that survived into

Left: A 15th-century fresco by Masolino da Panicale

The *Triumph of the Cross* above the high altar dates to the 12th century. The 12 doves symbolize the Apostles

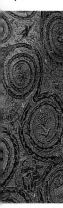

the Christian era. The bull was one of Mithraism's main symbols, hence the beast portrayed on the altar being killed by the god Mithras, along with the figures of torch-bearers and a snake, a symbol of regeneration. The cult was finally suppressed in AD 392.

This subterranean area of the church also includes part of a **Roman house** in which a *mithraem*, or place of worship, had been installed in the central room, probably towards the end of the second century. Such temples were meant to replicate Mithras' cave, so doors would have been blocked or narrowed to a slit to allow sunlight to strike the cult's icons and images. Benches were installed to enable the initiates to take meals and worship communally.

The house itself has been proved to be older, archeologists having discovered date-stamps corresponding to the reign of Domitian (AD 90–96) on the steps of the ancient staircase. In their day, these steps led from the ground-floor level of the house into its basement. Excavations suggest that the temple was walled up close to the year of Mithraism's fourth-century suppression, but that the basement continued to be used for a further six centuries.

The layout of the second structure here corresponds in part to that of a *horrea*, or warehouse, and may well have been a grain store, although some early theories suggest it may have been the site of workshops belonging to the imperial mint, the *Moneta Caesaris*. Newer theories suggest the site contains two buildings, one a commercial premises, the other a house built over these premises that belonged to a wealthy Roman Christian. This Christian, so the theory goes, went by the name of Clemente, and founded a church on the site dedicated to his saintly namesake.

TAKING A BREAK

There are many small bars on Via di San Giovanni in Laterano where you can stop for a cup of coffee, a cool drink or a quick bite to eat.

🚼 206 A4 ✉ Via di San Giovanni in Laterano ☎ 06 7045 1018
🕐 Church: daily 9–12:30, 3–6; closed during services. Temple: Mon.–Sat. 9–12:30, 3–6, Sun. 10–12:30, 3–6 🚇 Colosseo 🚌 75, 85, 87, 117, 175, 186 to Piazza del Colosseo or 85, 117, 850 to Via di San Giovanni in Laterano 🎫 Church: free. Temple and excavations: inexpensive

SAN CLEMENTE: INSIDE INFO

Top tip Remember that San Clemente is closed at lunchtime until mid-afternoon and access to the church is not permitted during services.

In more detail If the main door of the upper church is open, try to look outside at the *quadroporticus*, the distinctive square colonnaded courtyard that fronts the main facade. Such courtyards were once common features of early Roman basilica churches – rectangular churches with simple naves and no transepts – but are now rare.

San Giovanni in Laterano

San Giovanni in Laterano, not St. Peter's, is the cathedral church of Rome; St. Peter's lies in the Vatican, a separate sovereign state. Even without its exalted status, however, this great church would be worth visiting, both for its soaring facade and the beauty of its interior, cloister and baptistery.

San Giovanni in Laterano has venerable origins. It was in a Roman palace on the site that Constantine, the first Christian emperor, met Pope Miltiades in 313, and here that Constantine raised the city's first officially sanctioned church (over what had been the barracks of his personal guard). From earliest times it housed the *cathedra*, or throne, of the Bishop of Rome. The church's importance continued for centuries – for example, popes were crowned here until the 19th century. During this time, the original church was destroyed by the Vandals, and subsequent churches on the site were repeatedly replaced or restored following fires and earthquakes.

In the portico at the foot of the immense **facade** (built in 1735) stands an ancient statue of Constantine, while to its right are the church's main bronze **doors**, which were brought from the Curia, or Senate House, in the Roman Forum (▶ 50–55). The church's restrained **interior** (1646–50) is largely the work of the baroque architect Borromini, who thoughtfully retained the nave's earlier gold-hued and beautifully ornate **ceiling**. The ceiling aside, the interior contains relatively little in the way of great art, but you shouldn't miss the

---

SAN GIOVANNI IN LATERANO: INSIDE INFO

Top tips While visiting San Giovanni you might wish to visit the **flea market** (open Mon.–Sat., 10–1) held along nearby Via Sannio, a right turn just through Porta San Giovanni.

• If you balk at the long walk back to the city center from San Giovanni, consider taking the Metro from nearby Giovanni Metro station (just beyond Porta San Giovanni).

In more depth Stand with your back to San Giovanni's facade. The building ahead of you and a little to the left contains the **Scala Santa**, or Holy Staircase, 28 wood-covered marble steps reputedly removed from Pontius Pilate's palace in Jerusalem. Constantine's mother is said to have brought them to Rome. Since then, as the steps Christ ascended during His trial, they have been an object of veneration for the pilgrims who climb them on their knees.

Left: A 15th-century fresco by Masolino da Panicale

the Christian era. The bull was one of Mithraism's main symbols, hence the beast portrayed on the altar being killed by the god Mithras, along with the figures of torch-bearers and a snake, a symbol of regeneration. The cult was finally suppressed in AD 392.

This subterranean area of the church also includes part of a **Roman house** in which a *mithraem*, or place of worship, had been installed in the central room, probably towards the end of the second century. Such temples were meant to replicate Mithras' cave, so doors would have been blocked or narrowed to a slit to allow sunlight to strike the cult's icons and images. Benches were installed to enable the initiates to take meals and worship communally.

The *Triumph of the Cross* above the high altar dates to the 12th century. The 12 doves symbolize the Apostles

The house itself has been proved to be older, archeologists having discovered date-stamps corresponding to the reign of Domitian (AD 90–96) on the steps of the ancient staircase. In their day, these steps led from the ground-floor level of the house into its basement. Excavations suggest that the temple was walled up close to the year of Mithraism's fourth-century suppression, but that the basement continued to be used for a further six centuries.

The layout of the second structure here corresponds in part to that of a *horrea*, or warehouse, and may well have been a grain store, although some early theories suggest it may have been the site of workshops belonging to the imperial mint, the *Moneta Caesaris*. Newer theories suggest the site contains two buildings, one a commercial premises, the other a house built over these premises that belonged to a wealthy Roman Christian. This Christian, so the theory goes, went by the name of Clemente, and founded a church on the site dedicated to his saintly namesake.

TAKING A BREAK

There are many small bars on Via di San Giovanni in Laterano where you can stop for a cup of coffee, a cool drink or a quick bite to eat.

➕ 206 A4 ✉ Via di San Giovanni in Laterano ☎ 06 7045 1018
🕐 Church: daily 9–12:30, 3–6; closed during services. Temple: Mon.–Sat. 9–12:30, 3–6, Sun. 10–12:30, 3–6 🚇 Colosseo 🚌 75, 85, 87, 117, 175, 186 to Piazza del Colosseo or 85, 117, 850 to Via di San Giovanni in Laterano 💶 Church: free. Temple and excavations: inexpensive

---

SAN CLEMENTE: INSIDE INFO

Top tip Remember that San Clemente is closed at lunchtime until mid-afternoon and access to the church is not permitted during services.

In more detail If the main door of the upper church is open, try to look outside at the *quadroporticus*, the distinctive square colonnaded courtyard that fronts the main facade. Such courtyards were once common features of early Roman basilica churches – rectangular churches with simple naves and no transepts – but are now rare.

San Giovanni in Laterano

San Giovanni in Laterano, not St. Peter's, is the cathedral church of Rome; St. Peter's lies in the Vatican, a separate sovereign state. Even without its exalted status, however, this great church would be worth visiting, both for its soaring facade and the beauty of its interior, cloister and baptistery.

San Giovanni in Laterano has venerable origins. It was in a Roman palace on the site that Constantine, the first Christian emperor, met Pope Miltiades in 313, and here that Constantine raised the city's first officially sanctioned church (over what had been the barracks of his personal guard). From earliest times it housed the *cathedra*, or throne, of the Bishop of Rome. The church's importance continued for centuries – for example, popes were crowned here until the 19th century. During this time, the original church was destroyed by the Vandals, and subsequent churches on the site were repeatedly replaced or restored following fires and earthquakes.

In the portico at the foot of the immense **facade** (built in 1735) stands an ancient statue of Constantine, while to its right are the church's main bronze **doors**, which were brought from the Curia, or Senate House, in the Roman Forum (➤ 50–55). The church's restrained **interior** (1646–50) is largely the work of the baroque architect Borromini, who thoughtfully retained the nave's earlier gold-hued and beautifully ornate **ceiling**. The ceiling aside, the interior contains relatively little in the way of great art, but you shouldn't miss the

SAN GIOVANNI IN LATERANO: INSIDE INFO

Top tips While visiting San Giovanni you might wish to visit the **flea market** (open Mon.–Sat., 10–1) held along nearby Via Sannio, a right turn just through Porta San Giovanni.
• If you balk at the long walk back to the city center from San Giovanni, consider taking the Metro from nearby Giovanni Metro station (just beyond Porta San Giovanni).

In more depth Stand with your back to San Giovanni's facade. The building ahead of you and a little to the left contains the **Scala Santa**, or Holy Staircase, 28 wood-covered marble steps reputedly removed from Pontius Pilate's palace in Jerusalem. Constantine's mother is said to have brought them to Rome. Since then, as the steps Christ ascended during His trial, they have been an object of veneration for the pilgrims who climb them on their knees.

Right: Baroque architect Francesco Borromini remodeled much of San Giovanni's sumptuous interior

papal altar and canopy (begun in 1367) at the main crossing, where, until recently, only a pope could officiate. It reputedly holds the skulls of saints Peter and Paul and part of a wooden table said to have been used by St. Peter.

San Giovanni's real glory is its **cloister** (1215–32), entered off the church's left (north) side, a tranquil corner with dozens of variously shaped columns, many adorned with exquisite Cosmati work (an inlay of colored stones and marbles).

Outside the church to its rear – you need to exit the building and bear left – is Constantine's San Giovanni in Fonte, or **Baptistery of St. John**, a building whose octagonal plan provided the blueprint for baptisteries across Italy for centuries to come. Some of the building has been altered over the years, but significant older parts survive, notably the fifth-century mosaic in the north apse and the Chapel of St. John (461–68), which preserves its original doors.

Above: Numerous statues adorn San Giovanni's soaring facade, a prominent feature of Rome's skyline

---

✚ 206 C3 ✉ Piazza di San Giovanni in Laterano ☎ 06 6988 6433
🕐 Church: daily 7–7, Apr.–Sep.; 7–5:45, Oct.–Mar. Cloister: daily 9–5.
Baptistery: daily 8–12:30, 5–7, Apr.–Sep.; 9–1, 4–6:30; Oct.–Mar. Scala Santa:
daily 6:30–noon, 3–6:30 🍴 Cafés in Via di San Giovanni in Laterano 🚇 San
Giovanni 🚌 4, 16, 30B, 85, 87, 186, 810, 850, 360 🎟 Church, Scala Santa,
Baptistery: free. Cloister: inexpensive

The cloister provides a small oasis of tranquillity

At Your Leisure

❶ Piazza Venezia

Piazza Venezia is the key to central Rome, a huge traffic-filled square from which some of the city's major streets strike off to the four points of the compass. But while you will probably pass through the piazza many times, it is not a place with many important things to see – save for the huge white edifice on its southern flank, the **Monumento a Vittorio Emanuele II** occupying much of the Capitoline Hill. This marble monolith, built between 1885 and 1911, commemorates the unification of Italy and the country's first king, Vittorio Emanuele. It is also called the Altare della Patria, or Altar of the Nation – the tomb of Italy's Unknown Soldier is here – but Romans know it more colloquially as the "typewriter" or "wedding cake" after its huge marble tiers.

On the square's west side stands the **Palazzo Venezia** (1451), which for 200 years between 1594 and 1797 was the property of the Venetian Republic – hence its name and the name of the square. The *palazzo* is known for the balcony from which Mussolini once harangued crowds in the square below – the dictator kept an office in the building – and for the underrated **Museo di Palazzo Venezia**, used for temporary exhibitions and noted for its permanent collection of medieval paintings, textiles, ceramics, jewelry and other decorative arts. If it's open, you should also look into **San Marco**, a church best known for its beautiful gilt ceiling and magnificent ninth-century apse mosaic.

Museo di Palazzo Venezia
🕂 199 E1 ✉ Via del Plebiscito 118
☎ 06 699 94319 or 06 699 94318
🕐 Tue.–Sun. 9–2 (hours vary for temporary exhibitions) 🍴 Cafés in Via delle Botteghe Oscure 🚇 Cavour
🚌 All services to Piazza Venezia
🎟 Moderate

❸ Musei Capitolini

On the left (north) side of Piazza del Campidoglio stands the **Palazzo Nuovo**, whose inner courtyard contains the colossal Roman statue of a river god, Marforio, a favorite with

Fragments of a massive statue of the Emperor Constantine II in the courtyard of the Palazzo dei Conservatori

photographers. Inside the portico is a celebrated **equestrian statue** of Marcus Aurelius (AD 161–80); it originally stood in the piazza outside, but was brought inside after restoration for safekeeping (the statue outside is a copy). It is the only such statue to survive from this period, and throughout the Middle Ages was repeatedly referred to by artists and

4 Fori Imperiali

The Fori Imperiali, or Imperial Forums, are five forums built when lack of space in the Roman Forum forced emperors from Julius Caesar onward to look elsewhere for their

writers.

Other rooms in the gallery contain a wealth of antique sculpture, the highlights of which are statues of the *Dying Galatian* and the *Capitoline Venus*, both Roman copies of Greek originals.

Across the piazza, the **Palazzo dei Conservatori** houses the rest of the museums' collections – which were begun in 1471 by Pope Sixtus IV – mainly further outstanding pieces of sculpture. Highlights include the Spinario (a first-century BC bronze of a boy) and the famous statue of the She-Wolf, probably an Etruscan bronze dating from the fifth or sixth century BC. The palace also contains a Pinacoteca, or picture gallery, with important Renaissance and other paintings, among them works by Caravaggio, Veronese, Tintoretto, Rubens, Van Dyck and Bellini.

🔁 199 F2 ✉ Piazza del Campidoglio 1 ☎ 06 3974 6221 🕐 Tue.–Sun. 10–9 🍴 Cafés in Via di Teatro del Marcello 🚇 Colosseo 🚌 44, 46, 64, 70, 81, 95, 87 and all other services to Piazza Venezia 💷 Expensive, but free on the last Sun. of the month

grandiose architectural schemes. Much of their area was lost when Mussolini forced the huge Via dei Fori Imperiali road through their heart in the 1930s. Guided tours of the site led by an archeologist are now available, though you can also easily admire the forums while walking down Via dei Fori Imperiali.

Walking away from Piazza Venezia on this street, the first forum you come to on the left is the **Foro Traiano**, or Trajan's Forum (AD 104–13). This is the most impressive of the five, and contains their single greatest monument, the Colonna Traiano (➤ 68). In its day, this forum was so vast and splendid it was considered one of the world's architectural wonders. Today, it's a sunken space of shattered columns and crumbling walls: only the forum's

Little remains visible today of the once vast Foro Traiano

Roman-era markets, the **Mercati Traianei**, entered some distance away on Via IV Novembre, preserve anything of their original grandeur.

Alongside Trajan's Forum to the right is the **Foro di Augusto**, or Augustus' forum (begun in 42 BC), part of an immense rebuilding project initiated by Augustus that would lead to his famous boast that "I found Rome brick and left it marble." The most striking ruins here are the distinct remains of the Temple of Mars Ultor. Across the road lie the **Foro di Cesare**, or Caesar's Forum, the first of the Imperiali Fora, built by Julius Caesar between 54 and 46 BC. Only small

areas of the site have been excavated, much of which lies beneath Via dei Fori Imperiali. There is even less to see of the remaining forums: the **Foro di Nerva** (AD 96–98), whose best surviving relic is a frieze on the colonnade at the corner of Via Cavour and Via dei Fori Imperiali, and the **Foro di Vespasiano** (AD 71–75), also known as the Foro della Pace, whose former library contains the present-day church of Santi Cosma e Damiano.

Mercati Traianei
➕ 205 E5   **✉** Via IV Novembre 94   **☎** 06 679 0048   **🕐** Tue.–Sun. 9–6, Apr.–Sep.; Tue.–Sun. 9–4:30, Oct.–Mar.   **🚇** Cavour or Colosseo   **🚌** 64, 70, 170   **💰** Moderate

5 Colonna Traiano

Trajan's Column rises as a lonely, majestic sentinel from the ruins of Trajan's Forum. Built in AD 113, it was raised to mark two victorious military campaigns over the Dacians, a tribe that lived in what is now Romania. Like triumphal arches, such columns were typical of Roman victory monuments, and also like triumphal arches invariably contained friezes and reliefs recording details of a campaign's battles and events. Here, the reliefs run in a remarkable spiral – more than 200 yards of exquisitely carved marble containing a continuous 155-scene sequence with more than 2,600 figures portrayed two-thirds actual life size. The importance of the column is in the intense detail of these scenes, detail which has allowed scholars to learn much about the mechanics of the Roman military machine.

One reason for the survival of the column is that it formed the bell-tower of a Christian church, San Nicola de Columna. When this was demolished in the ninth century the column became the first archeological monument to be designated for protection by Rome's papal rulers. The structure is composed of 29 vast drums of marble – eight for the base, nineteen for the column and two for the summit pedestal. Inside, the drums contain a spiral staircase carved from the solid stone, a miracle of Roman engineering, but a miracle withheld from public view, for the column can only be admired from the outside. The figure crowning the summit is St. Peter, added in 1588, replacing a bronze statue of Trajan, whose ashes once resided in a golden urn at the column's base.

➕ 205 D5   **✉** Via dei Fori Imperiali   **🚇** Cavour   **🚌** 64, 70, 170

St. Peter's Chains

San Pietro in Vincoli was built in 432, reputedly on the site where St. Peter was condemned to death during the persecutions of Nero. The church takes its name from the highly venerated chains (*vincoli*) that you see in a casket under the main altar. There are actually two sets of chains: one is believed to have been used to bind Peter in Jerusalem, the other thought to have been used to shackle him in Rome's Mamertine prison. When the two were eventually united they miraculously fused together.

8 San Pietro in Vincoli

It takes only a couple of minutes to walk to this church from the Colosseum, and only a little longer to see its main attraction – an imposing **statue of Moses** (1503–13), one of Michelangelo's sculptural master-pieces. The statue was conceived as part of a 42-figure ensemble designed to adorn the tomb of Pope Julius II, one of Michelangelo's principal patrons. In the event the project was never realized, although it would torment Michelangelo for much of his life – he referred to it as this "tragedy of a tomb." Instead he was distracted by other works such as the Sistine Chapel – another Julius commission – and then after Julius' death deprived of funds by popes who saw little glory in funding their predecessor's obsession.

The statue of Moses hints at what might have been, a monumental figure captured at the moment he receives the tablet of the Ten Commandments (shown here under his right arm). Michelangelo left a famous signature in the statue's beard – his profile – and gave Moses a wonderfully equivocal expression as he watches the Israelites dance around the golden calf, his look of divine illumination at receiving the tablets mixed with fury at his people's faithlessness and idolatry. Note, too, the figure's horns, which

represent beams of light, features ascribed to Moses in the iconography of many medieval paintings and sculptures. The main flanking statues are also by Michelangelo and repre-sent Rachel and Leah, symbols of the active and contemplative life. The other figures, which are noticeably less successful, are the work of Michelangelo's pupils.

🔢 205 F5 ✉ Piazza di San Pietro in Vincoli 4a ☎ 06 488 2865 ⏰ Daily 7–12:30, 3:30–7 🍴 Nerone (➤ 73) Ⓜ Colosseo or Cavour 🚌 75 to Via Cavour or 75, 85, 87, 117, 175 or 186 to Piazza del Colosseo 🎟 Free

Michelangelo's masterpiece in San Pietro in Vincoli depicts Moses receiving the Ten Commandments

9 Domus Aurea

The Domus Aurea, or Golden House, was built as a colossal pleasure dome by Nero after the fire in AD 64 during

Beneath the Colle Oppio, a peaceful park in the center of Rome, lies the Domus Aurea

which the emperor famously "fiddled while Rome burned." It centered on the present-day site of the Colle Oppio, but extended across a quarter of the ancient city, embracing much of the Esquiline, Palatine and Coelian hills. Parts of the much-reduced complex (now underground) are open, having been closed to the public for many years. To visit, you must join a guided tour and reservations are essential.

The house's scale and splendor must have been almost beyond imagining. Most surfaces were covered in gold leaf, hence its name. Ceilings were carved with ivory and held concealed vents that sprayed a fine mist of scent or flower petals into the rooms below. The approach was just over a mile long and flanked by triple colonnades, while the gardens featured an artificial lake overshadowed by a 115-foot statue of Nero – the largest statue ever made in antiquity, larger even than the now lost Colossus of Rhodes.

Enthusiasm for the palace died with Nero in AD 68. Pressure of space then meant that much of the building was sacrificed in favor of projects such as the Colosseum and a huge bath complex – Rome's first – built by Trajan in 104. So much was lost, in fact, that it was only in 1490 that excavations first brought a portion of its remains to light. Among other things, the discovery revealed magnificent frescoes that greatly influenced Renaissance artists such as Raphael, whose Stanze in the Vatican borrowed heavily from the wall paintings (➤ 150–151). Another magnificent work of art found in the area was the *Laocoön*, one of the greatest of all ancient statues (➤ 148).

Today, visitors can see ancient wall paintings, together with many of the brick-vaulted chambers, rooms and passageways, most of which would once have been faced with marble.

Off the Beaten Track

The little-known park of **Villa Celimontana** south of the Colosseum (entered from Via della Navicella) is a good place to escape from the rigors of sightseeing. The area around the park is also relatively quiet and unexplored, with interesting churches such as Santa Maria in Domnica and Santo Stefano Rotondo (➤ 16–17), and little lanes such as Viale del Parco and Clivo di Scauro which lead to Santi Giovanni e Paolo.

original Seven Hills. It takes its name from one of the hill's two summits, the *Cispius* and *Oppius*. Although just across the street from the Colosseum, it is little used by visitors, but not by locals, who make

Much of the surroundings, including Trajan's baths, have never been excavated, offering the tantalizing prospect that many more masterpieces still lie concealed.

✚ 206 A4 ✉ entrance to Colle Oppio, Via Labicana 136 ☎ Advance ticket sales 06 481 5576. Reservations 06 3974 9907 🕐 Daily 9–8 🚇 Colosseo 🚌 30B to Via Labicana or services to Piazza del Colosseo (➤ 60) 💷 Expensive

🔟 Colle Oppio

The Colle Oppio is central Rome's most convenient park, a pretty area of grass, walkways, trees and archeological remains spread over the slopes of the Esquiline Hill, one of Rome's

full use of its café and quiet corners, particularly on Sundays. The park's loveliest area of grass, only faintly shaded by slender palms, is the section right by the entrance across from the Colosseum.

The park makes a pleasant way of reaching Santa Maria Maggiore (➤ 118–119) or the Palazzo Massimo alle Terme (➤ 120–123) avoiding the busy Via Cavour and other roads. One important word of warning, though: avoid the park at night.

✚ 206 A4 ✉ Via Labicana 136 🚇 Colosseo

For Kids

The Forum may be a little too ruined for young imaginations to deal with but the scale of the **Colosseum** and its gladiatorial associations (➤ 56–60) should fire youngsters' minds. Children should enjoy also the dank and mysterious Mithraic bowels of **San Clemente** (➤ 61–63), and curiosities such as the huge hands and feet in the courtyard of the **Musei Capitolini** (➤ 66–67) and Bernini's eccentric elephant outside the church of Santa Maria sopra Minerva (➤ 94). The **Colle Oppio** park is a favorite among families – buy kids an ice cream or drink at the park café. On Sundays, street performers can often be found on the nearby Via dei Fori Imperiali.

Where to...
Eat and Drink

Prices

Expect to pay per person for a meal, excluding drinks and service

$ under –€20 $$ €20–€40 $$$ over €40

The area of Rome that embraces the Capitoline Hill, Colosseum and Roman Forum is almost entirely given over to monuments, and the number of restaurants is correspondingly small. Though most are aimed at tourists, there are a handful of good places in the side streets close to the main sights.

Antico Caffè del Brasile $

This traditional bar serves superlative coffee, for the owners roast the blends themselves. Its chief claim to fame is that Pope John Paul II came here to buy his coffee when he was still Cardinal Wojtyla. In days past, huge sacks of coffee sat below vast roasting machines to the rear. E.U. directives meant these had to go, but if some of the Brasile's authentic charm has gone, the quality – and range – of coffees and hot chocolate to buy or drink on the premises is still outstanding. The bar is on a side street off Via Cavour.

➕ 205 F5 ⊠ Via dei Serpenti 23 ☎ 06 488 2319 🕲 Mon.–Sat. 6:45 a.m.–8:30 p.m.; Sun. a.m. Closed 1 week in Aug.

Cavour 313 $

This popular and long-established wine bar is little patronized by non-Romans despite being less than a minute's walk from the entrance to the Roman Forum. First impressions inside are of rather plain and uninspiring wood-dominated decor. But don't be put off: the atmosphere is informal and friendly; the many good hot and cold snacks are well-priced, and there's a wide choice of more than 500 wines (some by the glass) to choose from.

➕ 205 F5 ⊠ Via Cavour 313 ☎ 06 678 5496 🕲 Lunch: daily 12:30– 2:30 p.m., mid-Jun. to Sep.; Mon.–Sat. Oct. to mid-Jun. Dinner: daily 7:30–12:30. Closed Aug.

Charly's Saucière $$

The name doesn't sound Italian, and this is in fact one of Rome's very few French restaurants. An unpromising notion maybe, but this pleasant and discreet little place just south of the church of San Giovanni in Laterano has been doing good business for many years. Swiss dishes, including fondues, also feature among the menu's list of classic and immaculately prepared French staples such as fine meats, soufflés and pâtes. Puddings are often outstanding. French wines, of course, predominate on the wine list. This is a good place for a more formal dinner than nearby Pasqualino (▶ 73).

➕ 206 C3 ⊠ Via di San Giovanni in Laterano 270 ☎ 06 7049 5666 🕲 Lunch: Tue.–Fri. 12:45–3. Dinner: Mon. and Sat. 8–midnight. Closed 2 weeks in Aug.

Leonina $

You can tell you're in the presence of something special by the regular long lines at Leonina. People here are waiting for some of Rome's best pizza al taglio, or pizza by the slice. Prices for what is usually the most inexpensive of snacks are a little higher here than elsewhere, but then so is the quality of the pizza; there's also a far greater and more exotic choice of toppings than usual. Via Leonina runs parallel to Via Cavour just west of the Cavour Metro station: it's a brief walk from San Pietro in Vincoli, a slightly longer one from the Roman Forum.

Nerone $–$$

Nerone, less than a minute's walk from the Colosseum, is the perfect spot for an inexpensive and relaxed trattoria meal. *Antipasti* (starters) here are especially good – a buffet table is laden with Roman and Abruzzese specialties (the owners come from the Abruzzo, the mountainous region east of Rome). The dining area amounts to a couple of plain rooms, and in summer you can sit outside at a few tables on the pavement with a corner of the Colle Oppio park just across the road.

🚇 **206 A5** 🖂 **Via delle Terme di Tito 96 (corner of Viale del Monte Oppio)** ☎ **06 481 7952** 🕒 **Mon.–Sat. noon–3, 7–11**

Pachi $

A Neapolitan pizzeria at the western (Forum) end of Via Cavour, Pachi provides a good lunch or inexpensive dinner option and an alternative to the nearby 313 Cavour (▶ 72). It's a big place, however, and when business is slow the vividly colored interior can seem empty and soulless. This said, the pizzas are a cut above the usual, and there's a good selection of alternative dishes.

🚇 **205 E5** 🖂 **Via Cavour 315** ☎ **06 6920 2164** 🕒 **Tue.–Sun. noon–3:30, 7–midnight**

Pasqualino $–$$

Pasqualino has been around for many years and doesn't seem to have changed its menu, serving staff or simple trattoria approach to cooking and eating in decades. There is frequently a big foreign presence here, including lively groups of trainee priests from the nearby Irish College, but also enough locals and local color to make this a thoroughly Roman experience. A good place to stop for lunch after seeing the Colosseum, just two minutes' walk away, or for an informal dinner.

🚇 **206 A4** 🖂 **Via dei Santi Quattro 66** ☎ **06 700 4576** 🕒 **Lunch and dinner daily. Closed 2 weeks in Aug.**

Tempera $

Don't be tempted into the over-priced cafés or snack bars on Piazza Venezia. Instead, walk just round the corner to this *birreria*, or beer hall. The term is slightly misleading for what is in reality more of a large, pleasant bar and simple restaurant. You could just have a beer here: it's worth a visit simply to admire the original art nouveau interior. Romans pack the place at lunchtime to take advantage of the handful of inexpensive but well-prepared pasta and other dishes (though it is little known to visitors to the city). Service is canteen style, and the seating is at simple wooden tables. The atmosphere is lively but not intimidating.

🚇 **206 A4** 🖂 **Via di San Marcello 19** ☎ **06 679 5310** 🕒 **Lunch: Mon.–Fri. 12:30–2:30. Dinner: Mon.–Fri. 7:30–10:30, Sat. 7:30–midnight. Closed 2 weeks in Aug.**

Trattoria Sora Lella $$

Sora Lella lies on the Isola Tiberina (Tiber Island) between the Capitoline Hill area and the Trastevere district. It is well worth the detour from either location, as the accomplished, authentic Roman cooking is a cut above what you'd expect of somewhere that affects the informal atmosphere of a simple trattoria. Sora Lella was a much-loved actress, and the restaurant was named in her honor by her son, Aldo Trabalza, after her death in 1993. Her portrait occupies pride of place alongside the bar.

🚇 **204 C4** 🖂 **Via di Ponte Quattro Capi 16, Isola Tiberina** ☎ **06 686 1601** 🕒 **Mon.–Sat. 1–2:30, 8–11. Closed Aug.**

Where to... Shop

This is not an area of the city for shoppers to visit with any great expectations, though you may stumble across the occasional artisan's workshop, gallery, antiques shop or specialty store in the side streets off Via Cavour (the best hunting grounds are Via dei Serpenti, Via del Boschetto and Via Madonna dei Monti). One such is **La Bottega del Cioccolato**, a chocolate shop at Via Leonina 82 (tel: 06 482 1473).

Otherwise most of the stores on the streets around Rome's ancient monuments are local food and general stores for those who live around Via Cavour (by the Forum) and in the residential enclave between the Colosseum and San Giovanni in Laterano.

Where to... Be Entertained

Ancient monuments and cultural life generally don't mix in Rome. Outdoor concerts were once held in the Terme di Caracalla (Baths of Caracalla) south of the Colosseum, but for a variety of reasons, most significantly the preservation of the ruins, these have been suspended indefinitely. Similar restrictions mean that no productions are held at the Colosseum, Roman Forum or other sites.

MUSIC AND THEATER

The **Teatro di Marcello** provides a summer venue for classical concerts organized by the **Associazione Il Tempietto** (Via del Teatro di Marcello 44, tel: 06 7720 9128, e-mail: tempietto@alt.it). Between November and July the association's concerts move indoors to the church of **San Nicola in Carcere** almost immediately to the south of the Teatro. Tickets are available from both venues about two hours before each performance.

San Giovanni in Laterano is one of only a handful of churches to maintain a choir and present a sung Mass. The church is also a good place to hear organ music; the superb Luca Blasi organ is usually played during and after the 10 a.m. Sunday Mass. Contact visitor centers or the church for further details. The tiny church of **San Teodoro** in Via San Teodoro on the western flank of the Palatine Hill is also used as a concert venue by the choral association "Agimus," short for the **Associazione Giovanile Musicale** (tel: 06 3600 1824).

Theater and dance productions are held at the **Teatro Colosseo**, east of the Colosseum at Via Capo d'Africa 5a (tel: 06 700 4932).

NIGHTLIFE

The only central club to speak of in this area is **Jam Session** (Via del Cardello 13, tel: 06 6994 2419, Thu–Sun. 11 p.m.–4 a.m.), a small underground dance and live music club on a tiny street off the western (Forum) end of Via Cavour. However, you may also hear jazz and blues played at **ControLocale** in the grid of streets east of the Colosseum at Via SS Quattro Coronati 103 (tel: 06 700 8944). If you've been out late and need a drink or bite to eat, **La Base** at Via Cavour 274 (tel: 06 474 0659) stays open until 5 a.m. every morning.

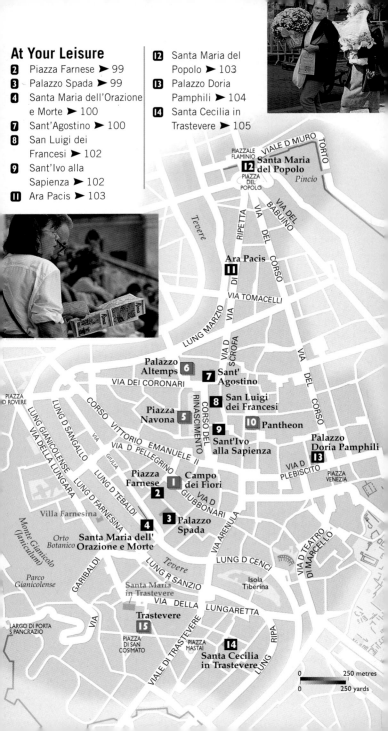

PIAZZALE FLAMINIO

VIALE D MURO TORTO

12 Santa Maria del Popolo

PIAZZA DEL POPOLO

Pincio

VIA DEL BABUINO

RIPETTA

VIA DEL CORSO

VIA DEL

Tevere

11 Ara Pacis

VIA TOMACELLI

LUNG MARZIO

VIA D SCROFA

6 Palazzo Altemps

VIA DEI CORONARI

7 Sant' Agostino

CORSO VITTORIO EMANUELE II

5 Piazza Navona

CORSO DEL RINASCIMENTO

8 San Luigi dei Francesi

10 Pantheon

VIA DEL CORSO

PIAZZA D ROVERE

LUNG GIANICOLENSE

LUNG D SANGALLO

VIA DELLA LUNGARA

CORSO VITTORIO EMANUELE II

GIULIA

VIA D PELLEGRINO

9 Sant'Ivo alla Sapienza

Palazzo Doria Pamphili

VIA D PLEBISCITO

13

LUNG D TEBALDI

1 Piazza Farnese

Campo dei Fiori

2

VIA D GIUBBONARI

PIAZZA VENEZIA

Villa Farnesina

LUNG D FARNESINA

3 Palazzo Spada

VIA ARENULA

VIA D TEATRO DI MARCELLO

Monte Gianicolo (Janiculum)

Orto Botanico

4 Santa Maria dell' Orazione e Morte

Tevere

LUNG R SANZIO

LUNG D CENCI

Isola Tiberina

Parco Gianicolense

GARIBALDI

Santa Maria in Trastevere

VIA DELLA LUNGARETTA

Trastevere

15

PIAZZA DI SAN COSIMATO

VIALE DI TRASTEVERE

PIAZZA MASTAI

14 Santa Cecilia in Trastevere

LUNG

RIPA

LARGO DI PORTA S PANCRAZIO

0   250 metres

0   250 yards

The first day of this two-day itinerary includes many highlights of medieval and Renaissance Rome – as well as one of the city's grandest ancient monuments – and is followed by a quieter day in Trastevere and the old Ghetto district. If you are short of time, you can condense the itinerary into a single day by visiting Piazza Navona, Palazzo Altemps and the Pantheon in the morning, and the Palazzo Doria-Pamphili and Trastevere in the afternoon.

The Heart of Rome in Two Days

Day One

Morning
Breakfast in **Campo dei Fiori** (➤ 80–81), before exploring its wonderfully evocative morning food and flower market (left). Then head off to **Piazza Farnese** (➤ 99), the Via Giulia – one of Rome's most elegant streets – and (perhaps) the small **Palazzo Spada** art gallery (➤ 99–100).

Walk back to **Piazza Navona** (➤ 82–85), a baroque showpiece second only to St. Peter's, meander the side streets off the square – notably Via della Pace – and stop for a coffee in one of its cafés.

Just north and east of Piazza Navona lie the churches of **Sant'Agostino** (➤ 100–101), home to a Raphael fresco, and **San Luigi dei Francesi** (➤ 102), graced with three major paintings by Caravaggio.

Lunch
Try Cul de Sac or Bar della Pace if you only want a snack lunch (➤ 108), La Carbonara (➤ 107) for an inexpensive meal al fresco or La Rosetta for a splurge (➤ 108).

Afternoon
Visit **Palazzo Altemps** (➤ 86–89), one of Rome's most dazzling museums, where some of the greatest classical Roman sculpture is on display. Then make your way to the **Pantheon** (right, ➤ 90–94), the most perfectly preserved of all Rome's ancient monuments.

Spend the rest of the afternoon exploring Via del Corso, one of the city's main shopping streets, and the streets to its west where you will find many interesting little specialty stores. Alternately, visit **Ara Pacis** (➤ 103), a Roman monument covered in marble reliefs, and the art-filled church of **Santa Maria del Popolo** (➤ 103–104).

Day Two

Morning
Allow an hour or so to see the rich collection of paintings at the **Palazzo Doria Pamphili** (➤ 104–105), plus some extra time to join a guided tour of the palace's private apartments.

Walk to Trastevere (above) by way of Santa Maria in Cosmedin and the Ghetto (➤ 176–179). Alternately, take a bus to Trastevere from Via del Plebiscito just off Piazza Venezia.

Lunch
You can take lunch in any number of places on your walk to Trastevere: try Sora Margherita in the Ghetto (➤ 108) or Augusto in Trastevere (➤ 107).

Afternoon
Spend time simply exploring **Trastevere's** pretty streets and squares (right, ➤ 95–98), before making your way to **Santa Maria in Trastevere**, which reopens at 4 p.m.

Trastevere has lots of places to eat, so you may wish to extend the day and stay in the area for dinner without returning to your hotel. Do this either by walking up to the **Gianicolo Hill** above Trastevere for good views of the city, or by visiting the church of **Santa Cecilia in Trastevere** (➤ 105–106).

Campo dei Fiori

Campo dei Fiori, or the "Field of Flowers," is a place you will probably return to more than once during your stay. One of Rome's prettiest piazzas, it is the site of a wonderful outdoor market with picturesque palaces and houses providing the backdrop for a colorful medley of stands selling fruit, flowers and fish.

Take time to wander around these stands and enjoy the street life: the old knife-sharpeners, the redoubtable Roman matriarchs trimming vegetables, the fishmonger bawling his wares, and the local housewives driving a hard bargain with knowing vendors. When you have had your fill of sights, sounds and smells, pick one of the small cafés around the square and watch proceedings over a cappuccino.

In its earliest days the square really was a field of flowers: until the Middle Ages it formed a meadow that fringed the first-century BC Theatre of Pompey. Then it was built over and quickly became a bustling focus of city life. All manner of famous names were associated with the surrounding district: Lucretia Borgia was born locally, her brother Cesare was assassinated nearby, and the artist Caravaggio murdered a rival after losing a tennis match in the square. Lucretia's father, Alessandro, better known as Pope Alexander VI, would also have been familiar with the area, for one of his mistresses, Vanozza Cattenei, ran some of the inns and brothels for which the district became celebrated.

Today, there's relatively little to see here apart from the market and the statue at its heart (▶ Inside Info). However, be

Top: The Campo is a popular place at night

Above: Vendors in Campo dei Fiori, Rome's prettiest market

Right: Market vendors on the Campo swap stories in a quiet moment

Below: Fine foods at fair prices

sure to explore some of the interesting streets nearby, notably Via dei Cappellari, or "Street of the Hatters," a shadowy lane filled with furniture workshops and premises of other artisans. Also walk the short distance to Piazza Farnese to admire the square and its palace (➤ 99), and then continue to Via Giulia, one of Rome's most exclusive residential streets, to look at the church of Santa Maria dell'Orazione e Morte (➤ 179).

TAKING A BREAK

The Campo is full of small cafés and restaurants: one of the nicest is the **Caffè Farnese** (Via dei Baullari 106–107) just off the square on the corner with the grander Piazza Farnese. One of the best places for lunch or dinner is the old-fashioned **Grappolo d'Oro** (➤ 107), a few steps off the square.

✚ 198 C2 ✉ Piazza Campo dei'Fiori 🚌 46, 62, 64 to Corso Vittorio Emanuele II or 44, 56, 60, 65, 75, 170 to Via Arenula

CAMPO DEI FIORI: INSIDE INFO

Top tips The Campo's cafés make a perfect place for breakfast; the market is also at its least crowded early on (it runs daily except Sunday from about 6 a.m. to 2 p.m.).
• As in any busy part of the city, be sure to keep a tight grip on your valuables.
• The Campo is also popular at night: the Vineria wine bar (No. 15) and the American-run Drunken Ship (No. 20–21) in the piazza's western corner are the liveliest bars.

In more detail At the heart of Campo dei Fiori stands a cowled and rather **ominous-looking statue**, easily missed amid the debris of the market. This depicts Giordano Bruno, a 16th-century humanist and scholar who was burned at the stake on this spot in 1600 for the crime of heresy. His secular outlook suits the square, which to this day remains unusual among Roman piazzas in having no church.

Piazza Navona

None of Rome's many squares is as grand or theatrical as Piazza Navona. The magnificent piazza, one of the city's baroque showpieces, is dominated by three fountains, a ring of ocher-colored buildings – many hung with flowers in the summer – and an almost constant throng of visitors, artists and vendors.

Right: Street vendors and artists contribute to the piazza's lively atmosphere

You will probably be tempted back here many times during your visit, although whether your budget will stretch to too many drinks at the piazza's pretty but expensive cafés is another matter. You don't need to spend money, however, simply to enjoy the area, which is an irresistible meeting and people-watching place at most times of the day and night.

The piazza's distinctive elliptical shape betrays its origins, for the square corresponds almost exactly to the outline of the race track and stadium built on the site by Emperor Domitian in AD 86. This was known as the Circus Agonalis, a name which by the Middle Ages had been modified to *in agone* and the dialect *'n 'agone* before arriving at the present "Navona."

Catching up with the news by the Fontana del Nettuno, one of the piazza's trio of fountains

All manner of activities took place here over and above games and races, not least the martyrdom of Sant'Agnese (Saint Agatha), a 13-year-old girl killed in AD 304 for her refusal to renounce her Christian beliefs and marry a pagan. She was thrown into one of the brothels close to the stadium and then paraded naked in the Circus, only for her nakedness to be covered by the miraculous growth of her hair. The simple oratory eventually built on the site of her death was superceded by the present church of **Sant'Agnese in Agone** on the piazza's western edge in the mid-17th century.

One of the architects involved in the church was Borromini, the great but troubled rival of Rome's other baroque superstar, Gian Lorenzo Bernini, who designed the piazza's central fountain, the **Fontana dei Quattro Fiumi** (1648), or Fountain of the Four Rivers. The fountain's four major statues represent the four rivers of Paradise, the Nile, Ganges, Plate and Danube, and the four known corners of the world – Africa, Asia, Europe and America. Note the dove on the top of the obelisk, a symbol of Pope Innocent X Pamphili, who commissioned the work.

Innocent was also responsible for other major changes to the square, notably the creation of the Palazzo Pamphili (left of Sant'Agnese), now the Brazilian Embassy, changes that largely put an end to the horse racing, jousting and bullfights that had taken place in the square for much of the Middle Ages. At times the piazza was also flooded, allowing the city's aristocrats to be pulled around the resultant artificial lake in gilded carriages, an echo of the so-called *naumachia*, the mock seabattles staged by the ancient Romans under similar circumstances.

Bernini's Fontana dei Quattro Fiumi (detail, right) lies at the heart of the piazza

✚ 198 C3 ✉ Piazza Navona Ⓢ Spagna 🚌 70, 81, 87, 90, 186, 492, to
Corso del Rinascimento or 46, 62, 64 to Corso Vittorio Emanuele II

TAKING A BREAK

There is little to choose between most of the piazza's cafés,
though those on its eastern flanks enjoy a little more sun. Two
of the best-known bars are **Ciampini** (No. 94–100) and **I Tre
Scalini** (➤ 108), the latter celebrated for its sensational chocolate chip ice cream (*tartufo*). Don't forget the ever-popular **Bar
della Pace** (➤ 108) nearby.

Piazza Navona
is a popular
place for an
after dinner
stroll

The Fontana del
Nettuno, at the
northern end of
the piazza

PIAZZA NAVONA: INSIDE INFO

Top tips Be warned that drinks at cafés around Piazza Navona are some of the
most expensive in the city. But remember that once you've paid for your drink
you can sit at your table as long as you wish.
• Piazza Navona is busy with sightseers by day, but still busier by night, so **leave
time for an after dinner stroll** past the floodlit fountains and the many artists and
caricaturists who set up shop here.

In more detail An often-told tale relates how Bernini deliberately designed one
of the statues on his central fountain so that it appeared to be shielding its eyes
or recoiling in horror at Sant'Agnese, the church of his great rival, Borromini. It's
a nice story, but in fact the fountain was created before the church.

Hidden gems Most visitors overlook Piazza Navona's two lesser fountains. At
the piazza's northern end stands the **Fontana del Nettuno**, or Fountain of Neptune,
which shows the marine god grappling with a sea serpent. At the southern end is
Giacomo della Porta's **Fontana del Moro** (1575), or Fountain of the Moor, whose
central figure – despite the fountain's name – is actually another marine god: the
erroneous name probably comes from the name of the sculptor, Antonio Mori,
who added the dolphin from a design by Bernini.

Palazzo Altemps

The Palazzo Altemps and its sister gallery, the Palazzo Massimo alle Terme (➤ 120), form the magnificent setting for the cream of Rome's state-owned antiquities. The Roman sculptures here are some of the city's finest, and are superbly displayed in a beautifully restored Renaissance palace.

The Palazzo Altemps was begun around 1477, but took its name from Cardinal Marco Sittico Altemps, its owner after 1568. Altemps was a collector of antiquities and would have been pleased at what has become of his palace, for it now houses some of the most sublime sculptures of the classical age. These sculptures form part of the collection of the Museo Nazionale Romano, whose previously poorly displayed exhibits were split between several new homes at the end of the 1990s.

The palace and its exhibits spread over just two floors, and unlike many similar museums don't dull the senses with endless rows of anonymous busts and second-rate statues. Everything here is outstanding, with just a handful of exhibits in each room – some rooms have just one or two sculptures – with the result that each masterpiece has the space it needs to shine. As an added bonus, the palace itself has some beautifully decorated and frescoed rooms and chambers, not least the small church of Sant'Aniceto and the stunning painted loggia on the second floor.

After a small medley of rooms around the ticket hall you walk into the palace's airy central courtyard, flanked at its top and bottom (north and south ends) by two statue-filled arcades. Start your exploration by turning left, but note that although the rooms are numbered and named on the gallery plan, their open-plan arrangement encourages you to wander among the exhibits at random.

Room 7, the Room of the Herms, houses the first of the gallery's major works, two first-century figures of **Apollo the Lyrist**, both from the Ludovisi collection, a major group of sculptures amassed by Ludovico Ludovisi, a Bolognese nephew of Pope Gregory XV. The collection – purchased by the Italian government in 1901 – forms the core of the Altemps' displays. Another work from the collection, the **Ludovisi Athena**, dominates Room 9, a statue distinguished by the finely carved tunic and the snake twisting to stare at the goddess. Room 14 contains a wonderful sculptural group portraying Dionysius and satyr with a panther, full of beautifully carved details such as Dionysius' ringleted hair and clasped bunch of grapes.

Left: Portrait busts of the caesars line the beautiful painted loggia on the second floor

The palazzo is built around a central courtyard

The gallery's real stars are on the second floor. To reach them, cross back over the courtyard and climb the monumental staircase close to where you first entered. This will bring you to the south loggia, where you should hunt out a second-century **sarcophagus** embellished with scenes of Mars and Venus, significant because it was drawn and much admired by Renaissance artists such as Raphael and Mantegna. Room 19 at the far end of the loggia is known as the Painted Views Room – for obvious reasons.

In the next room (Room 20, the Cupboard Room), you come face to face with two sensational statues: the **Ludovisi Orestes and Electra**, a first-century group by Menelaus (the artist's signature can be seen on the supporting plinth), and the **Ludovisi Ares**, a seated figure (possibly Achilles) with sword and shield; the sculpture is probably a Roman copy of a Greek original and was restored by Bernini in 1622.

The gallery's finest works occupy the next room (Room 21, The Tale of Moses Room), which contains little more than two monolithic heads and a deceptively humble-looking relief. The heads are the Ludovisi Acrolith (left of the relief) and the **Ludovisi Hera**. The latter was one of the most celebrated and admired busts of antiquity, and has been identified as an idealized portrait of Antonia Augusta, the mother of Emperor

Claudius, who was deified by Claudius after her death and held up as an exemplar of domestic virtue and maternal duty.

Less striking, but more precious to scholars because of its unusual nature and probable age, is the central relief, the **Ludovisi Throne** discovered in 1887 in the grounds of the Villa Ludovis. Although some controversy surrounds the piece, most critics believe it is a fifth-century BC work brought to Rome from one of the Greek colonies in Calabria, southern Italy, after the Romans conquered much of the region in the third century BC. The scene portrayed on the front of the "throne" probably shows the birth and welcome to land of Aphrodite (literally "born of the foam"). Panels on the throne's sides show two young girls, both seated on curious folded cushions, one nude and playing a double-piped flute, the other clothed and sprinkling grains of incense from a box on to a flaming brazier.

The Ludovisi Throne is one of the gallery's finest pieces. Its front panel (below) depicts the birth of Aphrodite

Three further exceptional sculptures dominate the large room (Room 26) at the end of palace's west flank, a large salon with ornate fireplace once used for entertaining palace guests. At its heart stands the *Galatian Soldier and His Wife Committing Suicide*, one of the most dramatic and visceral sculptures in Western art. It was found with the *Dying Galatian* statue, now in the Musei Capitolini (► 66–67), and probably

belonged to a group of linked statues based on three bronzes commissioned by Attalus I, king of Pergamum, to commemorate his victory over the Galatians. The marble copies here and on the Capitoline were commissioned by Julius Caesar to celebrate his victory over the Gauls. Like the Ludovisi Throne, the statue was found during construction of the Villa Ludovisi on land that once belonged to Julius Caesar. Finally, don't miss the room's superb helmeted head of Mars and the **Grande Ludovisi Sarcophagus**, a virtuoso sculpture portraying a battle scene divided into three: the victors at the top; the combatants at the center; and the vanquished at the bottom.

TAKING A BREAK

Stop for a coffee at the ever-popular **Bar della Pace** (► 108), just off Piazza Navona.

➕ 198 C4 ✉ Piazza di Sant'Apollinare ☎ 06 683 3566 🕐 Tue.–Sat. 9–7, Sun. 9–8 🚌 70, 81, 87, 116, 186, 492 and 628 to Corso del Rinascimento 🎫 Moderate. Combined pass available

PALAZZO ALTEMPS: INSIDE INFO

Top tips If you come to Rome outside the summer months, try to **visit the Palazzo Altemps after dark**: the superb lighting in the gallery adds immense drama to many of the exhibits.

• Invest in the **gallery guide and plan** published by Electa-Soprintendenza Archeologica di Roma (available in English): it is beautifully illustrated and provides interesting background information to the main exhibits.

Pantheon

The Pantheon is the closest you'll come to a perfect Roman building. One of Europe's best-preserved ancient buildings, its majestic outlines have remained almost unchanged despite the passage of almost 2,000 years. No other monument presents such a vivid picture of how Rome would have looked in its ancient heyday.

The first sight of the Pantheon is one of Rome's most memorable moments. The initial impact is further reinforced when you move closer, for only then does the building's colossal scale become clear – few stone columns, in Rome or elsewhere, are quite as monolithic as the Pantheon's massive pillars. The building itself does not take long to admire, however – inside or out – for there's little specific to see, which means your best bet is to take in the former temple from the sanctuary of an outdoor café table in Piazza della Rotonda.

Temple to Church

The Pantheon you see today was built by Emperor Hadrian between AD 118 and 125. It largely superceded two previous temples on the site, the first having been built some 150 years earlier between 27 and 25 BC by Marcus Agrippa, the son-in-law of Emperor Augustus. This structure was damaged by a momentous fire that swept Rome in AD 80. A second temple, built by Emperor Domitian, suffered a similar fiery fate when it was struck by lightning in AD 110.

Given this history, the large dedication picked out in bronze letters across the building's facade is puzzling, for it clearly alludes to Marcus Agrippa: *m. agrippa l. f. cos tertium fecit* ("Marcus Agrippa, son of Lucius, made this in his third consulship"). This apparent anomaly is evidence of Hadrian's modesty, for he habitually retained the name of a building's original dedicatee on the Roman monuments he rebuilt or restored.

Subsequent rulers were less modest, as you can see from the faint two-line inscription below in much smaller letters: *pantheum vetustate corruptum cum omni cultu restituerunt* ("with every refinement they restored the Pantheon, worn by age"). This refers to renovations supposedly made by Emperors Severus and Caracalla in AD 202. Not only were the pair

Unknown Purpose

For so great a building it is remarkable that no one really knows the Pantheon's purpose. Its name suggests it was a temple devoted to "all the gods," but there is no record of any such cult elsewhere in Rome. Some theories suggest it was devoted to the 12 Olympian gods of ancient Greece, others that it was not a temple at all in the accepted sense, but rather a place where rulers would glorify themselves by appearing in the company of statues of the gods.

immodest in their claims, they were also dishonest, for it appears the restorations never took place.

Hadrian's involvement was confirmed in 1892, when archeologists – who until then had associated the building with Agrippa – found that many of the Pantheon's bricks contained the Emperor's personal seal. Hadrian's involvement probably included the building's design, the simple squares and circles of which created a structure of near-architectural perfection.

Plenty of Roman buildings shared the Pantheon's mixed fortunes, but few survived the passage of time in such pristine form. The reason for its excellent condition is that it became a Christian church in AD 608, when Rome's then ruler, the Byzantine emperor Phocas, presented the building to Pope Boniface IV. This was the first time a temple constructed for

The 30-foot *oculus* in the middle of the dome dramatically illuminates the interior of the Pantheon

pagan rites had been converted into a church – worship in such temples had previously been banned – and the change brought with it the ruling that to remove even a single stone from the site constituted a mortal sin.

Not all the building survived unscathed, however, as you'll see from the porch's exterior walls, which were once largely clad in white marble. The main body of the building to the rear was simply faced in stucco, a cost-saving way of imitating marble. Better preserved than the covering are the huge columns, most of which are fashioned from Egyptian granite, together with their capitals and bases, which were carved from finest Greek Pentelic marble. Even here, though, certain contingencies had to be made: one column, for example, was brought from Emperor Domitian's villa in Castelgandolfo in the hills above Rome in 1626; two more – needed to replace damaged pillars – came from the Baths of Nero in 1666.

Damage was not always accidental, however. Sometimes it was intentional, most notably when Emperor Constans II plundered the bronze gilding that covered many surfaces in 663–67. Most of the bronze found its way to Constantinople and was melted down and re-formed into coins. Something similar happened in 1626, when Pope Urban VIII was persuaded by Bernini, the celebrated architect and sculptor, to remove the ancient bronze gilding from the portico's wooden beams. Over 200 tons of metal were removed, most of which went to make Bernini's huge *baldacchino*, or altar canopy in St. Peter's (► 156–160). Enough metal was left over, it's said, to provide Urban with some 80 new cannons for the Castel Sant'Angelo.

The Pantheon's dome is one of the marvels of Roman engineering. It becomes progressively thinner and uses lighter materials toward its top

Italy's kings and queens are buried in the Pantheon

Dome and Interior

Walking into the interior produces a doubletake, for looking up at the great coffered dome reveals a 30-foot hole, or *oculus*, in the middle of the ceiling. This was a deliberate part of Hadrian's design, intended to allow those inside the building a direct contemplation of the heavens. It is also a dramatic source of light, casting a powerful beam of sunlight into the marble-covered interior on sunny days and providing a beautiful glimpse of the starlit sky on clear evenings. On startling occasions, it also allows in birds and rain.

The dome is the Pantheon's greatest glory, measuring more than 144 feet in diameter – greater than the dome of St. Peter's – exactly the same as the height of the building from floor to *oculus* (the interior is a perfect hemisphere). This was the world's largest concrete dome until 1958, when it was superseded by the CNIT building in Paris.

The dome's distinctive coffering, or *lacunas*, was made by pouring material into molds, just one of the cupola's many engineering subtleties. What you can't see is the way in which the dome's skin becomes thinner as it approaches its apex – from 23 feet to a little more than 3 feet thick – so reducing its overall weight. Neither can you see the way in which progressively lighter materials were used: concrete and travertine at the base, volcanic tufa midway up and featherlight pumice close to the *oculus*.

Lower down, little of the marble veneer you see on the walls is original, although it is thought to correspond closely to Hadrian's original decorative scheme. Much of the pavement, however, although extensively repaired, is believed to be original. Around the walls are seven alternating rectangular and

Missing Statues

Among the treasures lost from the Pantheon over the centuries is a statue of Venus that once stood outside Agrippa's original version of the temple. The statue was celebrated for the earrings with which it was adorned, made by cutting in half a pearl that Cleopatra left uneaten after a famous bet she made with Mark Antony that she could spend 10 million *sesterces* on a single meal.

semicircular niches, originally designed to hold statues, but now given over in part to the tombs of the kings and queens of Italy's short-lived monarchy (1870–1946). The third niche on the left contains the tomb of the painter Raphael (1483–1520), who was exhumed in 1833 and reburied here in an ancient Roman sarcophagus.

TAKING A BREAK

The **Tazza d'Oro** café (Via degli Orfani 84, tel: 06 678 9792) just off Piazza della Rotonda is considered by many to serve the best coffee in Rome. But bear in mind that unlike the cafés in the square you can't sit down and there is no view of the Pantheon.

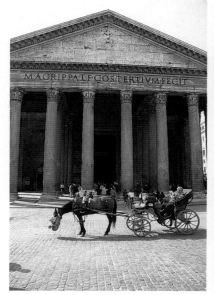

The Pantheon's main facade

✚ 199 D3 ⊠ Piazza della Rotonda ☎ 06 6830 0230 ⏰ Mon.–Sat. 9–6:30, Sun. 9–1 🚇 Spagna 🚌 119 to Piazza della Rotonda, or 46, 63, 62, 64, 70, 81, 87 and all other services to Largo di Torre Argentina 💰 Free

---

PANTHEON: INSIDE INFO

Top tips The Pantheon is almost always **closed on Sunday afternoon**.
- Don't look for the ticket office: the Pantheon is a church and **entrance is free**.
- **Come in the rain** to enjoy the remarkable spectacle of water pouring through the hole in the Pantheon's roof.
- The Pantheon can be seen quickly and easily in conjunction with two other smaller sights: the Caravaggio paintings in **San Luigi dei Francesi** (➤ 102) and the Gothic church of **Santa Maria sopra Minerva**, founded in the eighth century over a Roman temple to Minerva. Outside the church, look out for Bernini's elephant statue supporting an ancient Egyptian obelisk. Inside, be sure to see the frescoes of the *Annunciation* and *Assumption* by Filippino Lippi, the statue of *The Redeemer* by Michelangelo to the left of the high altar, and the tomb of Fra Angelico, patron saint of painters, who is buried in a passage at the end of the north (left) nave.

In more detail The date on which the Pantheon was consecrated as a church – November 1, 608 – is interesting, for it marked the beginning of All Saints' Day, or the Day of the Dead. In another allusion to all the saints, as opposed to all the gods, the church was christened and dedicated to Santa Maria ad Martyres, the Virgin and the Christian Martyrs. Countless martyrs' bones and relics were brought here from catacombs around the city to mark the event.

Trastevere

Trastevere means "over the Tevere," and refers to a quaint enclave of the city on the southern bank of the Tiber (Tevere), an area that until recently was both the most traditional part of central Rome and the heart of its eating and nightlife district. Although no longer at the cutting edge, its cobbled streets and tiny squares are still picturesque places to explore and eat, either by day or night.

Trastevere is full of small bars and restaurants

Trastevere has few hotels, so chances are you will be coming here on foot or by bus. It's not far to walk from most of central Rome, and the routes you would take from places such as the Capitoline or Campo dei Fiori run through interesting parts of the city such as the Ghetto, the Isola Tiberina and the cluster of churches and temples around Piazza Bocca della Verità (➤ 177). If you want to conserve your energy and catch a bus, there are plenty of choices, as Ponte Garibaldi, the main bridge linking the rest of Rome to Piazza Sonnino, one of Trastevere's main squares, is a major city thoroughfare.

As for what you should see, there are two main sights – the fine church of **Santa Maria in Trastevere**, the focus of the area's central square, and the **Villa Farnesina**, which contains rooms and ceilings adorned with frescoes by Raphael and others. Lesser attractions include the **Orto Botanico** (➤ 98), but in the end, this is a place to explore and admire at random, particularly the web of streets sandwiched between Via Garibaldi and Viale Trastevere.

Santa Maria in Trastevere

There's nearly always something happening in Piazza Santa Maria in Trastevere: kids playing football, old men chatting, lovers holding hands, though late at night the atmosphere becomes seedier. Even when there are no people to watch, you can simply enjoy the facade of the church that dominates the square. Santa Maria in Trastevere was reputedly founded in 222, which – if true – would make it one of the city's oldest churches. It was first properly documented in 337, when a church was begun here by Pope Julius I on the site where it was believed that a miraculous fountain of oil had flowed on the day of Christ's birth.

The mosaic in the upper apse of Santa Maria in Trastevere depicts Christ and the Virgin enthroned

Gianicolo Hill

If you have the legs for a longer walk, then aim for the trees and greenery etched on the skyline above Trastevere. This is the Gianicolo, or Janiculum Hill, one of Rome's original Seven Hills, and views of Rome from here make the climb worthwhile. Walk up Via Garibaldi and look at the **Fontana Paola** (1610–12), a monumental fountain created for Pope Paul V, and then see the late 15th-century church of **San Pietro in Montorio** at the top of Via Garibaldi, supposedly built over the spot on which St. Peter was crucified (scholars believe he was actually martyred closer to the present-day site of the Vatican). In an adjoining courtyard stands the **Tempietto**, a tiny masterpiece of Renaissance architecture designed by Bramante, the architect partly responsible for St. Peter's.

If you still have energy to burn, walk to the **Villa Doria Pamphili**, Rome's largest park, a huge area of paths, pines, lakes and open spaces.

Santa Maria in Trastevere's beautiful facade mosaics show the Virgin flanked by 10 female figures

The present church dates from the 12th century and was begun by Pope Innocent II, a member of a prominent local family. Its most arresting features are its facade **mosaics** – many Roman churches would have once been similarly decorated – that portray, among other things, the Virgin flanked by 10 figures. Like the identity of the figures themselves, the identity of the mosaics' creator is not known. Pietro Cavallini is a possible candidate, since he was responsible for many of the even more spectacular mosaics inside the church. For instance, Cavallini's hand can be seen in the lively mosaics of the lower apse (1290), which portray scenes from the Life of the Virgin. The scenes in the upper apse are earlier (1140) and are executed in a more old-fashioned Byzantine style.

Don't miss the church's lovely inlaid medieval pavement and the nave's ancient columns, the latter brought here from the Terme di Caracalla, a sprawling Roman baths complex 15 minutes' walk beyond the Colosseum.

Be prepared for the unexpected in this part of town

Trastevere is still a largely residential district

TRASTEVERE: INSIDE INFO

Top tips Try to see Santa Maria in Trastevere at night, when its facade and mosaics are usually **floodlit** and dazzling.
• Trastevere is generally safe, but you should take care late at night in the darker and more outlying streets.

Villa Farnesina

From the church, walk northeast on Via della Scala and continue on Via della Lungara, not an exciting walk, but worth making for this beautiful Renaissance villa, built in 1511 for Agostino Chigi, a wealthy Sienese banker. Its highlight is the **Loggia of Cupid and Psyche** on the first floor, adorned with frescoes (1517) designed by Raphael but largely painted by Giulio Romano and others. Upstairs is the **Sala delle Prospettive**, a room entirely covered in bewitching frescoes containing views of Rome and clever *trompe l'oeil* tricks of perspective. The adjoining room, formerly a bedchamber, contains vivid 16th-century frescoes by Sodoma.

A stone's throw from the Villa you'll find the **Orto Botanico**, situated at the end of Via Corsini, a turn off Via della Lungara just south of the villa. Opened in 1883, its 30 acres occupy the former gardens of the Palazzo Corsini, and spread up the slopes of the Gianicolo Hill to the rear. It is famed for its palms and orchids, but is also a lovely place to take a shady time out from sightseeing.

TAKING A BREAK

The **Sala di Tè Trasté** (Via della Lungaretta 76, tel: 06 589 4430), a civilized pocket of Trastevere calm, serves coffee, cakes and snacks in a comfortable, modern setting.

Santa Maria in Trastevere
✚ 201 E1 ✉ Piazza Santa Maria in Trastevere ☎ 06 581 4802 🕐 Tue.–Sun. 7:30 a.m.–9 p.m, Mon. 7:30–12, 4–9. 🚌 H, 8, 44, 75 and 780 to Viale di Trastevere 🎫 Free

Villa Farnesina
✚ 198 A2 ✉ Via della Lungara 230 ☎ 06 6880 1767 🕐 Mon.–Sat. 9–1
🚌 23 and 280 to Lungotevere della Farnesina or H, 8 and 780 to Viale di Trastevere 🎫 Moderate

At Your Leisure

2 Piazza Farnese

Piazza Farnese lies just a few steps from Campo dei Fiori, yet it's hard to think of two more contrasting Roman squares. Campo dei Fiori will always be interesting because of its market, but it is shabby and cramped. Piazza Farnese is broad and august, graced with elegant fountains, and unlike the Campo, which has no buildings of note, is dominated by the magnificent **Palazzo Farnese**. The palace, which has housed the French Embassy since 1871, is closed to the public. You can still admire the exterior, though, commissioned in 1515 by Cardinal Alessandro Farnese (later Pope Paul III), and catch a glimpse through the huge windows of Annibale Caracci's ceiling frescoes (1597–1603) when the interior is illuminated at night. Much of the stone for the palace was pilfered from the Colosseum and used here by the Tuscan architect Antonio da Sangallo the Younger. When Sangallo died in 1546 he was replaced on the project by Michelangelo, who designed much of the palace's cornice, many of the upper windows and the loggia. For one of Rome's grandest buildings, the French government pays the lowest rent in the city: set, before the advent of the Euro, at one lira every 99 years. The Italians pay a similarly nominal sum for their embassy in Paris.

The **fountains** in the square were originally massive baths of Egyptian granite from the Terme di Caracalla. They were brought to the piazza in the 16th century by the Farnese family, who used them initially as a *dias* or platform from which to admire the square's various entertainments (look out for the carved lilies, the Farnese family symbol). They were turned into fountains in 1626.

✚ 198 B2 ✉ Piazza Farnese
🚌 46, 62, 64 to Corso Vittorio Emanuele II or 44, 56, 60, 65, 75, 170 to Via Arenula

3 Palazzo Spada

There are three modest reasons to visit the Palazzo Spada, situated just a couple of minutes' walk from Campo dei Fiori. The first is the palace itself, built for Cardinal Girolamo Capo di Ferro in 1548. Much of the building's charm derives from the distinctive facade, added between 1556 and 1560, which is covered in beautifully patterned stucco work. The second is an architectural *trompe l'oeil*, or visual trick, created in 1652 by the consumate craftsman Francesco Borromini. It involves what appears to be a long columned corridor between two courtyards. In fact it's a passage less than 30 feet long. The illusion is achieved by the deliberate narrowing of the corridor and foreshortening of the

columns. The third reason to visit the palace is its small collection of paintings, among them works by Andrea del Sarto, Titian, Albrecht Dürer, Jan Breughel the Elder and Guido Reni's portrait of his patron, Cardinal

Bernardino Spada, who acquired the palace in 1632.

🚩 198 C2 ✉ Vicolo del Polverone 15B ☎ 06 686 1158 🕐 Tue.–Fri. 8:30–7:30, Sat.–Sun. 8:30–6:30 🍴 Cafés in Campo dei Fiori and Piazza Farnese 🚌 8, 44, 46, 60, 62, 64, 65, 70, 87, 170 and other services to Via Arenula 🎟 Moderate

🄳 Santa Maria dell'Orazione e Morte

After looking at Piazza Farnese, walk along Via dei Farnesi. This soon brings you to **Via Giulia**, laid out by Pope Julius II between about 1503 and 1513, and still one of the city's most elegant and coveted residential thoroughfares. It's well worth admiring, though perhaps not along its full length, for it runs for more than half a mile toward St. Peter's.

Even if you don't go down the street, devote a couple of minutes to the church on the junction of Via Giulia and Via dei Farnesi. Look for the unmistakable facade, decorated with stone skulls and, to the right of the church looking down Via Giulia, the figure of a beaked bird – Osiris, the Egyptian god of death. A cheering inscription relating to the skulls

reads, in translation: "Me today, thee tomorrow."

Santa Maria dell'Orazione e Morte (Our Lady of Oration and Death) was once the headquarters of a religious confraternity, the Compagnia della Buona Morte, or the "Company of the Good Death." Its charitable duties included collecting the unclaimed bodies of the poor and providing

Borromini's architectural *trompe l'oeil* in the Palazzo Spada creates the illusion of a long corridor in a passage just 30 feet long

them with a Christian burial. The corpses were once stored in three large tunnels running down to the Tiber from the church. All but one were sealed up during construction of the river's modern embankment.

🚩 198 B2 ✉ Via Giulia 🕐 Open for Mass Sun. morning 🚌 23, 65, 116, 280

🄶 Sant'Agostino

The church of Sant'Agostino (1479–83) lies tucked away in the streets just north of Piazza Navona.

The exterior is plain and unprepossessing, although the facade was one of the earliest Renaissance frontages in the city. The interior, which was extravagantly refurbished in 1750, is more promising and holds some unlikely treasures for so modest a church. The first is a Michelangelo-influenced fresco of the **Prophet Isaiah** (1512) by Raphael, commissioned by humanist scholar, Giovanni Goritz, as an adornment to his tomb (the painting is on the third pillar of the left, or north, side of the church).

The first chapel on the same side features Caravaggio's outstanding

The *Madonna del Parto* by Jacopo Sansovino in the church of Sant'Agostino

painting, **Madonna di Loreto** (1605). Turn around, and against the west wall – the wall with the entrance door – stands a statue by Jacopo Sansovino. Known as the **Madonna del Parto**, or Madonna of Childbirth (1521), it is much venerated by pregnant women or couples wanting a child.

🔲 198 C4 ✉ Via di Sant' Agostino
☎ 06 6880 1962 🕐 Daily 8–noon,
4–7:30 🍴 Cafés in Piazza Navona
🚍 70, 81, 87, 116, 186, 492 and 628 to
Corso del Rinascimento 🎟 Free

For Kids

Children should enjoy the sights and sounds of the **Campo dei Fiori** market (▶ 80–81) and the artists and occasional street performers entertaining the crowds in **Piazza Navona** (▶ 82–85). They'll also relish the ice cream at I Tre Scalini (▶ 108) or a trip to Bertè (Piazza Navona 108, tel: 06 687 5011), one of Rome's oldest toy stores. Città del Sole (Via della Scrofa 66, tel: 06 6880 3805), near Piazza Navona is also good for toys.

A walk around the **Isola Tiberina** may be a winner, and the **Orto Botanico** (Largo Cristina di Svezia 24, off Via Corsini, tel: 06 686 4193) provides plenty of outdoor playing space (much favored by local moms with children) but no playing equipment. The Villa Sciarra, however – to the southwest of Trastevere – has a playground and mini-roller coaster.

8 San Luigi dei Francesi

The French national church (1518–89) in Rome is easily seen on the short walk between Piazza Navona and the Pantheon, and is well worth stopping for the five minutes it takes to see its principal attractions: three superlative paintings by Caravaggio. The three pictures are located in the last (fifth) chapel on the left as you face the altar. All three are late works (1597–1602), and all demonstrate the dramatic handling of light and shade, or *chiaroscuro* (literally "clear and dark") for which Caravaggio was

famed. They all deal with the same theme – the life of St. Matthew – and portray the *Calling of St. Matthew* (the saint hears God's summons while collecting taxes); *St. Matthew and the Angel* (the altarpiece); and *The Martyrdom of St. Matthew*.

198 C3 Piazza di San Luigi dei Francesi at the corner of Via Giustiniani and Via della Scrofa 06 6882 8271 Hours vary, but generally Mon.–Wed., Fri. and Sat. 8–12:30, 3:30–7; Sun. and Thu. 8–12:30 Cafés in Piazza Navona or Piazza della Rotonda 70, 81, 87, 116, 186, 492, 628 to Corso del Rinascimento Free

Francesco Borromini's spiral cupola at Sant'Ivo alla Sapienza was inspired by the sting of a bee

9 Sant'Ivo alla Sapienza

The fact that Sant'Ivo is rarely open matters little, for the church's main attraction is its extraordinary spiralling dome and lantern, the work of Borromini, a leading baroque architect and rival of Gian Lorenzo Bernini. Borromini received his commission from Pope Urban VIII, a member of the powerful Barberini family, and it is said the architect based his spiky and eccentric dome on the family's symbol, the bee, taking the bee's sting as his inspiration. You'll catch a glimpse of the dome if you walk from the Pantheon to

A bas-relief from the Ara Pacis portraying the earth goddess Tellus

Piazza Navona via Piazza Sant'Eustachio. For a closer look you need to enter the Palazzo alla Sapienza, part of the papal university first founded in 1303 (roughly translated, *sapienza* means "wisdom" in Italian).

➕ 199 D3 ✉ Corso del Rinascimento 40 ☎ No phone ⏰ Usually only open Sun. 10–noon 🍴 cafés in Piazza Navona or Piazza della Rotonda 🚌 70, 81, 87, 116, 186, 492 and 628 to Corso del Rinascimento 🎟 Free

🔟 Ara Pacis

There's no convenient way to see this Roman monument, which lies in a slightly isolated position across the Tiber and to the northeast of the Castel Sant'Angelo. It's well worth making a detour, however, for the "Altar of Peace" (13–9 BC) contains some of the city's best-preserved Roman bas-reliefs. The altar was commissioned by the Senate to commemorate Emperor Augustus' military victories in France and Spain. The most striking of several sculpted friezes shows the procession that accompanied the altar's consecration and includes the figures of Augustus, a number of high-ranking Roman officials and members of Augustus' family.

➕ 199 D5 ✉ Via di Ripetta ☎ 06 3600 3471 ⏰ Tue.–Sat. 9–7, Sun. 9–1, Oct.–Mar.; Tue.–Sat. 9–5, Sun. 9–1, Apr.–Sep. (currently closed for restoration) 🚌 81, 926 🎟 Moderate

Off the Beaten Track

If you want to escape the hordes, visit Trastevere's peaceful botanical gardens, **Orto Botanico** (► 98), off Via Corsini. Alternately, make your way to the **Villa Doria Pamphili**, a huge park on the western flanks of the Gianicolo. It is a long walk to the latter, however, so take either a cab or bus 870 from the western end of Corso Vittorio Emanuele II.

🔟 Santa Maria del Popolo

This church receives fewer visitors than it deserves, mainly because it lies on the northern fringe of the old city. Founded in the 11th century – allegedly over the tomb of Emperor Nero – it was much restored in later centuries by leading architects such as Bramante and Bernini. Inside, there are four outstanding artistic treasures. The first is a series of

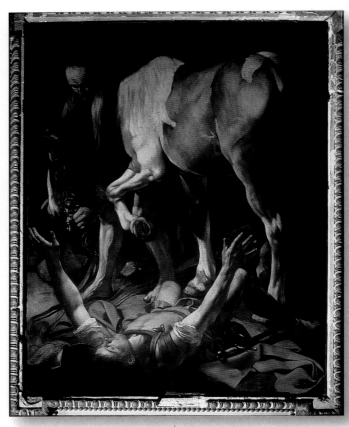

Caravaggio's *Conversion of St. Paul*, one of the artistic treasures in the church of Santa Maria del Popolo

frescoes (1485–89) behind the altar by the Umbrian Renaissance painter Pinturicchio; the second is a pair of tombs (1505–07) in the choir by Andrea Sansovino; the third is a pair of paintings by Caravaggio, *The Conversion of St. Paul* and *Crucifixion of St. Peter* (1601–02) in the first chapel of the left transept; and the fourth is the Cappella Chigi (1513), a chapel commissioned by the wealthy Sienese banker Agostino Chigi. The last is noteworthy because virtually all its component parts were designed by Raphael.

➕ 201 F5 ✉ Piazza del Popolo 12
☎ 06 361 0836 🕐 Daily 7–7
🍴 Rosati (▶ 138) 🚇 Flaminio
🚌 117, 119 to Piazza del Popolo
🎟 Free

🔟 Palazzo Doria Pamphili

You'd never imagine looking at the Palazzo Doria Pamphili's bland and blackened exterior that inside it contained a multitude of beautifully decorated rooms, several of which provide a sumptuous setting for one of Italy's most important private art collections.

There's no shortage of great paintings in Rome, but what makes the collection here so appealing is the beauty of its palatial setting. You could spend an hour or so with the paintings, and then – if you're not sated by the gallery's surfeit of decoration – join one of the guided tours around parts of the palace normally closed to visitors. These tours require an additional admission fee on top of an already expensive ticket to see the pictures and are conducted in Italian. Neither fact should put you off, as Rome offers few opportunities to see behind the scenes of so grand a private palace.

The palazzo is one of Rome's largest, with well over 1,000 rooms, five courtyards and four colossal staircases. Its size – in an age when the upkeep of such buildings is astronomical – is all the more remarkable given that it's still owned, and in part occupied, by the Doria Pamphili family. This venerable papal dynasty was created when two families were united by marriage: the Doria, an important Genoese merchant dynasty, and the Pamphili (or Pamphilj), a pillar of the Roman aristocracy.

The family's **paintings** are arranged somewhat haphazardly on part of the second floor, with Flemish and Italian works hung alongside one another – the arrangement preferred by Prince Andrea Doria IV in 1760: a handlist is available to make sense of the paintings, which are numbered rather than labeled. The collection's most famous work is Velázquez's penetrating ***Portrait of Innocent X*** (1650), a pope of notoriously weak character. Innocent is said to have remarked of the likeness that it was "too true, too true." Most of the great names of Italian art are also represented, including Caravaggio (*Rest on the Flight into Egypt* and *Mary Magdalene*), Raphael (*Double Portrait*), Titian (*Salome with the Head of John the Baptist*) and many more.

The **guided tours** of the palace apartments take you, among other places, to the Saletta Rossa, or Red Room, whose walls are covered in painted *Allegories of the Elements and Seasons* by Jan Brueghel the Elder; the club-like Fumoir, or Smoking Room – created for the English wife of a Doria scion in the 19th century; the Winter Garden conservatory; and the Green Room, home to paintings that include Renaissance masterpieces by Lorenzo Lotti (*Portrait of a Man*) and Filippo Lippi (*Annunciation*).

🚹 199 E3 ✉ **Piazza del Collegio Romano 2** ☎ **06 679 7323** ⏰ **Gallery: Fri.–Wed. 10–5. Apartments: Fri.–Wed. 10:30–noon** 🚇 **Barberini** 🚌 **60, 62, 81, 85, 95, 160, 492 and all other services to Piazza Venezia** 🎟 **Gallery: expensive. Apartments: inexpensive.**

🄵 Santa Cecilia in Trastevere

This church sits slightly west of Viale di Trastevere and the rest of Trastevere, but can easily be included as part of a Trastevere stroll or a walk from the other side of the Tiber by way of the Isola Tiberina. Much of its appeal is wrapped up in the story of its dedicatee, St. Cecilia, who is said to have lived with her husband Valerio, an important Roman patrician figure, in a house on the site in the fourth century. Valerio joined his chaste wife as a Christian, only to be rewarded with martyrdom. Cecilia's own martyrdom was protracted: attempts to scald and suffocate her failed and she finally

succumbed to three blows to her neck, but only after converting many onlookers and singing throughout her ordeal – one of the reasons why she is the patron saint of music.

The present church is a mixture of styles, ranging from the 12th-century portico with its Roman columns to the 18th-century facade and chill baroque interior. Several fine works of art survived the alterations over the years, notably a **statue of St. Cecilia** by Carlo Maderno. The sculptor was apparently present when the saint's tomb was opened (for reasons unknown) in 1599, her body having previously been moved from the catacombs outside the city on the orders of Pope Paschal I in the ninth century. Maderno made a drawing of her reputedly uncorrupt body, and in his statue clearly depicted the three cuts left by the Roman executioner's unsuccessful attempts to cut off Cecilia's head. Today, the saint's tomb is in the church's crypt.

Above the church's altar is a lovely Gothic *baldacchino*, or **altar canopy** (1293), the work of Arnolfo di Cambio. The apse to its rear is adorned with a glowing ninth-century **mosaic** which shows Pope Paschal I presenting Cecilia and her husband Valerio to Christ. The cloister features celebrated but faded frescoes of the **Last Judgment** (1293) by the Roman painter and mosaicist Pietro Cavallini, an important contemporary of Giotto.

🕂 204 C4 ☒ Piazza di Santa Cecilia in Trastevere ☎ 06 589 9289 🕓 Church: daily 10–noon, 4–5:30 (hours can vary). Cavallini frescoes: Tue., Thu. 10–11:30 🚌 56, 60, 75, 710, 780 🚊 8 to Viale di Trastevere

14

The late 16th-century statue of St. Cecilia by Carlo Maderno in the church of Santa Cecilia in Trastevere

Where to...
Eat and Drink

Prices
Expect to pay per person for a meal, excluding drinks and service
$ under €20 $$ €20–€40 $$$ over €40

Augusto $
Where once Rome was filled with old-fashioned trattorias straight out of a 1950s Fellini film, these days such charming restaurants are a dying breed. Augusto is one of the few survivors, serving basic but authentic Roman dishes at quite reasonable prices in one of Trastevere's prettier and quieter piazzas. Tables on the square during summer. No credit cards.

➕ 198 B1 ☒ Piazza de' Renzi 15
☎ 06 580 3798 🕐 Lunch: Mon.–Sat. 12:30–3. Dinner: Mon.–Fri. 7:30–11, Sat. 12:30–3. Closed mid-Aug. to mid-Sep.

Da Baffetto $
Baffetto is a Roman institution: a tiny pizzeria of almost caricatured old-style appearance with excellent pizzas (and a handful of other dishes), brusque but efficient service (you're not encouraged to linger), a fast and furious atmosphere, and very lengthy lines unless you arrive early or late. A place to come for the genuine – if somewhat self-conscious – Roman pizzeria experience. No credit cards.

➕ 198 B3 ☒ Via del Governo Vecchio 114 ☎ 06 686 1617
🕐 Daily 6:30 p.m.–1 a.m. Closed 2 weeks in Aug.

La Carbonara $–$$
This popular Campo dei Fiori fixture is the best of the restaurants on the square and serves perfectly acceptable food at decent prices. The large number of outdoor tables means you shouldn't have to wait too long to be seated.

➕ 198 C2 ☒ Campo dei Fiori 23
☎ 06 686 4783 🕐 Mon., Wed.–Sun. 12:15–3, 7–11:30

Il Convivio $$$
The check may be a shock, but it's unlikely to be as high as in the city's other top-class restaurants, and here at least you're assured of a memorable meal with good service in tasteful and intimate surroundings. The menu changes according to season and the inclinations of the chef, the cooking combining a dash of traditional Roman cuisine with creative Italian-based cooking.

➕ 198 C4 ☒ Vicolo dei Soldati 31
☎ 06 686 9432 🕐 Lunch: Tue.–Sat. 1–2:30. Dinner: Mon.–Sat. 8–10:30. Closed 1 week in Aug.

Grappolo d'Oro $–$$
When *The New Yorker* magazine's former correspondent wrote his farewell to the city, he based the article on observations of and from this peerless traditional trattoria close to Campo dei Fiori. Little has changed here in decades, from the seemingly ageless waiters to the traditional cooking – try the delicious *ravioli alla Gorgonzola* or one of the various risottos. The only difference, inevitably, is that more visitors know about the place, so arrive early: reserving a table is hit or miss.

➕ 198 C3 ☒ Piazza della Cancelleria 80 ☎ 06 686 4118
🕐 Mon.–Sat. noon–3, 7:30–11

Il Leoncino $
Da Baffetto (see left) may be better known, but Il Leoncino, just a couple of blocks west of Via del Corso, offers just a Roman pizzeria experience – and is more likely to be busy with locals. Pizzas are made behind an old

marble-topped bar and cooked in wood-fired ovens.

🚹 199 D5 🖂 Via del Leoncino 28, off Piazza San Lorenzo in Lucina 🕾 06 687 6306 🕲 Lunch: Mon.–Tue., Thu.–Fri. 1–2:30. Dinner: Thu.–Tue. 6:30–midnight

Myosotis $$

The modern dining rooms and light, innovative cooking at Myosotis are something of a departure from Rome's often rather traditional and decoratively uninspired restaurants. Service is amiable, the atmosphere relaxed and the prices reasonable. Menus change with the season, but almost always include Roman classics such as *spaghetti alla carbonara* and a selection of fish.

🚹 199 D4 🖂 Vicolo della Vaccarella 3–5 🕾 06 686 5554 🕲 Mon.–Sat. 12:30–3, 7:30–11. Closed 3 weeks in Aug.

Paris $$–$$$

Paris serves some of the city's best traditional Roman-Jewish cuisine

(including deep-fried artichokes, pasta and chickpeas and salt cod). Other more conventional Roman and Italian dishes are also available. In fine weather there are a few tables outside, while the interior is a picture of simple elegance. A safe bet for a reliable meal in pleasant surroundings.

🚹 201 E1 🖂 Piazza San Calisto 7a 🕾 06 581 5378 🕲 Lunch: Tue.–Sun. noon–3. Dinner: Tue.–Sat. 7:45–11

La Rosetta $$$

Rome has several good fish and seafood restaurants, the best and most central being La Rosetta. Just a few steps from the Pantheon and Italian Parliament, the restaurant is a politicians' favorite. Prices are high – they usually are for fish – but meals here are invariably memorable and the elegant setting is perfect if you want to dress up. Reservations are required.

🚹 199 D3 🖂 Via della Rosetta 9 🕾 06 686 1002 🕲 Lunch: Mon.–Fri. noon–3. Dinner: Mon.–Sat. 8–11:30

Sora Margherita $–$$

The tiny, simple Sora Margherita in the Ghetto district serves reasonably priced, authentic Romano-Jewish cuisine. It's been run for years by the eponymous Margherita and her husband, opening for lunch only and surviving on local customers without even the need for a sign above the door (look for the red streamers at the entrance). No credit cards.

🚹 199 D1 🖂 Piazza delle Cinque Scole 🕾 06 686 4002 🕲 Mon.–Fri. noon–3:30. Closed Aug.

BARS AND CAFÉS

Bar della Pace $

Old Rome hands may be cynical about this place just off Piazza Navona, but they still come back. By day, the bar is a pretty place for a coffee, and by night it is one of the city's best, trendiest and buzziest spots. The co-owned pizzeria-trattoria alongside is also good.

🚹 198 C3 🖂 Via della Pace 3–7 🕾 06 686 1216 🕲 Daily 9 a.m.–2 a.m.

Cul de Sac $

This wine bar close to Piazza Navona serves a large selection of wines, as well as a good choice of (mostly cold) snacks and appetisers.

🚹 198 C3 🖂 Piazza Pasquino 73 🕾 06 6880 1094 🕲 Mon. 7 p.m.–midnight, Tue.–Sun. 12:30–3, 7–midnight

Il Goccetto $

An intimate and cosy wine bar close to Cul de Sac (see above) that takes its wine seriously. The setting, part of a grand medieval house, is lovely, with original frescoed ceilings.

🚹 198 A3 🖂 Via dei Banchi Vecchi 14 🕾 06 686 4268 🕲 Mon.–Sat. 11–2, 5:30–11. Closed 3 weeks in Aug. and Sat. lunch Jul. and Aug.

I Tre Scalini $

Tre Scalini would be just one more Piazza Navona bar were it not for its rightly celebrated *tartufo* ice cream.

🚹 198 C3 🖂 Piazza Navona 28–32 🕾 06 6880 1996 🕲 Thu.–Tue. 9 a.m.–1 a.m.

Where to... Shop

The heart of Rome is a large and varied area and the shopping opportunities here are correspondingly mixed and extensive. Small side streets often prove to be a happy hunting ground for specialties, notably Via dei Coronari (antiques), Via dei Giubbonari (inexpensive clothing and shoes), Via Giulia (art and antiques), Via dei Cappellari (furniture), Via dei Sediari (religious articles), and Via del Governo Vecchio, Via dei Banchi Nuovi and Via dei Governo (galleries, antiques and secondhand items). Trastevere has its share of small craft, antiques and specialty shops, but is not a major shopping area; it does, however, have a large general market in Piazza San Cosimato. The other main market in the area covered by this chapter is Campo dei Fiori (▶ 80–81).

ART AND ANTIQUES

Hendy

This lovely store near the Pantheon specializes in period Italian jewelry. Most items are early 20th century, but there are also older pieces.

◻ Piazza di Pietra 42
☎ 06 678 5804 ◎ Tue.–Sat. 10–7, Mon. 3:30–7

La Sinopia

The artifacts at La Sinopia, one of several antiques shops in this interesting street, are of high quality and though prices are fairly high too, they offer value for money.

◻ Via dei Banchi Vecchi 21c
☎ 06 687 2869 ◎ Mon.–Sat. 10–1, 4–7:30

BOOKS

Feltrinelli

Part of a large, modern, nationwide chain, Feltrinelli stocks a good range of English-language titles. It also sells plenty of cards, magazines and posters, as well as stylish toys and games.

◻ Largo di Torre Argentina 5a ☎ 06 6880 3248 ◎ Mon.–Sat. 9–8, Sun. 10–1:30, 4–7:30

Libreria del Viaggiatore

This bookstore specializes in travel literature, maps and guides, and stocks a selection of English-language titles.

◻ Via del Pellegrino 78
☎ 06 6880 1048 ◎ Tue.–Sat. 9–2, 4–8, Mon. 4–8

Rinascita

A serious, high-brow bookstore, Rinascita has more recently branched out into "softer" areas such as art books, comic books, videos and modern writing. English and other foreign-language titles are also available.

◻ Via delle Botteghe Oscure 1–3 ☎ 06 679 7637 ◎ Mon.–Sat. 10–8, Sun. 10–2, 4–8

CLOTHING

Davide Cenci

You won't be in Rome long before you realize that many of the city's older inhabitants like to adopt a particular classic style of dress. This large, rambling shop near Piazza Navona is where Romans have come since 1926 for Italian designed tweeds, stylish raincoats, crisp double-cuff shirts...

◻ Via Campo Marzio 1–7 ☎ 06 699 0681 ◎ Tue.–Fri. 9:30–1:30, 3:30–7:30, Sat. 10–7:30, Mon. 3:30–7:30

COSMETICS AND TOILETRIES

Antica Erborista Romana

This fascinating store has been selling herbal remedies and other herbal and natural products since the 18th century.

🏠 Via di Torre Argentina 15 📞 06 687 9493 🕐 Mon.–Fri. 8:30–1, 2:30–7:30, Sat. 9–1:30

Officina Profumo-Farmaceutico di Santa Maria di Novella

This is the Roman outlet for a Florence-based store that sells cosmetics, perfumes, herbal and other natural products, most of which are made using traditional methods originally devized by Dominican monks.

🏠 Corso del Rinascimento 47 📞 06 687 9608 🕐 Mon.–Sat. 9:30–7:30, Sun. 11–7:30

FOOD

Ai Monasteri

This intriguing store is just across the road from Officina Profumo-Farmaceutico di Santa Maria di Novella (see above) at the northern end of Piazza Navona. It sells a wide variety of honey, oils, jams, liqueurs

and other food products made, grown or gathered at Italian monasteries.

🏠 Corso del Rinascimento 72 📞 06 6880 2783 🕐 Fri.–Wed. 9–1, 4:30–7:30, Thu. 4:30–7:30

Innocenzi

If you're visiting Trastevere's Piazza San Cosimato market, be sure to drop into this wonderful cornucopia of ordinary and extraordinary foods from across the world.

🏠 Piazza San Cosimato 66 📞 06 581 2725 🕐 Fri.–Wed. 7–1, 4:30–8, Thu. 4:30–8

Moriondo e Gariglio

This family-run concern makes and sells outstanding chocolates in all shapes, sizes and varieties.

🏠 Via del Pie' di Marmo 21–22 📞 06 699 0856 🕐 Mon.–Sat. 9:30–1, 3:30–7:30

Valzani

A superb and long-established Trastevere institution celebrated for

its cakes, chocolates, pastries and other delicious treats for those with a sweet tooth.

🏠 Via del Moro 37b 📞 06 580 3792 🕐 Wed.–Sun. 9–8. Closed Jun.–Aug.

HOUSEHOLD

House & Kitchen

Unlike Spazio Sette (see below), this is a traditional store that sells a full range of kitchen utensils – basic and exotic – and other household goods.

🏠 Via del Plebiscito 103 📞 06 679 4208 🕐 Mon.–Sat. 9:30–8. Sun. 10:30–2, 3:30–7:30. Closed Sun., Jul. and Aug.

Ceramica Musa

A host of ceramic tiles, many based on old designs, are available at this colorful store to the north of the Pantheon.

🏠 Via Campo Marzio 39 📞 06 687 1242 🕐 Tue.–Fri. 9–1, 3:30–7:30, Sat. 9–1, Mon. 4–7:30. Closed Aug.

Ornamentum

Rome has several stores offering a beautiful range of furnishing and other fabrics, but none perhaps quite as sumptuous as Ornamentum on Via dei Coronari. This is the ultimate emporium for silks, damasks and other fabrics, as well as an enormous range of tassels, brocades and assorted furnishing accessories.

🏠 Via dei Coronari 227 📞 06 687 6849 🕐 Tue.–Fri. 9–1, 4–7:30, Sat. 9–1, Mon. 4–7:30. Closed Aug.

Spazio Sette

Old mixes with new at Spazio Sette, the city's best furniture, household and design store, where a huge range of consumer desirables is spread over three floors of a Renaissance palace complete with frescoed ceilings and pretty court-yard garden.

🏠 Via dei Barbieri 7 📞 06 686 9747 🕐 Tue.–Sat. 9:30–1, 3:30–7:30, Mon. 3:30–7:30

Where to...
Be Entertained

CLASSICAL MUSIC

One or two classical music organizations have their headquarters in the center of Rome (even if they stage their concerts elsewhere). One is the **Associazione Musicale Romana** (AMR) on Via dei Banchi Vecchi 61 (tel: 06 686 8441), which usually puts on **chamber concerts** in spring and early summer; tickets are available from individual venues. Another organization is the important **Oratorio del Gonfalone** (tel: 06 687 5952), which has its own orchestra and that usually performs at the Oratorio del Gonfalone in Via del Gonfalone, a tiny street between Via Giulia and

Lungotevere Sangallo. It specializes in small chamber recitals, but also presents concerts by visiting Italian ensembles.

Many of the city's major **church music** concerts – usually performed by visiting choirs – are staged in the central **Sant'Ignazio**, a large church in Piazza di Sant'Ignazio almost midway between the Pantheon and Via del Corso. Unfortunately, the building has poor acoustics – the best place to sit is as close to the front as possible, so you need to arrive early. Contact visitor centers (▶ 30) for details of upcoming concerts, or look for posters outside the church. Recitals are usually free.

Several churches in the area offer **organ recitals**, but you need to keep your eyes peeled for posters advertising concerts. A good bet is **San Giovanni de' Fiorentini** in Via Giulia where, after noon Mass on Sunday, you may be treated to the sound of the church's wonderful late 17th-century instrument. The AMR (see above) generally organizes an organ festival in the church during September.

NIGHTLIFE

Campo dei Fiori

Campo dei Fiori has become something of a focus for bars that come into their own at nightfall. The place that started the trend is the piazza's gritty **La Vineria** (Campo dei Fiori 15, tel: 06 6880 3268, open Mon.–Sat. 9:30 a.m.–3 p.m, 5 p.m.–1 a.m.), also known as Da Giorgio, as authentic a Roman wine bar as you could hope for. It makes few concessions to interior decoration – there is just one plain bar –

and the characters who collect here can be colorful, to say the least. The outside tables are a favorite rendezvous on summer evenings. Almost immediately alongside La Vineria is the **Drunken Ship** (Campo dei Fiori 20–21, tel: 06 6830 0535, open daily 5 p.m.– 2 a.m.), a boisterous and brash place much favored by young Romans and foreign visitors alike. It serves mostly beer rather than wine and is further distinguished from its adjacent rival by its bold design and the fact that it has DJs and music most evenings: happy hour usually runs from about 5 p.m. to 8 p.m.

Around Piazza Navona

For a somewhat calmer alternative to the bars on Campo dei Fiori, try **Cul de Sac** (▶ 108) and **Il Goccetto** (▶ 108) and the perennially hip **Bar della Pace** (▶ 108), perhaps the most popular place to hang out in this part of Rome. For something almost equally trendy but a little less busy, wander round the corner to **Bar del Fico** (Piazza del Fico 26–28, tel: 06 686 5205, open Mon.–Sat. 9 a.m.–2 a.m, Sun. noon–2 a.m.) It is a touch less expensive and in winter has outdoor heating so you can still sit outside.

Jonathan's Angels (Via della Fossa 16, tel: 06 689 3426, open Tue.–Fri. 5:30 p.m.–2 a.m, Sat. 2 p.m.–2 a.m, Mon. 8 p.m.–2 a.m.), just off Piazza Navona, is something else again, an eccentric but delightfully decorated bar, decked out with candles and plenty of kitsch and overpowering paintings – including portraits of the eponymous Jonathan and his motorcycle; barely a scrap of the interior lacks decoration of some sort – even the restrooms.

Also close to Piazza Navona is **Anima** (Via Santa Maria dell'Anima 57, tel: 06 686 4021, open daily 6 p.m.–4 a.m, Sep.–Jun.), a lively discobar – more bar than disco – with a crazy postmodern look and DJ house, jungle and hip hop to dance to.

Around Piazza Venezia

Irish bars are big in many Italian cities, and Rome is no exception. One of the biggest and best in the city is **Trinity College**, housed near the Palazzo Doria Pamphili (▶ 104–105). It occupies two floors of a beautiful Renaissance palace at Via del Collegio Romano 6 (tel: 06 678 6472, open daily noon–3 a.m.). Good and inexpensive Irish food is served along with the inevitable beers and stouts.

Trastevere

In Trastevere, the best of the night-time bars and pubs is **Della Scala** (Via della Scala 4, tel: 06 580 3610, open daily 4 p.m.–2 a.m.), a big and bustling place for beer, wine by the glass, cocktails and light meals and snacks. It is much patronized by the young and is definitely not the place for a quiet drink. For something quieter, try **Sacchetti** (Piazza San Cosimato 61–2, tel: 06 581 5374, open Tue.–Sun. 5:30 p.m.–midnight), a family-run bar with tables outside. It serves delicious ice cream and home-made cakes and pastries.

Best of the live jazz and blues joints is the long-established **Big Mama** (Vicolo San Francesco a Ripa 18, tel: 06 581 2551, open daily 9:30 p.m.–1:30 a.m, Oct.–Jun.). It describes itself, with some justification, as the "Home of Blues in Rome," staging around 200 concerts a year. Stars of today and yesteryear perform alongside up-and-coming Italian musicians.

Testaccio

Though Trastevere is still lively at night and has many good bars and clubs, it is no longer as trendy as it was a few years ago. The axis of night-time action has now shifted to **Testaccio**, a traditional working-class district farther south. In summer the district buzzes with clubs, bars and outdoor venues, but it's peripheral to the city center, so you'll need to take a bus or taxi to get there.

Venues of the moment change with some regularity, but you can always be sure to find something to suit your tastes. Two of the more permanent fixtures for live music and dancing are **Akab** (Via di Monte Testaccio 69, tel: 06 574 4485, open: Wed.–Sat. 10 p.m.–4 a.m.) and **Caffè Latino** (Via di Monte Testaccio 63, tel: 06 5728 8556, open Tue.–Sun. 10 p.m.–3 a.m.).

L'Alibi (Via di Monte Testaccio 40–7, tel: 06 574 3448, open Wed.–Sun. 11 p.m.–4:30 a.m.), a primarily (though not exclusively) gay club, is one of the most established venues in this part of the city

MOVIE THEATERS

Trastevere has one of Rome's few English-language movie theaters, the three-screen **Pasquino** (Piazza Sant'Egidio 10, tel: 06 580 3622), but the theaters are small and probably only worth a visit if you're desperate to see a movie.

Northern Rome

Getting Your Bearings

This chapter encompasses two contrasting areas of Rome. The first is around Termini, the city's main train station, an unlovely part of the city you'd avoid were it not for a superb museum and major church; the second is around Piazza di Spagna, an area full of wonderful streets, fantastic stores, memorable views and compelling museums and galleries.

The mid-20th century architecture of Termini train station has its admirers, but the area around the station is all hustle, traffic, buses and budget hotels. In truth, there is little here to tempt you into staying longer than it takes to see the distinguished church of Santa Maria Maggiore and the magnificent collection of Roman statues, mosaics and wall paintings at Palazzo Massimo alle Terme.

Once your sightseeing in this part of the city is finished, you could catch the Metro from Repubblica to Spagna station to visit Piazza di Spagna, a means of avoiding a mostly uninteresting and far from pretty 19th-century part of the city. Alternately, you could walk from the Palazzo Massimo alle Terme toward Via Vittorio Veneto (often known simply as Via Veneto), famous in the 1950s and 1960s as the focus of Rome's *dolce vita* days of hedonism and high living. Today, sadly, it lives largely on its past reputation. You could also take in the works of art at Palazzo Barberini, as well as the interior of Santa Maria della Vittoria, home to a notorious Bernini sculpture.

By the time you reach the Trevi Fountain, the most spectacular of the city's many fountains, you have re-entered Rome's old historic core and are close to its most exclusive shopping district, the grid of streets centred on Via Condotti. You could easily spend a couple of hours here window shopping, perhaps followed by a lazy half-hour people watching in Piazza di Spagna. Literary pilgrims may want to visit the small museum on the piazza devoted to the poets John Keats and Percy Bysshe Shelley. Then climb the Spanish Steps for views across Rome, and, if the weather's fine, walk northwest from Piazza di Spagna along Viale della Trinità dei Monti. This street offers more fine views and leads into a more open part of the city, allowing you to strike onto the Pincio Hill, and from there into the park and gardens of the Villa Borghese. A walk of a half mile or so through the park brings you to the Borghese gallery and museum, home to superb sculptures by Bernini and paintings by Caravaggio, Raphael and other major painters. If you don't want to walk, take a cab or bus 116 from Piazza di Spagna.

Previous page: Bernini's *Apollo and Daphne* in the Galleria Borghese
Top left: Apse mosaic depicting Mary and Jesus in Santa Maria Maggiore

★ Don't Miss

At Your Leisure

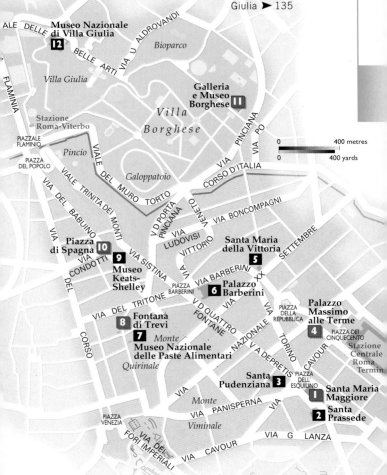

This itinerary, which takes you to some of the most famous sights in Rome's more easterly and northern margins, requires you to travel a little farther from the city center than on previous days.

Northern Rome in a Day

8:30 a.m.

Make your way to Piazza dei Cinquecento on foot, or by bus, Metro or taxi, and then walk the short distance to **Santa Maria Maggiore** (➤ 118–119). Explore the magnificently decorated church, especially its mosaics, and then visit the small nearby churches of **Santa Prassede** (➤ 132) and **Santa Pudenziana** (➤ 132).

9:15 a.m.

Walk to the **Palazzo Massimo alle Terme** (➤ 120–123) and allow a couple of hours to explore the museum's superb collection of classical sculpture and rare Roman mosaics and wall paintings (left).

11:00 a.m.

Walk west toward Piazza di Spagna, perhaps stopping off en route to visit **Santa Maria della Vittoria** (➤ 132–133), home to Bernini's erotic sculpture of St. Teresa, and the **Palazzo Barberini** (➤ 133–134), where works by Raphael, Caravaggio and Titian, among others, are on display.

12:30 p.m.

Make your way to the **Trevi Fountain** (right, ➤ 124–125), immortalized in Fellini's movie, *La Dolce Vita*, then continue north toward Via Condotti and Piazza di Spagna. If you have time, visit the **Museo Nazionale delle Paste Alimentari** (➤ 134).

1:00 p.m.

Stop for a either a snack lunch or a restaurant meal in the streets around the Trevi Fountain and Piazza di Spagna.

2:00 p.m.

After lunch you might stop for a coffee in the historic Antico Caffè Greco (➤ 138). Serious shoppers will want to spend plenty of time in the area around **Via Condotti** (or return another day), others can visit the **Museo Keats-Shelley** (➤ 135). Everyone should walk to the top of the celebrated **Spanish Steps** (➤ 126–127).

3:00 p.m.

Meander through the shaded parkland of the Villa Borghese to the **Galleria Borghese** (➤ 128–131), filled with sculptural masterpieces such as Bernini's *Pluto and Proserphine* (left), as well as magnificent works by Caravaggio and others. If the walk is too far, you can take a taxi from Piazza di Spagna. Remember you need a reservation for the Galleria.

5:30 p.m.

After seeing the Galleria you'll be stranded a long way from from the city center. If you don't want to walk back through the Villa Borghese, catch a taxi. Otherwise you can walk east to Via Po, where the 52 or 53 bus will take you back to central Rome. For Termini, catch the number 910 bus.

Santa Maria Maggiore

Santa Maria Maggiore is the most important – and possibly the oldest – of some 80 churches in Rome dedicated to the Virgin Mary. Its surroundings are not the prettiest in the city, but the ancient basilica's richly decorated interior is one of the most sumptuous in Italy.

According to legend, the church was built after the Virgin appeared to Pope Liberius in a vision on August 4, 356 and told him to build a church on the spot where snow would fall the following day. Snow duly fell, despite the fact that it was the middle of summer, leading not only to the foundation of a church, but also to the instigation of a feast day – Our Lady of the Snow – on August 5.

In truth, the church was probably founded in the middle of the fifth century on the ruins of a Roman building dating back to the first century, possibly earlier.

This building was probably a temple to Juno Lucina, a mother goddess much revered by Roman women, and it is probably no accident that a pagan cult was replaced by its Christian equivalent: the new church was dedicated to the mother of Christ as Santa Maria ad Praesepe (St. Mary of the Crib). The church's maternal link was further reinforced by relics of Christ's Holy Crib, fragments of which were enshrined beneath the high altar.

Obelisks and pillars stand sentinel outside the church's north and south entrances, one a Roman copy of an Egyptian obelisk (in Piazza dell'Esquilino) removed from the Mausoleo di Augusto, the other a column removed from the Basilica di Massenzio in the Roman forum. The south entrance is the usual entry point for visitors.

Much has been added to the church since the fifth century, not least its immense amount of decoration, but the original basilica-shaped plan survives, a design probably adapted directly from the site's earlier Roman structure. Almost the first thing to strike you inside is the magnificent coffered **ceiling**, reputedly gilded with the first gold to be shipped from the New World, a gift from Ferdinand and Isabella of Spain to Pope Alexander VI.

The colossal columns supporting the ceiling lead the eye upward to a superb 36-panel sequence of **mosaics**, fifth-century works portraying episodes from the lives of Moses, Isaac, Jacob and Abraham. A later but equally magnificent mosaic (1295) depicting the Coronation of the Virgin adorns the apse, the area behind the high altar, and is the work of Jacopo Torriti. Complementary swirls of color decorate parts

Mass has been celebrated in Santa Maria Maggiore for more than 1,500 years

Ancient marbles from the Palatine Hill were used to decorate the Cappella Sistina, Santa Maria Maggiore's most ornate chapel

of the church floor, examples of Cosmati inlaid marble work dating from the middle of the 12th century.

Among the interior's most impressive additions are a pair of large facing chapels: the **Cappella Sistina** (on the right as you face the altar) and the **Cappella Paolina** (on the left), completed for popes Sixtus V and Paul V in 1587 and 1611 respectively. Little in either is individually outstanding, but the overall decorative effect is overwhelming.

TAKING A BREAK

If you want a leisurely drink, the best advice is to continue on toward Piazza di Spagna. **Monti DOC** (➤ 142), however, is a good local choice.

🔲 203 E1 ✉ Piazza di Santa Maria Maggiore and Piazza dell'Esquilino ☎ 06 483 195
🕐 Daily 7–7 🚇 Termini or Cavour 🚌 70, 71, 75, 204 🎟 Free

SANTA MARIA MAGGIORE: INSIDE INFO

Top tip Santa Maria Maggiore is in a relatively unappealing part of the city close to the Termini train station, but can be easily combined with a visit to the nearby Palazzo Massimo alle Terme. Unlike many churches in the city, it remains open all day.

Hidden gem Look out for the **tomb of Cardinal Consalvo Rodriguez** in the chapel to the rear right (south) of the high altar as you face it. The cardinal died in 1299, and the tomb was completed soon after. Its sculptor is not known, but the beautiful inlaid marble is the work of Giovanni di Cosma, one of the family first responsible for this distinctive "Cosmati" decorative style.

Palazzo Massimo alle Terme

The Palazzo Massimo alle Terme houses part of the Museo Nazionale Romano, one of the world's greatest collections of ancient art. One of the city's newest museum spaces, it provides a magnificent showcase for some of the most beautiful sculptures, paintings and mosaics of the Roman age.

The Palazzo lies close to Rome's unlovely Termini station, but don't be put off. Once inside the superbly restored 19th-century building you're confronted by beauty at every turn. The gallery spreads over three floors: the first two levels (first and second floor) are devoted largely to sculpture, the top (third floor) mostly to mosaics and a series of frescoed Roman rooms moved from sites around the city. Such painted rooms are extremely rare, most frescoes of this age having long been lost to the elements. They are also surprisingly beautiful, so be certain to leave enough time to do them justice.

The wall paintings from the Villa di Livia are part of the rare collection of frescoes and mosaics on the third floor

These mosaics and paintings distinguish the Palazzo Massimo from its sister museum, the Palazzo Altemps (► 86–89), which is smaller and devoted more to sculpture, and in particular to the outstanding sculptures of the Ludovisi collection.

Beyond the ticket hall and vestibule, bear to your right for the first of the first floor's eight rooms, which are arranged around the palace's interior central courtyard. Ahead of you, along the courtyard's right-hand side, runs a gallery – one of three – filled with portrait busts and statues that served as funerary or honorary monuments in the last years of the Republican era (the end of the second and beginning of the first century BC). Room I opens to the right, where the highlight among several busts and statues of upper-class Roman figures is the **General of Tivoli**. It was probably the work of a Greek sculptor and is thought to have been executed between 90–70 BC, at a time when the Romans were conducting numerous military campaigns in Asia.

Room III contains a collection of Roman coins, while the highlight of Room V is a virtuoso statue of **Emperor Augustus** – note the exquisite detail of the emperor's toga. Different in style, but no less compelling, is Room VII's statue of **Niobede**, one of the mythical daughters of Niobe murdered by Apollo and Artemis. The statue shows Niobede trying to remove an arrow shot by Artemis. Other rooms and galleries on this floor contain many more similarly outstanding sculptures, as well as small areas of wall painting that whet the appetite for the exhibits on the museum's top floor (see below).

Sculptures on the next (second) floor move chronologically through the Roman era, picking up the thread of the floor below in Room I with work from the era of the Flavian emperors – Vespasian, Titus and Domitian (after AD 69). The following 14 rooms contain exhibits spanning the next 400 years.

Interspersed with these are rooms arranged by theme, notably Room VI, which is devoted to the idealized sports and other statues that once adorned ancient Rome's gymnasiums and sports arenas. Here you'll find the gallery's most famous statue,

Bottom: The Palazzo Massimo contains a wealth of fine Roman sculpture

the ***Discobolo Lancellotti***, or Lancellotti Discus-Thrower (mid-second century AD), the finest of several Roman copies of a celebrated fifth-century BC Greek bronze original. This original was widely celebrated by classical writers as a perfect study of the human body in motion.

A very different but equally beguiling statue resides in Room VII, devoted to gods and divinities, and shows L'Ermafrodito Addormentato, or ***Sleeping Hermaphrodite*** (second century AD). Like the Discus-Thrower, the sculpture is the best of several known copies made from a popular Greek original created some 400 years earlier. The statue's sensuous appearance made it a popular adornment for gardens and open spaces in the grand houses of private individuals. A far cruder statue depicting a **masked actor in the guise of Papposileno** is the most striking figure in Room IX, which is given over to the theater and performing arts.

Discobolo Lancellotti, a Roman copy of an earlier Greek bronze, dates from the second-century AD

Much of your time in the gallery should be spent on the top (third) floor. Its first highlight is Room II, which is given over to exquisite wall paintings removed from the **Villa di Livia**, a villa belonging to Livia Drusilla, mother of Emperor Augustus (who reigned 27 BC–14 AD). The murals portray a lovely garden scene, rich in greens and blues and filled with

PALAZZO MASSIMO ALLE TERME: INSIDE INFO

Top tips The gallery is not difficult to navigate, but the **gallery guide** (see below) contains a good plan of each floor.
• The gallery shop has many beautiful gifts and books, so bring money and credit cards in case you're tempted.

In more detail The beauty of the Palazzo Massimo – unlike many galleries of antiquities – is that it's not crammed with endless rows of dull statues: quality rather than quantity has been its guiding principle. There are relatively few works, and each is well labeled and well presented. Should you want to know more, it's well worth investing in the excellent guides to the gallery published by Electa-Soprintendenza Archeologico di Roma. Copies in English are generally available from the gallery shop.

finely painted birds, flowers and trees, suggesting the original room was part of a summer house.

From here, walk back through Room I and along the floor's right-hand (north) gallery to rooms III to V. These contain wall paintings removed from the **Villa della Farnesina**, uncovered in 1879. Probably from a villa originally built for the wedding of Augustus' daughter, Giulia, these are the most important Roman paintings of their kind and embrace several distinct styles, from traditional Greek-influenced landscapes and mythological scenes to Egyptian-style friezes and architectural motifs. You rarely see such paintings, making their delicacy, skill and sublime coloring all the more surprising and memorable. Much the same can be said of the many **mosaics** exhibited on this floor, whose beauty and detail are in marked contrast to later – and supposedly more sophisticated – medieval mosaics across the city.

TAKING A BREAK

Places to stop for a drink or snack on the Piazza della Repubblica are somewhat uninspiring, but if you walk a little farther on Via Vittorio Emanuele Orlando you'll find **Dagnino** (Galleria Esedra, tel: 06 481 8660), a lovely old-fashioned pastry shop selling Sicilian specialties.

A collection of mosaics is housed on the third floor

➕ 203 E2 ✉ Piazza dei Cinquecento 67 ☎ 06 4890 3500 🕐 Tue.–Sat. 9–6:45, Sun. 9–7:45 🍴 No museum café: cafés and McDonald's nearby in Piazza della Repubblica 🚇 Termini 🚌 64 and all other services to Piazza dei Cinquecento, Repubblica 💰 Expensive. Combined pass available ➤ 190

Trevi Fountain

The Trevi Fountain, or Fontana di Trevi, is the most beautiful of Italy's many fountains. It is perhaps most famous for its tradition – throw a coin in the waters and you will return to Rome – and for actress Anita Ekberg's nocturnal visit in Federico Fellini's classic movie, *La Dolce Vita*.

One of the Trevi Fountain's main attractions is that you stumble across it almost by accident. There it is as you turn from one of the three streets that lend the fountain its name (*tre vie* means "three streets") into the small piazza, a sight the writer Charles Dickens memorably described as "silvery to the eye and ear."

The fountain's waters were originally provided by the Acqua Vergine, or *Aqua Virgo*, an aqueduct begun by Agrippa in 19 BC to bring water to the city from the hills outside Rome. It took its name from the legend that it was a young girl (*vergine*) who showed the original spring to a group of Roman soldiers. Today, the fountain disgorges a colossal 21 million gallons of water daily; in its Roman heyday the aqueduct could carry more than 26 million gallons of water an hour.

The first major fountain to take advantage of this watery bounty was built in 1453 by Pope Niccolò V, who financed the project with a tax on wine. This led irate Romans of the time to sneer that the pontiff had "taken our wine to give us water." The present fountain was begun by another pope, Clement XII, in 1732 – an inscription above the fountain's main arch records the fact – and inaugurated 30 years later by Clement XIII.

The Fontana's designer – probably Nicola Salvi – came up with the novel idea of draping the fountain over the entire wall of the Palazzo Poli, thus adding to its monumental scale and dramatic impact. The fountain's central figure represents Neptune, or Oceanus. In front stand two tritons (1759–62) by sculptor Pietro Bracci: the one on the left as you face the fountain represents the stormy sea (symbolized by the agitated horse), while the figure on the right blowing into a conch shell represents the sea in repose.

Anita Ekberg in
La Dolce Vita

Few visitors to the fountain can resist the temptation to cast a coin into the waters. The tradition echoes the practice of the ancient Romans, who often threw coins into certain fountains to appease the gods, and later of early Christians, who would scatter coins onto the tomb of St. Peter and other prominent saints and martyrs.

TAKING A BREAK

For superlative ice cream head to the **Gelateria di San Crispino** (➤ 138). Or stop for a coffee at **Antico Caffè Greco** (➤ 138) – you'll pay a price to drink here as it is one of Rome's most historic cafés.

🔲 199 F4 ☒ Piazza di Trevi 🔁 Barberini 🚌 52, 53, 61, 62, 71, 80, 95, 116 and 119 to Via del Tritone 💵 Free

TREVI FOUNTAIN: INSIDE INFO

Top tips Come to admire the fountain **late in the evening,** when the crowds are thinner and the fountain is usually floodlit.
• The fountain area is especially busy on Sunday, when many Romans make it a place to meet for a chat. If you'd rather not share in the boisterous atmosphere, come on another day.

In more detail The **figures in the rectangular niches** either side of Neptune are allegorical figures symbolising "Health" (with a relief above it of the young girl showing soldiers the source of the Acqua Vergine's spring) and "Abundance" (with a relief depicting Agrippa approving the aqueduct's design).

Piazza di Spagna

The Piazza di Spagna is one of Rome's great outdoor salons, a beautiful square that dominates the city's most elegant shopping district and whose famous Spanish Steps provide a magnet for visitors at all hours of the day and night.

The Spanish Steps and the church of Trinità dei Monti

The steps are the piazza's most celebrated sight. More properly known as the Scalinata della Trinità dei Monti, they consist of a majestic double staircase that cascades down the slopes of the Pincio Hill from the church of **Trinità dei Monti**. Built between 1723 and 1726, they provide not only one of Rome's most famous architectural set-pieces – especially in spring, when huge pots of azaleas adorn the steps – but also a forum that has proved a favored meeting place for Romans and visitors alike for several centuries.

Both the square and the steps take their name from the Palazzo di Spagna, built in the 17th century as the Spanish Embassy to the Holy See. Before that, the area was known as the Platea Trinitatis, after the Trinità church. Many foreign visitors made the area their home during the 18th-century heyday of the Grand Tour. The English, in particular, were passionate admirers, so much so that the district became known as the "English ghetto" and boasted a famous café, the Caffè degli Inglesi, a favorite drinking den for expatriates. That particular establishment is no more, but there are two other historic cafés on or near the square: Babington's Tea Rooms (to the left of the steps as you face them), founded in the late 19th century by two English women, and the Antico Caffè Greco in Via dei Condotti (► 138), founded in 1760 and patronized by the likes of Goethe, Casanova, Shelley, Byron, Baudelaire, Wagner and Liszt.

Another visitor to the area's cafés would probably have been the English poet John Keats, who lodged – and died – in a house to the right of the Spanish Steps. Today, the building is given over to a **museum** (► 135) devoted to the poet and other literary exiles, including Shelley.

At the foot of the Spanish Steps is the charming, tiny **Fontana della Barcaccia**, literally the "Fountain of the Rotten (or Worthless) Boat." Its name derives from the centerpiece, a half-sunken boat with water spilling lazily from its sides. The fountain's low level and less than spectacular display are the result of the low pressure of the Acqua Vergine aqueduct (► 124) that feeds it. The baroque design – possibly based on an earlier Roman model – was probably a joint effort on the part of Pietro Bernini and his more famous son, Gian Lorenzo Bernini. It was commissioned in 1629 by Pope Urban VIII, a member of the Barberini family, whose sun and bee dynastic emblems adorn the stonework.

TAKING A BREAK

Both **Babington's** (► 138) and the **Antico Caffè Greco** (► 138) are pretty but expensive and only worthwhile if you want to savor their historic ambience. Better choices of cafés and bars can be found close by: try **Ciampini al Café du Jardin** (► 138).

Piazza di Spagna is a meeting place for Romans and visitors alike

🚩 199 F5　✉ Piazza di Spagna　🚌 119

PIAZZA DI SPAGNA: INSIDE INFO

Top tips Climb to the top of the Spanish Steps from Piazza di Spagna for **good views**. Watch for pickpockets if the square is crowded.

• The Trinità church, begun in 1502, has immense scenic appeal but nothing inside that really merits a visit.

Galleria e Museo Borghese

The Borghese gallery and museum may be relatively small, but the quality of its paintings and sculptures – notably works by Bernini, Canova, Raphael and Caravaggio – make it one of the jewels of Rome's rich artistic crown.

Wealthy Roman prelates and aristocrats over the centuries often amassed huge private art collections, many of which were later sold, broken up or passed to the city or Italian state. The finest of all such collections was accumulated by Cardinal Scipione Borghese (1579–1633), a nephew of Camillo Borghese, later Pope Paul V. Many works were sold to the Louvre in Paris in 1807, mostly under pressure from Napoleon, whose sister, the infamous Paolina, was married to Prince Camillo Borghese. Nevertheless, the surviving exhibits – which were bequeathed to the state in 1902 – make this the finest gallery of its kind in Rome, its appeal enhanced by a lovely setting, the beautifully restored Casino (1613–15), or summerhouse, of the Villa Borghese.

The collection is simply arranged over two floors and around some 20 gloriously decorated rooms, the lower floor being devoted mainly to sculpture, the upper floor to paintings. One of the gallery's most famous works greets you in the first room – Antonio Canova's erotic statue of **Paolina Borghese** in the guise of Venus. This is one of the most sensual sculptures of the Borghese or any other gallery, so sensual, in fact, that Paolina's husband, Camillo Borghese, forbade anyone to see it after its completion – even Canova. Paolina was a willing and knowing model, who when asked how she could possibly have posed naked for the work is said to have replied "the studio was heated." The next room introduces the work of Gian Lorenzo Bernini, the presiding genius – with chief rival Borromini – of the baroque in Rome. The room's principal sculpture is a statue of **David** (1623–24) in the process of hurling his slingshot stone at Goliath, the

Antonio Canova's erotic reclining statue of Paolina Borghese scandalized her husband

The 17th-century Casino Borghese provides a magnificent setting for the Borghese Gallery's works of art

face of which is said to be a self-portrait of the sculptor. It was commissioned by Scipione – the cardinal became one of Bernini's principal patrons – who is said to have held a mirror for Bernini while he worked on the self-portrait.

Room III contains what many consider Bernini's masterpiece, *Apollo and Daphne* (1622–25), which portrays the flight of Daphne from Apollo and captures the moment Daphne turns herself into a laurel tree to escape the god. An equally bewitching work awaits you in Room IV, ***Pluto and Proserphine*** (1622), renowned for the detail of Pluto's hand grasping Proserphine's thigh – rarely has the softness of flesh been so convincingly portrayed in stone. The following room contains a statue of a hermaphrodite, a Roman copy of a Greek original. You may already have seen a similar work in the Palazzo Massimo alle Terme (► 120–123). Room VI has more works by Bernini: a statue of Aeneas and Anchises (1613), probably carved by Bernini in collaboration with his

father when he was just 15, and the much later allegorical work *Truth* (1652), which remains unfinished.

In Room VIII you find another Roman original, a celebrated second-century statue of a **Dancing Satyr**. The room is better known, however, for the first of the gallery's important paintings, namely several major works by Caravaggio. Many of these were shrewdly snapped up by Scipione when they had been turned down by others as too shocking or iconoclastic. Caravaggio is said to have painted self-portraits in at least two of the pictures – as the *Sick Bacchus* (c1593) and as Goliath in *David with the Head of Goliath* (1609–10). His best works here though are the **Madonna dei Palafrenieri** (1605–06) and the **Boy with a Basket of Fruit** (1593–95), both notable for their superb sense of realism. The former picture shows the Virgin crushing a serpent, a symbol of evil and also of heresy, an allusion to the confrontation of the time between the Catholic and Protestant churches.

All manner of other exceptional paintings are collected on the gallery's upper floor. Among the finest is Raphael's **Deposition** (1507), just one of several works by the artist in the first main room. Other fine paintings

The lavish interior of the Galleria, once the Casino, or summerhouse, of the Villa Borghese, has been beautifully restored

Bernini's statue of David, one of the gallery's principal works

include works by Perugino, Andrea del Sarto, Correggio – an outstanding **Danaë** (1530–31) – Lorenzo Lotto, Bronzino and Giovanni Bellini. One of the best pictures is kept back for the gallery's last room: Antonello da Messina's **Portrait of a Man** (*c*1475), the prototype of this genre of portrait painting.

The Deposition by Raphael is one of the highlights of the Galleria Borghese

➕ 203 D4 ✉ Piazzale del Museo Borghese 5 ☎ 06 854 8577 (recorded information) 🕐 Tue.–Sun. 9–7 🍴 Gallery café Ⓜ Spagna or Flaminio 🚌 52, 53 and 910 to Via Pinciana or 116 to Viale del Museo Borghese 💶 Expensive

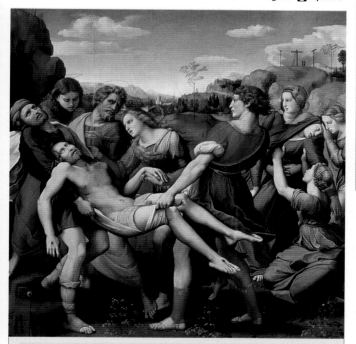

GALLERIA E MUSEO BORGHESE: INSIDE INFO

Top tip Numbers of visitors to the Galleria Borghese are limited, so reservations are required. Call 06 32810 to make reservations. Operators speak English. The booking service is open Monday to Friday 9–7, Saturday 9–1. Call well in advance, especially in high season (Easter–Sep.).

In more detail One of the Galleria Borghese's most mysterious and out-standing paintings is Titian's beautiful and little-understood *Sacred and Profane Love* (1514). Some claim its subject is actually Venus and Medea or Heavenly and Earthly Love: most critics, though, think it is an allegory of spring, and was inspired by the same strange dream romance, *Hypnerotomachia di Polifilo*, that provided Bernini with the idea for his eccentric elephant statue outside Santa Maria sopra Minerva (▶ 94).

At Your Leisure

❷ Santa Prassede

This tiny church on a side street immediately south of Santa Maria Maggiore is celebrated for its mosaics, in particular those of the Cappella di San Zeno, situated on the left near the church's entrance. The gold-encrusted chapel was commissioned in 822 by Pope Paschal I as his mother's mausoleum. The square halo of Theodora, Paschal's mother, in the mosaic left of the altar indicates that she was still alive when the work was commissioned. Other mosaics on the church's triumphal arch portray Christ flanked by angels in a heavenly Jerusalem, while those in the apse depict saints Prassede and Pudenziana. Prassede is said to have witnessed the martyrdom of 24 Christians who were then hurled into a well (marked by a marble slab on the church's floor). The saint then miraculously soaked up their blood with a single sponge.

➕ 206 A5 ✉ Via Santa Prassede 9a ☎ 06 488 2456 ⏰ Daily 7:30–noon, 4–6:30 (but hours may vary) 🚇 Termini 🚌 4, 9, 16, 70, 71, 75 and 204 to Piazza dell'Esquilino 🎟 Free

❸ Santa Pudenziana

Santa Pudenziana lies just a few moments' walk from Santa Prassede to the northwest of Santa Maria Maggiore. It is said to have been founded between 384 and 399 over the spot where St. Peter converted Prassede and Pudenziana, daughters of the Christian Senator, Pudes. One of the church's treasures is a reliquary containing part of the table on which the saint is believed to have said Mass.

The church's tiny facade dates from the 12th century, but has been much restored since – only the pretty frieze around the door is original. Inside, the highlight is an extraordinary mosaic from the early fourth-century church depicting Christ, the Apostles and two women thought to represent Pudenziana and her sister.

➕ 203 D1 ✉ Via Urbana 160 ☎ 06 481 4622 ⏰ Mon.–Sat. 7–7, Sun. 8:30–7 🚇 Termini or Cavour 🚌 4, 9, 16, 70, 71, 75 and 204 to Piazza dell'Esquilino 🎟 Free

❺ Santa Maria della Vittoria

Santa Maria della Vittoria seems like just one more modest baroque church (1608–20) but inside its decoration is some of the richest in the city. The last chapel on the left as you face the high altar contains one of Bernini's most celebrated sculptures, *The Ecstasy of St. Teresa* (1646). The work portrays the saintly Spanish writer, mystic and nun (1515–82) as she is "pierced" by the love of god – symbolized here by an

---

For Kids

The lively atmosphere at the **Trevi Fountain** (▶ 124–125) should appeal to children, and they may also enjoy the **Museo Nazionale delle Paste Alimentari** (▶ 134), dedicated to Italy's favorite food. Farther afield, the **Villa Borghese** has lots of attractions for youngsters: near the Viale delle Belle Arti entrance to the park are swings, paddleboats, pony rides and a train, while the old Villa Borghese zoo has been transformed into the **Bioparco** (Via del Giardino Zoologico 1; tel: 06 360 8211, open daily 9:30–6), which has many animals and specially organized activities for children. The **Museo di Zoologia** (Via Aldovrandi 18; tel: 06 321 6586, open Tue.–Sun. 9–5), alongside the zoo, has an impressive "Animals and their Habitats" exhibition. North of Piazza del Popolo is the **Museo dei Bambini** (Via Flaminia 80; tel: 06 3600 5488), aimed at the under-12s and full of educational and other hands-on exhibits.

Bernini's controversial *Ecstasy of St. Teresa* is one of the masterpieces of high baroque

leading patrician families. A magnificent baroque building in its own right, it is a major museum, housing the bulk of the collection of the Galleria Nazionale d'Arte Antica (the rest resides across the Tiber in the Palazzo Corsini). Long-term restoration keeps much of the huge palace complex closed, but you can see the palace's superb centerpiece, the **Gran Salone**, a vast and fantastically decorated room dominated

angel with an arrow. The statue's erotic overtones – the saint is said to be shown transported by an earthly rather than divine passion – have caused much controversy over the centuries. The surrounding chapel, the **Cappella Cornaro**, was commissioned from Bernini by Cardinal Cornaro, hence the eight statues of the cardinal's family admiring the statue as if from a theater box.

🚩 203 D2 ✉ Via XX Settembre 17
☎ 06 482 6190 🕐 Daily 7:30–noon, 3–6 (but hours may vary)
🚇 Repubblica 🚌 37, 60, 61, 62, 136, 137, 175, 492 or 590 to Via XX Settembre 🎟 Free

⑥ Palazzo Barberini

The Palazzo Barberini was begun in 1625 for Cardinal Francesco Barberini, a member of one of Rome's

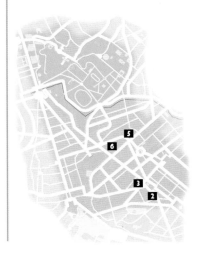

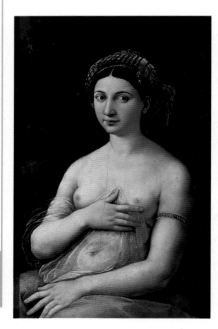

La Fornarina by Raphael, a painting which many believed to be a portrait of his lover

considered, probably erroneously, to portray the artist's mistress, the daughter of a baker (*fornaio* in Italian). Gossips of the time suggested Raphael's premature death (in 1520) was brought on by his lover's voracious sexual appetite.

➕ 203 D2 ✉ Via delle Quattro Fontane 13 ☎ 06 482 4184 🕐 Tue.–Sat. 9–7 (also Fri.–Sat. 7–10 p.m.) 🚇 Barberini 🚌 52, 53, 56, 58, 60, 61, 62, 95, 116, 119 and 492 to Fontana del Tritone 🎫 Moderate

7 Museo Nazionale delle Paste Alimentari

This excellently organized museum close to the Trevi Fountain is one of Rome's more unusual and rewarding, thanks to its unique theme – pasta. The displays in its 15 rooms cover every aspect of the food, from its history, cooking techniques and place in art to a collection of pasta-making equipment, models, dietary tips and photographs of famous people such as actress Sophia Loren enjoying Italy's national dish. Visitors are given a portable CD player with multilingual commentary to guide them around the exhibits.

➕ 202 C2 ✉ Piazza Scanderberg 117 ☎ 06 699 1119 🕐 Daily 9:30–5:30 🚇 Barberini 🚌 52, 53, 56, 60, 61, 62, 71, 95, 116 and 119 to Via del Tritone or Via del Corso 🎫 Expensive

by Pietro da Cortona's allegorical ceiling frescoes depicting *The Triumph of Divine Providence* (1633–39).

Other paintings are displayed chronologically in a series of beautiful rooms, and include major works by Caravaggio, El Greco, Tintoretto, Titian and many more. The single most famous picture is *La Fornarina*, attributed to Raphael, a work long

Off the Beaten Track

Much of the area surrounding Stazione Termini is given over to government offices or the buildings of the main city university and holds little visitor appeal. **San Lorenzo**, a traditional residential and student district, east of Termini, with a sprinkling of inexpensive restaurants and pizzerias is an exception (though probably not worth a separate trip). More worthwhile is the trip along Via Nomentana to the northeast to visit the **catacombs and churches of Santa Costanza** and **Sant'Agnese fuori le Mura**.

Around Piazza di Spagna, you can escape the crowds on **Via Margutta**, a pretty street filled with commercial art galleries, or in the web of **old streets** between Piazza del Parlamento and the ruins of the Mausoleo di Augusto, the circular mausoleum of the Emperor Augustus.

🄬 Museo Nazionale di Villa Giulia

The Villa Giulia, tucked away in the northern reaches of the Villa Borghese, is only worth the journey if you have a passion for the Etruscans, for a large part of the huge building is given over to the art and artifacts of that mysterious civilization. The collection is the greatest of its type in the world, but for too long has been neglected and left – often literally – to gather dust. Many of the rooms contain unexciting rows of urns and other funerary sculpture. Rather more inspiring are the museum's many exquisite pieces of gold and other jewelry, some of the larger sculptures, and the reconstructed Etruscan temple in the villa's extensive gardens.

🕇 202 A5 ⊠ Piazzale Villa Giulia 9 ☎ 06 320 1951 🕐 Tue.–Sun. 9–7 🚇 Flaminio 🚌 9, 13, 225 to Viale delle Belle Arti 🎟 Moderate

🄌 Museo Keats-Shelley

Literary pilgrims will enjoy this lovely old house to the right of the Spanish Steps, where the 25-year-old English poet John Keats died in 1821 after coming to Rome to seek a cure for tuberculosis.

Since 1909, the house has been lovingly restored and preserved as a small literary museum and library for scholars of Keats and his fellow English poet, Percy Bysshe Shelley, who also died in Italy when he drowned off the Tuscan coast. The fusty rooms are filled with old books, pamphlets and manuscripts, as well as literary mementoes such as Keats's death mask, a lock of the poet's hair, part of Shelley's cheekbone and a reliquary containing strands of John Milton's and Elizabeth Barrett Browning's hair.

🕇 199 F5 ⊠ Piazza di Spagna 26 ☎ 06 678 4235 🕐 Mon.–Fri. 9–1, 3–6; Sat. 11–2, 3–6 🚇 Spagna 🚌 117 and 119 to Piazza di Spagna 🎟 Inexpensive

The house in which English poet John Keats died is now a museum

Where to...
Eat and Drink

Prices

Expect to pay per person for a meal, excluding drinks and service
$ under €20 $$ €20–€40 $$$ over €40

Neither of the two main areas covered in this chapter – in and around Termini and Piazza di Spagna – are known for their restaurants: Termini is too downbeat, Piazza di Spagna too full of stores. Yet both have good places to eat in all price brackets and offer an excellent selection of bars for coffee and snacks, including some of Rome's most historic cafés. Both areas also have small places from another age – the discreet Beltramme, for example – and more modern establishments such as 'Gusto,

a restaurant that wouldn't be out of place in London, Sydney or New York.

Agata e Romeo $$$

The environs of Termini train station are an unlikely location for this excellent restaurant. The cooking is modern Roman mixed with pan-Italian and international dishes and gives the lie to the notion that creative cuisine, especially in Italy, is invariably pretentious or unsuccessful. Thus you might eat a traditional dish such as *baccalà* (salt cod), but salt cod that has been smoked and cooked with

an orange sauce; or be tempted by a flan of pecorino (sheep's cheese) with honey. The setting is simple but comfortable – brick arches and plain walls with the occasional painting. The wine list contains an interesting selection of regional Italian and other wines. Reservations are essential.

✚ 203 E1 ⊠ Via Carlo Alberto 45
☎ 06 446 5842 ⓔ Mon.–Sat.
1–2:30, 8–10:30. Closed Aug. and 1–2 weeks in Jan.

Est Est Est $

This pizzeria is a good place for an early and inexpensive supper if you have been shopping on the nearby Via Nazionale, are staying near Termini or don't mind the walk up from Piazza Venezia. It is one of Rome's oldest pizzerias, having retained its old-fashioned appeal despite several attempted makeovers. Pizzas, a selection of pasta dishes and inexpensive wine make this a reliable if unexciting standby. The name, incidentally, is

taken from a celebrated central Italian wine.

✚ 203 D1 ⊠ Via Genova 32 ☎ 06 488 1107 ⓔ Tue.–Sun. 7–11:30 p.m. Closed 3 weeks in Aug.

Fiaschetteria Beltramme $–$$

You could easily miss this historic but humble-looking trattoria, incongruously located on one of the smart streets near Via Condotti. That may be the idea, for this is a deliberately understated place frequented by locals, artists, storekeepers, society ladies and – on one famous occasion – by the pop star Madonna. The interior is little more than a long single room whose walls are topped with wicker-covered wine bottles and almost completely covered in paintings, bought or donated by locals over the years. Food is simple, well cooked and thoroughly Roman. You can't make reservations, so turn up and hope. No credit cards.

✚ 199 E5 ⊠ Via della Croce 39
☎ No phone ⓔ Mon.–Sat. noon–3, 7:30–10:30

'Gusto $-$$

'Gusto follows the trend of large, modern eateries that began to appear in London and Paris in the 1990s, and the Romans seem to love the result. The atmosphere is chic, sophisticated but also informal, and the decor a mix of designer neutrals, wicker, steel and wood. Downstairs in the busy split-level eatery you can sample pizzas, generous salads and other light meals (be prepared for lunchtime crowds of local office and other workers), while upstairs in the restaurant there is a more ambitious and eclectic menu, combining Italian traditions and stir-fry Asian cooking. Quality is good (rarely more), but you're here for the atmosphere as much as the food.

✚ 199 D5 ☒ Piazza Augusto Imperatore 9 ☎ 06 322 6273 ⓦ Tue.–Sun. 1–3, 7.30–1

Margutta $-$$

Margutta has been in business for many years, which is no small achievement given that it is a vegetarian restaurant, something that until recently was barely known in Italy. The stylish dining area is airy and filled of modern art, a nod to the restaurant's position on Via Margutta, home to many of the city's leading commercial art galleries. The food is always imaginative, never dull, and the wines, beers and ciders served are all organically produced. At lunch there's a good set-price all-you-can eat buffet menu. You can also drop by most of the day for a tea or snack in the bar area.

✚ 202 B2 ☒ Via Margutta 118 ☎ 06 3265 0577 ⓦ Daily 12:30– 3.30, 7:30–11

Otello alla Concordia $-$$

In summer, you need to reserve well in advance to secure a table outside in the courtyard-garden of this attractive restaurant. If you are unsuccessful, don't worry because the interior is almost as pleasant: a long plain room with a wonderful old wooden ceiling. The lively restaurant was one of the favorites of film director Federico Fellini, who lived close by on Via Margutta. The cooking is thoroughbred Roman – ask for house special *spaghetti all'Otello* to sample one of the classic Italian tomato and basil sauces.

✚ 199 E5 ☒ Via della Croce 81 ☎ 06 679 1178 ⓦ Mon.–Sat. 12:30–3, 7:30–11

Pizzare $

If the slick 'Gusto (see left) is not for you, this nearby pizzeria makes a cheerful and more traditional alternative. Not entirely traditional, however, for the pizzas here are Neapolitan – fatter and fluffier than their thinner-crusted Roman rivals. You can choose from around 40 different pizza toppings, as well as a variety of *antipasti* (starters) and tasty salads.

✚ 199 D5 ☒ Via di Ripetta 14 ☎ 06 321 1468 ⓦ Daily 12:30–3.30, 7:30–midnight. Closed 1 week in Aug.

La Terrazza $$$

La Terrazza is the highly regarded restaurant of the exclusive Eden hotel (▲ 36), and combines modern Mediterranean cooking with a magnificent view across the city from its terrace dining room. The food here is always excellent, sometimes exceptional, but you should be prepared for the occasional culinary experiment that doesn't quite come off. Typical simpler dishes might include smoked scallops with a salad of wild leaves and asparagus, or sea bass with black olives and oregano.

Service at La Terrazza is far more formal than at Agata e Romeo (▲ 136), its rival in this price bracket, so to feel comfortable, dress up for the occasion. The prices here are also rather higher, although the special lunch and set-price menus help to keep a brake on spending.

✚ 202 C3 ☒ Via Ludovisi 49 ☎ 06 474 3551 ⓦ Daily 12:30–2.30, 7:45–10:30

BARS AND CAFÉS

Antica Enoteca $

This wine bar opened in 1842 and has been restored to retain its pretty old-world appearance. You can order wine by the glass or bottle – or buy bottles of fine wines to take home – and choose nibbles from a cold buffet. Or you can eat in the restaurant to the rear.

🚇 199 E5 ⊠ Via della Croce 76b ☎ 06 679 0896 🕑 Wine bar: daily 11:30 a.m.–midnight. Restaurant: daily 12:30–3 p.m., 7–10:30

Antico Caffè Greco $

The long-established Caffè Greco is Rome's most famous café, and since it was founded in 1740 has played host to the likes of Casanova, Wagner, Lord Byron, Shelley, Stendhal and Baudelaire. Though it has had its ups and downs in recent years (and may no longer be the city's best café), it is still worth the price of a cappuccino to enjoy the venerable interior and savor its historic atmosphere. Locals stand; tourists tend to crowd the sofas. Expect to pay slightly over the odds.

🚇 199 E5 ⊠ Via Condotti 86 ☎ 06 678 5474 🕑 Daily 8 a.m.–9 p.m.

Babington's $-$$

Babington's was founded by two British women at the end of the 19th century and has affected the look and feel of a British tea room ever since. You can sip fine teas (reputedly the best in the city) and nibble dainty cakes here, but the high prices for such simple offerings reflect its smart Piazza di Spagna location.

🚇 199 F5 ⊠ Piazza di Spagna 23 ☎ 06 678 6027 🕑 Daily 9–8:30

Ciampini al Café du Jardin $

You will escape the crowds in Piazza di Spagna at this lovely café near the Villa Medici, but you won't escape the area's relatively high prices. However, it's worth paying a little more for the setting – a calm outdoor area with a pond and creeper-covered walls – and the superlative views. The café serves sandwiches, light pasta meals, snack lunches, breakfast, ice cream and cocktails.

🚇 199 E5 ⊠ Piazza Trinità dei Monti ☎ 06 678 5678 🕑 Thu.–Tue. 8–1 (closes earlier in spring and fall). Closed Nov.–Mar.

Dolci e Doni $

Take a cake break just a few steps from Piazza di Spagna in this chic pastry shop and tearoom. Or you can indulge in a breakfast, brunch or light lunch.

🚇 199 E5 ⊠ Via delle Carrozze 85b ☎ 06 678 2913 🕑 Daily 8–8. Closed 2 weeks in Aug.

Gelateria di San Crispino $

Walk just a few paces from the Fontana di Trevi and you arrive at this temple to *gelato*. Most Romans say it sells the city's best ice cream and sorbets; some insist that they are the best in Italy, which is close to saying the best in the world. There are no cones here, just cups: San Crispino's perfectionist owners, brothers Giuseppe and Pasquale Alongi, claim that cones, with their artificial additives, interfere with the purity and flavor of their fresh fruit and myriad other iced delights. Flavors change according to what is seasonally available. This is a place not to be missed.

🚇 199 F4 ⊠ Via della Panetteria 42 ☎ 06 679 3924 🕑 Wed.–Mon. noon–midnight

Rosati $

Rosati is one of Rome's great cafés – not as old as the Caffè Greco (see left), but equally beloved over the years by artists, politicians and writers such as Alberto Moravia and Italo Calvino. Its Piazza del Popolo location is superb, its position having long put it in competition with Canova, the piazza's other historic café.

🚇 202 A4 ⊠ Piazza del Popolo 5 ☎ 06 322 5859 🕑 Daily 7:30 a.m.– 11:30 p.m.

Where to... Shop

The grid of streets at the foot of the Spanish Steps is the epicenter of Roman chic and the only area that matters for shoppers in search of designer labels and luxury goods. Although Via Condotti (or Via dei Condotti) is the best-known street, the parallel streets of Via Frattina and Via Borgognona are almost equally full of familiar designer names. Smaller side streets in the vicinity are also increasingly full of smart boutiques selling shoes, exclusive lingerie, leather goods and other accessories. Some streets in the area also have particular specialties: Via della Croce, for example, has a scattering of good food shops, while Via Margutta is home to many commercial art galleries and antiques shops. Via del Corso and

Via del Tritone are lined with mid-market clothing, shoes and accessory stores, that provide an excellent alternative to the Via Condotti designer stores.

The area around Piazza Vittorio Emanuele south of Termini is a different world. It is home to many of Rome's most recent immigrants, and as a result is full of specialty food and other stores selling Chinese, Korean, Somalian and other Asian and African goods. The piazza is also the site of central Rome's main food and general market (Mon.–Sat. 6–2). The square and the surrounding streets are filled with colorful stands selling fruit, vegetables, inexpensive shoes, clothing and household goods.

DESIGNER STORES

The outlets of principal Italian and international designers are listed below by street. Note, however, that new outlets open regularly in these streets and stores often change their

locations. Opening hours for the designer stores are generally Tuesday to Saturday 10–7:30 or 8, Monday 1 or 2:30 to 7:30 or 8.

Via Condotti

Giorgio Armani
🖂 Via Condotti 77 🕾 06 699 1460

Gucci
🖂 Via Condotti 8 🕾 06 678 9340

Max & Co
🖂 Via Condotti 46 🕾 06 678 7946

Max Mara
🖂 Via Condotti 17–19a 🕾 06 6992 2104

Prada
🖂 Via Condotti 92–5 🕾 06 679 0897

Salvatore Ferragamo
🖂 Via Condotti 65 and 73 🕾 06 679 1565

Valentino
🖂 Via Condotti 13 🕾 06 678 5862

Via Frattina

DKNY
🖂 Via Frattina 44 🕾 06 6992 3472

Max Mara
🖂 Via Frattina 28 🕾 06 679 3638

Via Borgognona

Dolce e Gabbana
🖂 Via Borgognona 7d 🕾 06 678 2990

Fendi
🖂 Via Borgognona 36–40 🕾 06 679 7641

Gianfranco Ferrè
🖂 Via Borgognona 5b, 6 and 6a 🕾 06 679 7445

Gianni Versace
🖂 Via Borgognona 25 🕾 06 696 661 5037

Gianni Versace Versus
🖂 Via Borgognona 33–34 🕾 06 678 3977

Other designers with outlets in and around Via Condotti and Piazza di Spagna include **Missoni** (Piazza di Spagna 78, tel: 06 679 2555); **Krizia** (Piazza di Spagna 87, tel: 06 679 3772); **Valentino-Oliver** (Via del Babuino 61, tel: 06 3600 1906); **Emporio Armani** (Via del Babuino 140, tel: 06 3600 2197); and **Armani Jeans** (Via del Babuino 70a, tel: 06 3600 1848).

ANTIQUES

Antichità

Serious antiques hunters prepared to pay for quality will have a field day in Via del Babuino and Via Margutta northwest of Piazza di Spagna. Antichità, which specializes in old fabrics and furnishings, is one of several tempting stores here.

🖂 Via del Babuino 83 ☎ 06 320 7585 ⏰ Tue.–Sat. 9–1, 3:30–7.30, Mon. 3:30–7

Bottega del Marmorato

Here you'll find all manner of ornaments in marble, including copies of ancient busts and other antiquities.

🖂 Via Margutta 53b ☎ 06 320 7660 ⏰ Mon.–Sat. 9–1, 3.30–7:30

Valerio Turchi

This is the place to come if you want to pick up genuine pieces of Roman statues, sarcophaghi or other remnants of the ancient city.

🖂 Via Margutta 91a ☎ 06 323 5047 ⏰ Tue.–Sat. 10:30–7, Mon. 3:30–7:30

BOOKS

Economy Book & Video Center

This American-run shop off Via Nazionale has Rome's best selection of English and other foreign-language books and videos.

🖂 Via Torino 136 ☎ 06 474 6877 ⏰ Tue.–Sat. 9–8, Mon. 3–8

The Lion Bookshop

The Economy's only serious rival when it comes to English-language books, this store has a pleasant reading room where you can linger with books over a cup of coffee.

🖂 Via dei Greci 33 ☎ 06 3265 4007 ⏰ Mon.–Sat. 10–7:30, mid-Jun. to Sep; Tue.–Sat. 10–7:30, Mon. 4:30–7:30, Oct. to mid-Jun.

DEPARTMENT STORES

Energie

Not a department store in the accepted sense, but if you're travelling with teenagers, or wish to buy what the fashion-conscious young Roman is wearing, then this large, loud and buzzing shop has a large selection of mid-range contemporary clothing.

🖂 Via del Corso 486 ☎ 06 322 7046 ⏰ Mon.–Sat. 9:30–8, Sun. 9:30–1, 4–8

La Rinascente

This is the only department store in central Rome worth a mention – but it's a good one. It sells mainly high-quality clothing, accessories, lingerie and general household and fashion items

🖂 Largo Chigi 20, near the corner of Via del Tritone and Via del Corso ☎ 06 679 7691 ⏰ Mon.–Sat. 9–9, Sun. 10:30–8

FOOD AND WINE

Buccone

This is one of the biggest and best places in Rome to buy wine – thousands of bottles line the huge shelves – and a wide range of other alcoholic drinks such as *grappa* and *amaro*. Wine is also available by the glass, and there is a small but excellent selection of fine foods.

🖂 Via di Ripetta 19 ☎ 06 361 2154 ⏰ Wed.–Sat. 9 a.m.–midnight, Mon.–Tue. 9–8:30, Sun. 10–7:30

Pasta all'Uova

Via della Croce does not have as many delicatessens as it once did, but there are still stores such as this, a little place that sells a variety of fresh and dried pasta. Many of the novelty pastas – unusual colors and designs – make inexpensive gifts.

🖂 Via della Croce 8 ☎ 06 679 3102 ⏰ Mon.–Wed., Fri.–Sat. 7.30–7:30, Thu. 8–3:30 (8–7:30 in summer)

HATS AND GLOVES

Sermoneta

Giorgio Sermoneta's intimate store has been selling just about every size, color and style of Italian glove for more than 35 years.

🖂 Piazza di Spagna 61 ☎ 06 265 0838 ⏰ Tue.–Sat. 10–7:30, Mon. 3:30–7:30

Borsalino

Hats, hats and more hats: the only place in Rome you need to visit if you are looking for something to wear up top.

🖂 Piazza del Popolo 20 ☎ 06 679 4192 🕓 Mon.–Sat. 9–8

HOUSEHOLD GOODS

Cucina

This store contains an extensive range of kitchen utensils, gadgets and household china.

🖂 Via del Babuino 118a ☎ 06 679 1275 🕓 Tue.–Sat. 9–7:30, Mon. 3:30–7:30

LINGERIE

La Perla

Many small stores around the Piazza di Spagna and Via del Corso sell only lingerie, but none quite offers the quality or style you'll find here.

🖂 Via Condotti 79 ☎ 06 6994 1933 🕓 Tue.–Sat. 9:30–7:30, Mon. 3:30–7:30

---

table linens. The goods are expensive, but of outstanding quality.

🖂 Via del Corso 381 ☎ 06 678 6862
🖂 Via Nazionale 84 ☎ 06 488 2641
🕓 Tue.–Sat. 9:40–7:30, Mon. 3:30–7:30

COSMETICS

Materozzoli

This refined store dates from 1870 and sells an enticing variety of top-of-the-line toiletries, perfumes, cosmetics and bathroom items.

🖂 Piazza San Lorenzo in Lucina 5 ☎ 06 6889 2689 🕓 Tue.–Sat. 10–1:30, 3:30–7:30, Mon. 3:30–7:30

SHOES

Fausto Santini

For something a little different, visit the store of the city's foremost shoe designer. Some of the designs are far-fetched, but none can be called boring, and the quality is good.

🖂 Via Frattina 120 ☎ 06 678 4114 🕓 Tue.–Sat. 10–7:30, Mon. 3:30–7:30

JEWELRY AND WATCHES

Bulgari

Whether or not you are going to buy anything – and you'll need an enormous credit card limit to do so – it is well worth looking at what is available at Bulgari, Rome's most expensive and exclusive jewelers.

🖂 Via Condotti 10 ☎ 06 679 3876 🕓 Tue.–Sat. 10–1:30, 3–7, Mon. 3–7

Swatch Store

This store is about as far removed as is possible from Bulgari in style and content, and sells a wide range of the familiar Swatch brand watches and straps.

🖂 Via Condotti 33a ☎ 06 679 1253 🕓 Mon.–Sat. 10–7:30, Sun. 10:30–1:30, 3:30–7:30

LINENS

Frette

Hotels or Italian households that have any pretension to style would not use anything but Frette bed or

---

Tod's

For years, no one took much notice of Tod's in Italy. But since they became coveted by the rest of the world – and the U.S. in particular – the locals are as keen as everyone else on the distinctive footwear.

🖂 Via Borgognona 45 ☎ 06 678 6828 🕓 Tue.–Sat. 10–7:30, Mon. 3:30–7:30

STATIONERY

Pineider

The pens and stationery here are the finest and most exclusive in the city.

🖂 Via dei Due Macelli 68 ☎ 06 678 9013 🕓 Tue.–Sat. 10–2, 3–7, Mon. 3–7

Vertecchi

This pretty store crammed with pens, paints, stationery and all manner of items covered in marbled paper is a good place for gifts.

🖂 Via della Croce 70 ☎ 06 679 0115 🕓 Tue.–Sat. 9–7:30, Mon. 3:30–7:30

Where to...
Be Entertained

CLASSICAL MUSIC

The **opera** season in Rome runs from November through May at the 19th-century auditorium, the **Teatro dell'Opera**, which lies just a few steps from Piazza dei Cinquecento at Via Firenze 72–Piazza Beniamo Gigli (tel: 06 481 601 or 06 481 7003). The reputation of Rome's opera house lags a long way behind that of La Scala in Milan, La Fenice in Venice and San Carlo in Naples, its lowly status not helped by years of mismanagement, union problems and enormous budget deficits. However, while performances may not be exceptional, it is often easier to obtain tickets here than in Milan or elsewhere. The box office is generally

open Monday to Saturday 10:30–5 on days when there is no performance or 10:45 a.m. to half an hour before the start of any performance. Phone toll free in Italy for information (tel: 800 01 66 65) between 10 a.m. and 1:30 p.m. Making a reservation by phone is all but impossible, so it is best to visit the box office in person. In the past, summer productions were held at a variety of outdoor venues, but these have changed repeatedly in the last few years. Contact the visitor center or the opera house direct for the latest information.

The Associazione Musicale Romana (▶ 111) puts on a **harpsichord festival** during May in the Villa Medici above the Spanish Steps (▶ 126).

NIGHTLIFE

If you are looking for places to drink in the evening, close to Santa Maria Maggiore lie two of Rome's oldest and best **Irish pubs**: the **Druid's Den** (Via San Martino ai Monti 28, tel: 06 488 0258, open Tue.–Sun. 8 p.m.–1 a.m.), and the **Fiddler's Elbow** (Via dell'Olmata 43, tel: 06 487 2110, open daily 4:30 p.m.–1 a.m. or later). They lie about a minute or so apart if you want to compare and contrast. If the thought of an Irish establishment doesn't appeal to you, try the more Italian **Monti DOC** (Via Giovanni Lanza 93, tel: 06 487 2696, open Mon.–Sat. 9–3:30, 6:30–1 a.m.), just to the south of Santa Prassede and Santa Maria Maggiore. This easygoing wine bar has a good selection of wines as well as snacks and meals.

In a similar vein is **Trimani** wine bar (Via Cernaia 37b, tel: 06 446 9630, open Mon.–Sat. 11:30–3, 5:30–midnight), close to the Piazza della Repubblica.

At the other end of the city, near Piazza del Popolo, you can drink and nibble snacks at **Lowenhaus** (Via della Fontanella 16d, tel: 06 323 0410, open Tue.–Sun. noon–2 a.m, Mon. 6 p.m.–2 a.m.). If pubs or pub-like bars are not for you, don't forget the various alternatives offered by wine bars in the area covered by this chapter, notably the Antica Enoteca (▶ 138) or Ciampini (▶ 138).

If you want to dance or listen to live music you have something of a problem. The only central club is the busy **Gregory's** (Via Gregoriana 54a, tel: 06 679 6386; Tue.–Sun. 5:30 p.m.–3 a.m.), a live jazz venue with drinks and snack food near Piazza di Spagna. As for dancing, one of the main clubs locally is **Piper**, one of the longest-running clubs in Rome. Frequent revamps have allowed it to ride out changes of fashion. It lies some distance from the center, northwest of Termini at Via Tagliamento 9 (tel: 06 855 5398, open Thu.–Sat. 11 p.m.–4 a.m.).

Vatican City

Getting Your Bearings

The Vatican – the world's smallest independent state – contains two of the highlights of any visit to Rome: the immense Basilica di San Pietro, or St. Peter's, and the vast Musei Vaticani, or Vatican Museums, home to one of the world's richest and largest collection of paintings, sculptures and other works of art accumulated by the papacy over the centuries.

The Vatican has a long history. Once, the hilly area of Rome west of the Tiber was a place of execution and later the site of imperial gardens and a circus, or race track, built for the emperors Caligula and Nero in the first century AD. In the fourth century, part of the area became the site for a huge basilica – the first

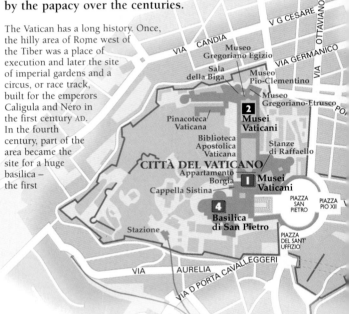

St. Peter's – built over or close to the tomb of St. Peter, who was crucified in the area sometime between AD 64 and 67.

By the 10th century, attacks by Lombards and Saracens had led to the building of a defensive wall around part of the district, and later to the use of the Castel Sant'Angelo – previously the mausoleum of Emperor Hadrian – as a papal fortress. After the sack of Rome in 1527, the area lost its strategic importance and the popes moved their residential palace and offices to the Lateran (San Giovanni in Laterano) and then the Quirinale (now government buildings).

By the 19th century, the papacy had controlled vast areas of central Italy, including Rome, for more than 1,000 years. Much of its domain, known as the Papal States, was given to the popes in the eighth century by the Frankish king Pepin the Short and his son Charlemagne. Following Italian unification in 1870, it was stripped of its territories and remained in a

⭐ Don't Miss

At Your Leisure

state of limbo until the Lateran Treaty of 1927, signed with Mussolini, formalized state and papal relations. It awarded the papacy full sovereignty of the Vatican State.

Today, the area has its own stores, banks, newspaper, helicopter pad and radio station. Most is out of bounds to the general public, with the important exceptions of St. Peter's, the Vatican Museums and – if you book visits in advance – parts of the Vatican Gardens. No documents are needed to enter these and no barriers exist between them and the city at large.

It should take just a couple of hours to see St. Peter's, though you may be tempted to linger in the dome, which offers the best views in Rome. Just before (or after) seeing St. Peter's you might spend an hour in the Castel Sant'Angelo – these days outside the Vatican – a fascinating Roman building overlaid with later fortifications and papal apartments.

Though you could see the highlights of the Vatican Museums – notably the Sistine Chapel and Raphael Rooms – in half a day, you could just as easily spend several days in the complex, particularly if you have an interest in any of the specialized collections. Its 12 museums contain Egyptian, Etruscan, Greek, Roman, medieval and Renaissance treasures. There are also countless beautifully decorated salons and corridors, plus a Pinacoteca, or art gallery, crammed with masterpieces by Raphael, Leonardo da Vinci and others.

Spend the morning at the Vatican Museums, concentrating on the Sistine Chapel, Stanze di Raffaello and Museo Pio-Clementino, and the afternoon exploring St. Peter's.

Vatican City in a Day

9:00 a.m.

The Vatican Museums are often crowded, so try to get there early and aim to see Michelangelo's superb frescoes (below) in the **Sistine Chapel** (➤ 152–153) as soon as you arrive.

10:00 a.m.

Spend an hour or so visiting the **Museo Gregoriano Egizio** (➤ 162), which houses the Vatican's Eyptian collection, and the **Museo Pio-Clementino** (➤ 148): devote most time to the latter, which contains the best of the Vatican's immense collection of classical sculpture.

11:00 a.m.

Move on to the Etruscan antiquities of the **Museo Gregoriano Etrusco** (➤ 162–163) and the **Sala della Biga** (➤ 163), which houses a rare Roman chariot. Then visit the second-floor **Galleria dei Candelabri, Galleria degli Arazzi** and the memorable **Galleria delle Carte Geografiche**

(➤ 149). The galleries occupy a series of long corridors adorned with statues, tapestries and beautiful painted maps (above).

Noon

Visit the **Stanze di Raffaello** (right, ➤ 150–151), a suite of rooms covered in paintings by Raphael, followed by the **Cappella di Niccolò V** (➤ 151) and **Appartamento Borgia** (➤ 163–164).

12:45 p.m.

The Vatican Museums have a cafeteria, or you could try Il Simposio or Taverna Angelica (➤ 167) or its Borgo alternatives, which would leave you in the proximity of Castel Sant'Angelo for the afternoon. Or you could buy picnic provisions in the food shops of Via Cola di Rienzo – make sure to arrive before 1 p.m., when most stores close – and walk south to eat lunch by the river or on the ramparts inside Castel Sant'Angelo.

2:00 p.m.

Explore **Castel Sant'Angelo** (➤ 165) and the nearby Ponte Sant'Angelo.

3:00 p.m.

Walk down Via della Conciliazione to Piazza San Pietro. Stroll around the piazza to admire its columns and the facade of **St. Peter's** (➤ 156–161), then explore the interior. Note that lines for the dome (right) may be long at peak times of the year.

5:00 p.m.

Catch a 64 bus back to the heart of Rome, or walk back via the Ponte Vittorio Emanuele II.

The Vatican Museums

Start a visit to the Vatican Museums by concentrating on the main highlights – the Museo Pio-Clementino, which contains the best of the Vatican's many classical sculptures; the frescoes in the Stanze di Raffaello, or Raphael Rooms; and the Cappella Sistina, or Sistine Chapel, celebrated for Michelangelo's famous ceiling paintings.

Visiting the museums can pose something of a challenge, and not just because they are so large: opening hours vary from year to year, as does the order in which you are able to walk around. One-way systems introduced at the busiest times of year can also make it difficult to retrace your steps. The most popular sights – the Sistine Chapel and Raphael Rooms – are also the ones that are farthest from the museum entrance. Try to see these first if you arrive early – you'll avoid the lines – otherwise head first for the Museo Pio-Clementino.

Museo Pio-Clementino and Galleries

Founded by Pope Clement XIV in 1771 and augmented by his successor Pius VI, this museum made use of the papacy's already immense collection of Greek and Roman antiquities. Here, as elsewhere, the order in which you move through the museum may vary: the highlights, however, are easily seen.

These start with the Vestibolo Rotundo, a hall leading to the Gabinetto dell'Apoxyomenos, dominated by the **Apoxyomenos**, the only known Roman copy of a fourth century BC Greek masterpiece. It shows an athlete scraping the sweat, dust and oil from his body in the wake of victory. Returning to the Vestibolo, you move left to the Cortile Ottagono, a small court-yard that contains some of the greatest of all classical statues. The most famous is the **Laocoön**, an intricately carved sculptural group dating from around 50 BC. Created by sculptors from Rhodes, it was found near the Domus Aurea (► 69–72) in 1506 and had a huge influence on Renaissance sculptors, especially Michelangelo. The sculpture shows a Trojan priest, Laocoön, and his two sons fighting with sea serpents.

Other works in the Cortile include the **Apollo del Belvedere**, a Roman copy of a fourth-century BC Greek bronze original. This masterpiece of classical sculpture, like the Laocoön, greatly influenced sculptors of the Renaissance and other eras. The statue of the young god Apollo originally held a bow in one hand and is thought to have held an arrow in the other. Also here is a statue of **Hermes**, another Roman copy of a Greek original, and the figure of **Perseus** by Antonio Canova. This 19th-century sculptor was hugely influenced by

The Galleria delle Carte Geografiche (above) is lined with beautiful 16th-century maps (detail, below)

the sculpture of the classical world and his statue here shows the clear influence of the nearby Apollo del Belvedere.

Beyond the Cortile lies the **Sala degli Animali**, a charming collection of ancient and 18th-century sculpted animals, the most distinguished of which is a Roman statue of the hero Meleager with a dog and the head of a wild boar. Moving on, you come to the Galleria delle Statue, where the highlights are the *Apollo Sauroktonos*, a Roman copy of a fourth-century BC original showing Apollo about to kill a lizard, and the famed **Candelabri Barberini**, a pair of second-century lamps discovered at the Villa Adriana in Tivoli (➤ 172). Close to the Sala degli Animali is the Sala delle Muse, which is dominated by the *Torso del Belvedere*, probably a first-century BC Greek work. The gigantic torso was much admired by Michelangelo, whose famous nudes, or "*ignudi*" in the Sistine Chapel frescoes were directly influenced by the figure.

Other statues worth hunting out include the *Venere di Cnido* (Venus of Cnidus) in the Gabinetto delle Maschere, a copy of a famous Greek nude rejected by the islanders of Kos because it was too erotic and eagerly purchased by the Cnidians. Also visit the **Sala a Croce Greca** to see the Sarcofago di Sant'Elena and Sarcofago di Constantina, the sarcophagi – respectively – of the mother and daughter of Emperor Constantine.

Moving on from this museum, you should at some point walk along the long galleries on the upper of the complex's two floors: one is the Galleria dei Candelabri e degli Arazzi, which is adorned with splendid tapestries, candelabra and other works. This leads into the highly memorable **Galleria delle Carte Geografiche**, a long corridor decorated with beautiful painted maps (1580–83) of the Papal States, much of Italy, and many of the main cities of each region.

➕ 200 B4 ✉ Vaticano ☎ 06 6988 4466 🕐 Mon.–Fri. 8:45–3, Sat. 8:45–12:30 (last ticket 1 hour before closing) 🚇 Ottaviano-San Pietro or Cipro-Musei Vaticani 🚌 23, 32, 49, 64, 81, 492, 991 💶 Expensive. Free last Sun. of the month (➤ 155)

Stanze di Raffaello

Raphael was an artist who died young – he was just 37 – and painted relatively little. This makes the Stanze di Raffaello, or Raphael Rooms, which are almost entirely covered in frescoes by the painter, one of Italy's most treasured artistic ensembles. The four rooms were commissioned from Raphael by Pope Julius II in 1508 and completed after the painter's death in 1520 by his pupils: they include scenes inspired by Leo X, who became pope while work was in progress.

A love of art starts young

The order in which you're allowed to see the rooms varies from month to month, but if possible try to see them in the order in which they were painted. This means beginning with the **Stanza della Segnatura** (1508–11), which served as Julius' library and was the place where he applied his signature (*segnatura*) to papal bulls (edicts). The frescoes here are the rooms' finest – many critics call them an even greater achievement than the Sistine Chapel. The four main pictures provide a celebration of the triumph of Theology, Philosophy, Poetry and Justice, fusing classical, religious, artistic and philosophical themes in a complicated allegorical mixture. It is well worth buying a guide to help decipher the paintings.

The next room to be painted was the **Stanza di Eliodoro** (1512–14), a private antechamber, or waiting room. Here the paintings are a form of visual propaganda for Julius and Leo,

Left: The Stanza della Segnatura contains the finest frescoes in the Stanze di Raffaello

Above: Many frescoes in the Stanza di Costantino were completed by Raphael's assistants

although their professed theme is the timely intervention of Divine Providence in the defense of an endangered faith. Thus the battle scenes in *The Expulsion of Heliodorus from the Temple* – a reworking of a Biblical story – are an allusion to Julius' skill in defending the Papal States from foreign interference. Similarly, the panel ostensibly showing Attila the Hun turning back from Rome actually contains a portrait of the new pope, Leo X (the figure on a donkey). Note the three-part fresco showing *The Deliverance of St. Peter from Prison*, the first time Raphael attempted to portray a scene set at night.

The third room chronologically was the **Stanza dell' Incendio** (1514–17), designed as a dining room for Leo X, who asked Raphael to paint a series of scenes that celebrated the achievements of two of his papal namesakes, Leo III and Leo IV. Thus the main frescoes portray the Coronation of Charlemagne (a ceremony conducted by Leo III in 800); the Oath of Leo III (when Leo denied accusations leveled at him by rivals); the Battle of Ostia (where Leo IV showed mercy to a defeated Saracen navy in 848, an allusion to Leo X's attempts to forge a crusade against the Turks); and the Fire in the Borgo (in which Leo IV – painted here as Leo X – extinguished a fire near St. Peter's by making the sign of the Cross).

Below: Works by Fra Angelico adorn the Cappella di Niccolò V, close to the Stanze di Raffaello

Much of the Stanza dell'Incendio was painted by pupils working from designs by Raphael, as were the four principal frescoes on the life of the Emperor Constantine in the last room, the **Stanza di Costantino** (1517–24).

Before moving on from the Raphael Rooms, be sure to see the nearby **Cappella di Niccolò V**, a small chapel covered in beautiful frescoes by Fra Angelico showing scenes from the *Lives of St. Stephen and St. Lawrence* (1447–51).

TAKING A BREAK

If you need a respite from sightseeing, visit the Vatican Museums' café or try **Non Solo Pizza** (➤ 167), a few blocks north of Piazza Risorgimento.

The Sistine Chapel

You will not want to miss the Cappella Sistina (Sistine Chapel), but expect substantial crowds, a busy atmosphere and considerable pressure to move on to make way for visitors behind you. This can make for a rather unsatisfactory visit, but detracts little from the majesty of Michelangelo's breathtaking frescoes.

The chapel was built for Sixtus IV between 1477 and 1481. It received its first pictorial decoration between 1480 and 1483, when the lower walls were frescoed by several of the leading artists of their day, notably Perugino, Domenico Ghirlandaio and Sandro Botticelli. A quarter of a century elapsed before Michelangelo was commissioned to fresco the chapel's ceiling, which up to that point had been adorned with a simple wash of blue covered in gold and silver stars.

Michelangelo supposedly proved reluctant to accept the commission, partly because he viewed painting as a lesser art than sculpture, and partly because he was more passionately concerned with creating a tomb for Julius (an immense project that was never completed). In any event, the ceiling occupied him for four years, work being completed in 1512. The frescoes – controversially restored between 1979 and 1994 – consist of nine main panels, beginning with the five principal events in the Book of Genesis: *The Separation of Light from Darkness, The Creation of the Heavenly Bodies, The Separation of Land and Sea, The Creation of Adam* and *The Creation of Eve.* These are followed by *The Fall* and *Expulsion from Paradise, The Sacrifice of Noah, The Flood* and *The Drunkenness of Noah.* Scattered around the ceiling are various painted prophets, sibyls, Old Testament characters, and 20 *ignudi*, or nude youths. In all, the painting covers an area of 10,000 square feet and contains more than 300 individual figures.

The ceiling on its own is a masterpiece, but the chapel contains a second, and probably greater fresco by Michelangelo, the huge **Last Judgment** (1536–41) that covers the entire wall behind the altar. Bear in mind while you admire the painting that it was painted a full 22 years after the ceiling frescoes, during which time Rome had been sacked by the forces of Emperor Charles V in 1527, an event which apparently deeply affected Michelangelo and effectively brought to an end the period of optimism of the Renaissance years.

Something of the darker forces affecting the city and the painter can be glimpsed in Michelangelo's uncompromising vision of a pitiless God venting his judgment on a cowering humanity. Those spared in this judgment are portrayed in the fresco rising to Paradise on the left, while those doomed by it are shown sinking to Hell on the right. The dead rise from their graves along the lower part of the painting, while Christ stands at its center, surrounded by the Virgin, Apostles and assorted saints. Of the 391 figures in the picture, only one is painted gazing directly at the onlooker – the famous damned soul hugging himself as he awaits his doom.

Michelangelo's celebrated ceiling frescoes are the most famous of the many fine paintings in the Sistine Chapel

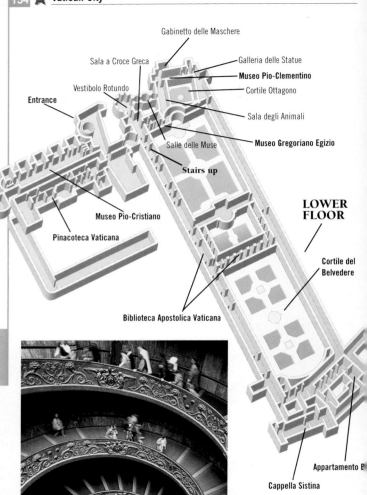

Gabinetto delle Maschere

Sala a Croce Greca

Galleria delle Statue

Museo Pio-Clementino

Vestibolo Rotundo

Cortile Ottagono

Entrance

Sala degli Animali

Salle delle Muse

Museo Gregoriano Egizio

Stairs up

LOWER FLOOR

Museo Pio-Cristiano

Pinacoteca Vaticana

Cortile del Belvedere

Biblioteca Apostolica Vaticana

Appartamento B

Cappella Sistina

Giuseppe Momo's monumental staircase at the entrance to the Vatican Museums

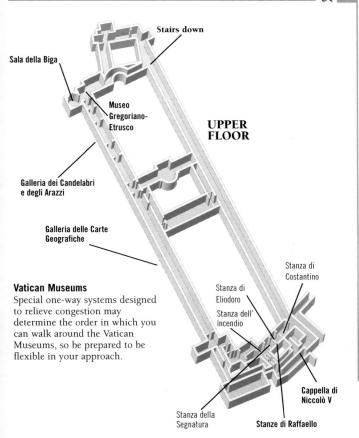

Stairs down

Sala della Biga

Museo
Gregoriano-
Etrusco

**UPPER
FLOOR**

Galleria dei Candelabri
e degli Arazzi

Galleria delle Carte
Geografiche

Stanza di
Costantino

Vatican Museums
Special one-way systems designed
to relieve congestion may
determine the order in which you
can walk around the Vatican
Museums, so be prepared to be
flexible in your approach.

Stanza di
Eliodoro

Stanza dell'
Incendio

**Cappella di
Niccolò V**

Stanza della
Segnatura

Stanze di Raffaello

THE VATICAN MUSEUMS: INSIDE INFO

Top tips If you're coming from St. Peter's note that it's a 10-minute walk to
the Vatican Museums' entrance: if you don't want to walk, take a bus or taxi to
Piazza del Risorgimento, not Piazza San Pietro.
• The Vatican Museums are **closed on Sunday except for the last Sunday of the
month**, when admission is free. Free admission, however, means that the
museums are at their busiest on this day. The museums are open on Mondays,
when most of Rome's state museums are closed.
• If you wish to visit the **Vatican Gardens** (Giardini Vaticani) you need to make a
reservation three or four days in advance. For more information call the Vatican
Museums (tel: 06 6988 4466).

In more detail It's well worth buying additional guides to the Raphael Rooms
and Sistine Chapel to help understand the wealth of allusion and meaning in
their paintings.

St. Peter's

The Basilica di San Pietro, or St. Peter's, is the world's most famous church, an important place of Catholic pilgrimage, and the one sight in Rome that you simply must see, even though there are few important works of art inside.

History of the Basilica

The church is built over the shrine of St. Peter, one of the Apostles and the first pope. The huge basilica you see today is not the original St. Peter's.

St. Peter himself was crucified during the persecutions of Emperor Nero somewhere between AD 64 and 76, probably on the hilly slopes above the present church, and his followers then buried him in a cemetery nearby. The position of his tomb is reputedly marked by the present-day high altar, a notion supported by extensive archeological work that has taken place around the site since 1939. Some sort of shrine to the saint probably existed by 200, but the first church for which records survive was raised in 326 by Pope Sylvester I during the reign of Constantine the Great, the first Christian emperor.

This church survived for well over 1,000 years. By 1452, however, its main fabric was in a parlous state, leading Nicholas V, pope at the time, to suggest the construction of a new basilica, funds for which would be collected from across the Christian world. Nicholas had 2,500 wagonloads of stone removed from the Colosseum and carried across the Tiber to prepare for construction. Building only began in 1506, however, and would proceed – with many false starts and alterations to the original plans – for the better part of 300 years.

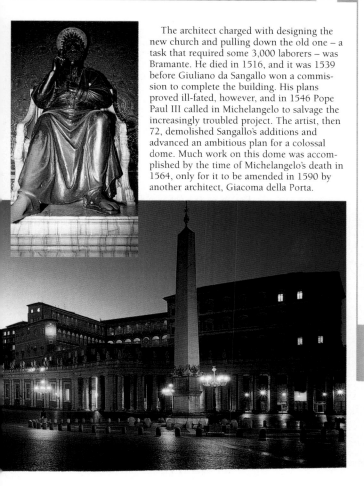

The architect charged with designing the new church and pulling down the old one – a task that required some 3,000 laborers – was Bramante. He died in 1516, and it was 1539 before Giuliano da Sangallo won a commission to complete the building. His plans proved ill-fated, however, and in 1546 Pope Paul III called in Michelangelo to salvage the increasingly troubled project. The artist, then 72, demolished Sangallo's additions and advanced an ambitious plan for a colossal dome. Much work on this dome was accomplished by the time of Michelangelo's death in 1564, only for it to be amended in 1590 by another architect, Giacoma della Porta.

Top: *St. Peter Enthroned*. The statue's right foot has been worn smooth by the kiss of pilgrims

Above: Piazza San Pietro provides a majestic setting for St. Peter's basilica

In 1605, Carlo Maderno was asked to redesign the church yet again, a scheme that involved, among other things, the construction of the present facade in 1612. Finishing touches were added by the great baroque architect Gian Lorenzo Bernini. The new church – a monument to architectural compromise – was eventually consecrated on November 18, 1626, precisely 1,300 years after the consecration of the original basilica.

The Piazza and Basilica

Bernini was responsible not only for last-minute refinements to the church, but also for **Piazza San Pietro** (1656–67), the enormous square (372 by 273 yards) that provides St. Peter's grand setting. The piazza's vast colonnades reach out in two half-circles, symbolizing arms stretching out to embrace

visiting pilgrims. The colonnades are four columns deep
and contain 284 columns. Be sure to hunt out the famous pair
of **stone discs**, one near each of the square's fountains. These
mark the focus of each colonnade's ellipse, and the point at
which the four sets of columns appear to line up as a single
pillar. The statues surmounting the colonnades represent 140
saints, while the colossal 350-ton obelisk at the center of the
piazza was brought to Rome from Egypt by Caligula in AD 37.
The orb at the top contains a fragment of the Holy Cross,
though it was once thought to contain the ashes of Julius
Caesar.

Turning to the **facade**, note the central balcony, from which
a new pope is proclaimed and where the pope proclaims new
sainthoods and delivers his "Urbi et Orbi" blessing on various
holy days. Note, too, the statues across the top of the facade,
which depict Christ, John the Baptist and 11 of the Apostles –
the missing disciple is St. Peter. The most celebrated of the
five portals ranged across the facade is the one on the extreme
right, the **Porta Santa**, which is opened only during Holy
Years, the most recent of which was the year 2000. The central
doors (1433–45), cast to commemorate the Council of
Florence in 1439, survive from the original St. Peter's. They
are among only a handful of treasures from the old basilica,
most of which were destroyed by Bramante, who earned the
nickname "*ruinante*" (the destroyer) as a result. On either side
of the portico stand statues of Constantine (1670) and
Charlemagne (1735), to the right and left respectively.

Inside, the first overwhelming impression is one of
immense size: the church measures 600 feet long, is almost
400 feet high at the dome, and can accommodate upward of
60,000 people. For many years it was the largest church in the
world, losing the title only when a copy of St. Peter's was built
in Yamoussoukro, in the Ivory Coast. Just inside the entrance,
look out for the series of brass line inscriptions on the marble
floor which set out the world's next 14 largest churches. Look
out, too, for the red porphyry disc a few yards from the
entrance which marks the spot where Charlemagne was
crowned Holy Roman Emperor in 800.

Below: Two vast colonnades flank Piazza San Pietro

Right: Piazza San Pietro and beyond from the dome of St. Peter's

Opposite: Michelangelo's statue of the Pietà, one of the treasures of St. Peter's

The genuine items of artistic merit found among the swathes of marble and decorative artifice are actually few in number, and take less time to see than you might imagine. The first of these is also the greatest: Michelangelo's statue of the **Pietà** (1498–99), which shows Mary cradling the dead Christ. Created when the sculptor was 23, it is Michelangelo's only signed work, the sculptor having reputedly added his name when he heard onlookers disputing the statue's authorship. The work is behind glass after being vandalized in 1972.

Farther down the church, the crossing is marked by the high altar – used only by the pope on special occasions – and a vast altar canopy, or **baldacchino** (1624–33), created by Bernini using bronze removed from the roof of the Pantheon. It was created for Urban VIII, a member of the Barberini family, hence the repeated appearance on the work of the Barberini symbol – the bee. Behind you on your right as you face the canopy is a 13th-century statue of **St. Peter Enthroned**, unmissable by virtue of its right foot, which has been caressed to smoothness following a 50-day indulgence granted by Pius IX in 1857 to anyone kissing the statue after confession. The statue's authorship is disputed: it was long thought to be a fifth-century work, but was later attributed to the 13th-century Florentine sculptor Arnolfo di Cambio.

In the apse beyond the high altar stands Bernini's elaborate **Cattedra di San Pietro** (1656–65), a bronze canopy built to encase a throne reputedly used by St. Peter (although probably dating from the ninth century). To its left and right lie two

Left: The sheer scale of Bernini's ornate *baldacchino* or altar canopy, impresses many visitors

Right: Part of the congregation at an outdoor Mass in Piazza San Pietro

important papal tombs: Bernini's **Monument to Urban VIII** (1627–47) on the right, which became the model for baroque tombs across Europe, and Guglielmo della Porta's **Monument to Paul III** (1551–75) on the left. The latter's female figures of Justice and Prudence are said to be modeled on the Pope's sister and mother respectively. Look also for Antonio del Pollaiuolo's **Monument to Pope Innocent VIII** (1498) – by the second main pillar of the nave on the right as you walk back toward the entrance. One of the artifacts saved from the old basilica, it shows Innocent twice – once sitting and once reclining.

Above: St. Peter's is renowned for its many tombs and monuments

All else in the basilica, however, pales into insignificance when set alongside the views from the **dome**. The entrance is at the end of the right-hand nave as you face the altar, from where you can take the lift or climb the steps to the first stage. From here, more steps lead to the higher drum and gallery, and then continue up to a steeper and narrower one-way staircase to the topmost lantern.

TAKING A BREAK

Da Guido (► 166) is a good choice for a simple snack or take-away sandwich.

🚹 200 B4 ✉ Piazza San Pietro, Città del Vaticano ☎ 06 6988 2019
🕐 Basilica: daily 7–7, Apr.–Oct.; 7–6, Nov.-Mar. Dome: daily 8 a.m.–5:45 p.m., Apr.–Sep.; 8–4:45, Oct.–Mar. 🚇 Ottaviano-San Pietro 🚌 62 to Via della Conciliazione, 64 to Piazza San Pietro or 19, 51, 81, 492, 982 to Piazza del Risorgimento 💷 Basilica: free. Dome, Grotte & Treasury: moderate.

ST. PETER'S: INSIDE INFO

Top tips A **rigid dress code** is enforced in St. Peter's, which is, of course, primarily a place of worship. Women should not wear shorts, short skirts or skimpy tops; they should also avoid displaying bare shoulders. Men should also avoid shorts and dress with decorum.

• The one thing you should definitely do when you visit St. Peter's is **climb the dome,** as the view of the city and surrounding countryside from the top is one of the finest in the city. Try to arrive early, as long lines develop, and pick a day when visibility is good.

In more detail There is plenty to see beneath St. Peter's, where you'll find the **Sacre Grotte Vaticane**, a crypt that contains the tombs of numerous popes. The entrance is by the pillar in the church's crossing with the statues of St. Peter and St. Longinus.

One to miss The Treasury contains gifts made to St. Peter's over the centuries, but its best artifacts have all been moved to the Vatican Museums.

At Your Leisure

🄯 Vatican Museums

The following museums and rooms within the Vatican Museums are some you might see on a longer or second visit. Entry details are the same as for the main museum complex (► 160). There are still more museums not discussed below: these include the **Museo Sacro** (sacred art from catacombs and early Christian churches in Rome); **Museo Storico** (coaches and weapons); **Museo Missionario Etnologico** (anthropological artifacts brought to Rome by missionary and other expeditions); **Museo Chiaramonti** (a huge quantity of Greek and Roman sculpture); and **Museo Gregoriano Profano** (a collection of secular or "profane" art – mostly more Greek and Roman sculpture).

Museo Gregoriano Egizio

The Vatican's Egyptian collection was founded by Pope Pius VII and collected in this nine-room museum by Pope Gregory XVI in 1839. It

The Museo Gregoriano-Etrusco exhibits some of the finest Etruscan artifacts

contains a wide range of mummies, monumental statues, headstones, papyri and sarcophagi from the third millennium BC to the time of Christ. Many were found in and around Rome itself, having been brought to the city from Egypt, which formed part of the Roman Empire for several centuries. Highlights include the sixth-century BC statue of Udyahorres-ne in Room I, the head of a statue of Pharaoh Monthuhotep II (2100–2040 BC) in Room V and the bronze incense burners in Room VI.

Museo Gregoriano-Etrusco

This 18-room museum is excellent if your interest in the Etruscans – who dominated central Italy before the rise of Rome – is not enough to take you all the way to the much larger Etruscan collection of the Villa Giulia (► 135). Like the Villa Giulia, this museum has its fair share of dull urns and vases, but it also contains some of the greatest of all Etruscan artifacts. The most celebrated of these is the *Mars of Todi* (Room III), a large bronze statue named after the Umbrian town in which it was found.

The Museo Gregoriano-Egizio houses the Vatican's Egyptian collection

disparate and unconnected first-century elements. Part of it may once have formed a votive offering, but for years was used as an episcopal throne in the church of San Marco. Niches around the walls contain accomplished Greek and Roman statues: some date back as far as the fifth century BC.

Appartamento Borgia
This suite of apartments was built for Pope Alexander VI, a member of the notorious Borgia family, during his papacy (1492–1503). Almost a palace within a palace, it proved so sumptuous that subsequent popes chose to use it as their principal lodgings for the next hundred years. Room I, the Sala delle Sibille, is where the infamous Cesare Borgia is said to have had Alfonso of Aragon, the husband of his sister, Lucretia Borgia, murdered. Today, the room is more remarkable for its frescoes, part of a fine series of paintings in the suite executed between 1492 and 1495 by the Umbrian artist Pinturicchio. The pictures cover a wide variety of themes, embracing religious, humanist and mythical subjects – the best are in Room V, the Sala dei Santi. Other rooms in this

Also worth special attention are the exhibits of Room II, most of which were taken from the **Regolini-Galassi Tomb** (c650 BC) uncovered in 1836 at Cerveteri just north of Rome. The Etruscans, like the Egyptians, buried the deceased with all manner of everyday items they might need in the afterlife, thereby providing archeologists with a graphic picture of their domestic and artistic habits.

Sala della Biga
This single marble-decked room features a Roman *biga*, or two-horsed chariot, reconstructed in 1788 from

complex are given over to the Collezione d'Arte Religiosa Moderna, a collection of modern religious art.

Biblioteca Apostolica Vaticana

The Vatican library easily rates as the world's most valuable collection of books and manuscripts. Books were accumulated by the popes for centuries, but only found a permanent home in 1474 during the papacy of Sixtus IV. Material has been systematically added to the library ever since, amounting to some 100,000 manuscripts, 70,000 archive volumes, 800,000 printed works, 100,000 prints and maps, and around 75,000 handwritten and illustrated books. Only a fraction of the collection is displayed here, but all the items are beautiful, and some – such as handwritten material by Michelangelo, Martin Luther, Petrarch and others – of immense historical importance.

Pinacoteca Vaticana

Even on its own, the Vatican's Pinacoteca, or art gallery, would be considered one of Rome's major collections of medieval, Renaissance and other paintings. Its 16 rooms offer a chronological insight into the development of religious art, and would be richer still had Napoleon not pilfered many of their treasures at the beginning of the 19th century.

Room I opens with 11th-, 12th- and 13th-century Tuscan and Umbrian works, followed by one of the gallery's highlights – Giotto's **Stefaneschi Triptych** (*c*1315). Commissioned by Cardinal Stefaneschi, it was originally intended for one of the principal altars in the old St. Peter's. Among the gallery's other star attractions are two majestic paintings by Raphael in Room VIII, a ***Transfiguration*** (1517–20) and the ***Madonna of Foligno*** (1512–13), as well as

The sculpted angels which line the Ponte Sant'Angelo, close to Castel Sant'Angelo, are known as the 'Breezy Maniacs'

For Kids

Children should relish the view from the top of the dome of **St. Peter's** (► 161), though they may find the climb to the top hard work. Only the fittest adults should even contemplate carrying small children up the steps. **Castel Sant'Angelo** (► 165), which not only looks like a "real" castle, but also has lots of spooky corridors and hidden corners, is almost guaranteed to intrigue youngsters.

In the Vatican Museums you need to be very selective if you have children with you: try them with the **Sala degli Animali** (► 149), the gallery of maps (► 149) or the mummies of the Egyptian museum (► 162).

Italian painters: Fra Angelico, Titian, Caravaggio, Veronese and many others.

3 Castel Sant'Angelo

There is no mistaking the Castel Sant'Angelo, whose dramatic round bulwarks rise on the banks of the Tiber just to the east of St. Peter's. Today, the castle is a museum, but it started life in AD 130 as a mausoleum for Emperor Hadrian. Its circular design – which formed the basis for all subsequent structures on the site – was copied from the Mausoleo di Augusto near the Capitoline Hill, which in turn was probably based on the design of Etruscan tombs. The mausoleum was used as a resting place for emperors until AD 271, when it was incorporated into the city's defenses. It then remained Rome's principal fortress for more than 1,000 years.

On entering the castle, you walk along deep, subterranean passages – part of the original Roman-era mausoleum – and then climb up to the ramparts, which offer excellent views across the city. Immediately below, look out for the Ponte Sant'Angelo, a bridge adorned with statues of angels sculpted according to a design by Bernini. The castle's various military and other exhibits are fairly dull, unlike the variety of beautifully decorated papal apartments and libraries woven into

Off the Beaten Track
For a glimpse of the inner sanctum of Vatican City (most of which is private to those working or living in this tiny state), reserve a place on one of the tours of the **Vatican Gardens** (➤ 155).

Outside Vatican City, the small grid of streets known as the Borgo – between Borgo Sant'Angelo and Via Crescenzio – is the least-visited enclave near St. Peter's.

Leonardo da Vinci's unfinished *St. Jerome* in Room IX. These are just four highlights among many, for the gallery contains works by most leading

the fortress's labyrinth of rooms and passageways.
🚼 198 A5 ⊠ Lungotevere Castello 50 ☎ 06 681 9111 🕐 Tue.–Sun. 9–8 🚍 23, 34, 49, 64, 70, 81, 87, 280, 492 🎟 Moderate

Where to...
Eat and Drink

Prices

Expect to pay per person for a meal, excluding drinks and service

$** under €20 **$$** €20–€40 **$$$ over €40

The area around St. Peter's and the Vatican suffers from a shortage of good restaurants compared to other parts of the city. Once, the grid of streets between Via della Conciliazione and Via Crescenzio, an area known as the Borgo, was filled with artisans' workshops and traditional little eating places. Most of these have gone now, or have been replaced by restaurants aimed specifically at the tourist market. A few old places remain, however, along with one restaurant – Les Étoiles –

that ranks among Rome's finest. There's a fair amount of choice if all you want is a quick snack, and an abundance of places on Via Cola di Rienzo – a street renowned for its food stores – to buy picnic supplies.

Da Guido $

This tiny, modest and still remarkably inexpensive restaurant is typical of the little eating places that once filled the streets of the Borgo close to St. Peter's. You can eat a simple snack, lunch or early supper here – the place is shut after 9 p.m. –

or simply buy a sandwich or filled roll to take out.

➕ 200 C4 **✉ Borgo Pio 13** **☎ 06 687 5491** **🕐 Mon.–Fri. 8 a.m.–9 p.m., Sat. 8–3:30. Closed Aug.**

Dal Toscano $$

This lively restaurant is convenient for the Vatican Museums, being just east of the museums' entrance on Via Germanico between Viale Ottaviano and Via Vespasiano. It's also popular with locals and families, so reservations are recommended, at least in the evenings. As the name suggests, this is not a place for Roman specialties, but rather the thick *bistecca alla fiorentina* (T-bone steaks), *ribollita* soups and other Tuscan staples.

➕ 200 C5 **✉ Via Germanico 58** **☎ 06 3972 5717** **🕐 Tue.–Sun. 12:30–3, 8–11**

Les Étoiles $$$

This is one of the great Roman restaurants for a treat or celebration. From the moment you enter the stylish dining room and see the view of St. Peter's you know you're in for something special. The Italian food and courteous service are as good as the view, and the menu changes from day to day; season to season, depending on the availability of produce and the mood of the head chef. The restaurant forms part of the Atlante Star hotel, and has a roof garden and outdoor terrace for dining in the summer.

➕ 201 D4 **✉ Via dei Bastioni 1** **☎ 06 687 3233** **🕐 Daily noon–3:30, 7:30–midnight**

Grotte di Castello $

The Grotte di Castello is a comfortable, usually uncrowded restaurant that lies close to both the Taverna Angelica (▲ 167) and Tre Pupazzi (▲ 167). In a departure from the usual Roman cuisine, it offers regional Umbrian cooking, as well as generous pizzas.

➕ 201 D4 **✉ Borgo Vittorio 92** **☎ 06 686 5143** **🕐 Tue.–Sun. 12:30–2:30, 7:30–10:30**

Non Solo Pizza $

Non Solo Pizza ("Not Only Pizza") serves pizza by the slice (and full pizzas after 7 p.m.) and a selection of Roman-style deep-fried delicacies: stuffed olives, rice and cheese balls, zuchini flowers and the like. It also serves a limited selection of inexpensive hot dishes, a good option for lunch after a visit to the Vatican Museums. The restaurant is in a side street a couple of blocks north of Piazza Risorgimento.

➕ 200 C5 🖾 Via degli Scipioni 95–97 ☎ 06 372 5820 ⏰ Tue.–Sun. 8:30 a.m.–9:30 p.m.

Osteria dell' Angelo $$

You need to reserve a table at this popular restaurant on a side street just north of the busy Viale delle Milizie. The sophisticated cooking goes beyond the usual local and Italian staples, while the decoration is dominated by sports photographs, a nod to the rugby-playing past of the owner, the eponymous Angelo. On warm summer evenings, you can eat outdoors.

➕ 200 C5 🖾 Via Giovanni Bettolo 24 ☎ 06 372 9470 ⏰ Lunch: Tue. and Sat. 12:45–2:30. Dinner: Mon.–Sat. 8–11

Pellachia $

If you're shopping for food or other goods on Via Cola di Rienzo, treat yourself to an ice cream at Pellachia, one of the best ice cream parlors in this part of Rome.

➕ 201 D/E5 🖾 Via Cola di Rienzo 103 ☎ 06 321 0807 ⏰ Tue.–Sun. 7 a.m.–1 a.m. Closed 1 week in Aug.

Il Simposio di Piero Costantini $–$$

Walk to the northwest corner of Piazza Cavour just east of the Castel Sant'Angelo for this striking wine bar, wine shop (downstairs) and restaurant. The wine bar has some spectacular wrought grape and vine motifs featuring grape and vine motifs. The restaurant offers first-class Italian food but at higher prices than in

more basic wine bars. The choice of wines is excellent – more than 2,000 Italian vintages by the bottle and a small selection by the glass.

➕ 198 B5 🖾 Piazza Cavour 16 (corner of Via Tacito) ☎ 06 321 1502 ⏰ Lunch: Mon.–Fri. 11:30–3. Dinner: Mon.–Sat. 6:30–midnight. Wine shop: Tue.–Sat. 9–1, 4:30–8, Mon. 4:40–8

Taverna Angelica $$

This, the best mid-range restaurant within easy reach of St. Peter's, lies on a tiny piazza on Borgo Vittorio in the heart of the Borgo. Despite its location, it is not a typical Roman trattoria. The modern interior is minimalist and the cooking light, innovative and biased toward fish and seafood (though non-fish dishes are also available). The wine list is good, and includes some by the glass. Space is limited, so be sure to make a reservation.

➕ 201 D4 🖾 Piazza delle Vaschette 14a ☎ 06 687 4514 ⏰ Lunch: Tue.– Sat. 12:30–2:30. Dinner: Mon.–Sat. 7:30–midnight. Closed 3 weeks in Aug.

Tre Pupazzi $–$$

If you can't get into Taverna Angelica (see left), try this 400-year-old place just around the corner to the east. It is far more traditional in appearance and cuisine, and serves good fish, pizzas and pasta dishes.

➕ 201 D4 🖾 Via dei Tre Pupazzi 1 ☎ 06 686 8371 ⏰ Mon.–Sat. 12:30–2:30, 7:30–11

Veranda $$–$$$

The Veranda forms part of the Hotel Columbus, close to St. Peter's and traditionally favored by visiting cardinals and other clergy. What sets this restaurant apart is not the food, which can sometimes be a little over adventurous, but its lovely terrace garden. This provides a tranquil and pleasant setting for eating outdoors when the weather is suitable.

➕ 200 C4 🖾 Hotel Columbus, Via della Conciliazione 33 ☎ 06 687 2973 ⏰ Daily 12:30–3, 7:30–11

Where to... Shop

The area surrounding the Vatican and St. Peter's is not the place to go for shopping. More or less the only things that you'll find for sale here are religious souvenirs and postcards. The Borgo's grid of streets still contains the occasional **artisan's workshop**, but nothing to compare with the number and variety of similar workshops on Via dei Cappellari and the other streets around Campo de' Fiori (▶ 109–110). One exception is **Italia Garipoli** (Borgo Vittorio 91a, tel: 06 6880 2196), which specializes in linens, drapes and other fabrics.

The area where you will find a good variety of stores is in the mainly modern streets north of Via

Crescenzio, and in particular Via Cola di Rienzo, one of the busiest shopping streets in northwest Rome. The street has a wide selection of stores selling mid-range clothing, shoes and other commodities, but is especially known for its *alimentari* – **food stores**. One of the best known is **Castroni** (Via Cola di Rienzo 196, tel: 06 687 4383; closed Sun.), which combines the basic Italian staples (cheese, hams, olive oils and so on) with food specialties from around the world. Or visit **Franchi** (Via Cola di Rienzo 200, tel: 06 686 4576; closed Sun.), one of Rome's most mouth-watering delicatessens, where you can buy picnic provisions or delicious sandwiches and snack lunches to take out, made to order by the counter staff.

Via Cola di Rienzo also has some surprises. Look out for **Costantini** (tel: 06 321 3210; closed Sun., Mon. morning and Aug.), a good wine shop to the south at Piazza Cavour 16

Where to... Be Entertained

Vatican Museums at **Alexanderplatz** (Via Ostia 9, off Via Leone, tel: 06 3974 2171, open Mon.–Sat. 9 p.m.–2:30 a.m.). This is considered Rome's best venue for live jazz; you can eat in the adjoining restaurant as you listen to the music (reservations recommended). Another good pub-club for live jazz, blues and rock is the longrunning **Fonclea** (Via Crescenzio 82a, tel: 06 689 6302, open daily 7 or 8 p.m.–2 a.m, admission often free except on Sat.). Similar music can be heard much farther north in the basement of the **Four Green Fields** pub (Via C Morin 38, off Via della Giuliana, tel: 06 372 5091, open daily 7:30 p.m.–2 a.m, admission generally free).

Since 1958 the **Pio auditorium** (Via della Conciliazione 4, tel: 06 6880 1044 for the box office), close to St. Peter's, has been the "temporary" main venue for concerts staged by Rome's foremost classical musical association, the **Accademia Nazionale di Santa Cecilia** (tel: 06 361 1064, or toll free in Italy 800 085 085). It has its own orchestra and also organizes concerts by visiting choirs, orchestras and other ensembles. Choral and organ music can be heard in St. Peter's, but the choir has a poor reputation; for information contact the Vatican visitor center (▶ 149).

Music of a different sort can be heard north of St. Peter's and two blocks north of the entrance to the

Excursions

Rome is so filled with museums, ancient monuments and other sightseeing temptations that many people on a short visit prefer to stay in the city, rather than visiting the nearby towns and sights. However, there are two interesting excursions that are easily made and offer an excellent counterpoint to the city and – should you need it – an escape from its often busy streets. The most popular is Tivoli, a town to the east of Rome, known for its gardens and the Villa Adriana, the ruins of Emperor Hadrian's vast private villa. The second is Frascati, a town nestled on the slopes of the Alban Hills, the volcanic peaks that rise just south of the city. Easily reached by train from Termini, the town is best known for its white wine, cooling summer breezes and lofty views of Rome.

Those with more time to spend exploring the area also might want to investigate Ostia Antica, Rome's old sea port, which today is an extensive archeological park west of the city. Farther up the coast to the north are Cerveteri and Tarquinia, two major Etruscan towns with large ancient necropoli, or tombs. Inland to the south lies Palestrina, known for its great pre-Roman temple. If you want a complete change, consider Orvieto, a fascinating Umbrian hill town with an outstanding cathedral, which can be reached from Rome by train in around 80 minutes. Contact the visitor center (► 30) for further details or for information on companies offering guided bus tours to these sights.

Tivoli

The ancient town of Tivoli – Roman *Tibur* – is the most popular one-day excursion from Rome. Some 22 miles from the city center, it's known for two principal sights: the Villa d'Este, a Renaissance villa renowned for its gardens, and the Villa Adriano, a vast Roman-era villa and grounds created by Emperor Hadrian. Also worth seeing are the more recent and more rugged grounds of the Villa Gregoriana.

Villa d'Este

The Villa d'Este began life as a Benedictine convent, but was converted into a country villa in 1550 for Cardinal Ippolito II d'Este. A wealthy collector and patron of the arts, he was also a scion of one of Italy's premier noble families – the son of Lucrezia Borgia. These days, the villa contains a lackluster collection of faded rooms and takes second place to its extraordinary, stylized – but extremely beautiful – gardens.

Some of the gardens' most eye-catching features are its fountains, of which the most impressive is the **Viale delle Cento Fontane**, or Avenue of One Hundred Fountains, with its countless jets of water. Also look out for Bernini's elegant Fontana del Bicchierone and the so-called Owl and Organ fountains, which – when they worked – could reproduce the sound of an organ and the screeching of an owl. The Fontana di Roma, or Rometta, is also worth seeking out because it features models of the Tiber, Tiber Island (➤ 178) and several of Rome's major ancient monuments.

The Viale delle Centro Fontane at the Villa d'Este

✉ Largo Garibaldi: entrance alongside the church of Santa Maria Maggiore ☎ 0774 312 070 ⏰ Daily 9–6:30, May–Sep.; Tue.–Sun. 9–one hour before sunset, Oct.–Mar. 💰 Gardens: moderate

Villa Gregoriana

The Villa Gregoriana is generally less crowded than the Villa d'Este and – although not particularly well maintained – is also perhaps more interesting and beautiful. Centered on a pair of waterfalls and a 200-foot gorge cut by the River Aniene, it lies in the town's northeast corner about 300 yards from the Villa d'Este. The park was created in 1831 when Pope Gregory XVI built tunnels to divert the waters of the Aniene to protect Tivoli from flooding. From the ticket office follow the posted path to the Grande Cascata, or Large Waterfall, which brings you to steps and a terrace overlooking the waterfall. Other paths nearby meander around the lush and often overgrown park, passing through the ruins of a Roman villa, among other things, and dropping down to the valley floor past ancient shrines and grottoes before a long climb up the other side of the gorge past the ruined Temple of Vesta.

✉ Largo Sant'Angelo at the junction of Viale Mazzini & Via Quintilio Varo
☎ 0774 311 249 ⏰ Daily 9 to one hour before sunset 💶 Inexpensive

Villa Adriana

Leave plenty of time for Villa Adriana as its site covers an area equal to that of ancient Rome, making it probably the largest villa ever created in the Roman world. It was begun in AD 125 and completed 10 years later by Emperor Hadrian. Many of its treasures, statues and stone have long gone, but the site remains a wonderfully pretty and romantic place, and enough survives of the villa's many buildings to evoke their original grandeur.

Hadrian reproduced or adapted the designs of many of the great buildings he had visited during his travels around the empire: the "Pecile" colonnade through which you enter, for example, reproduces the Stoa Poikile of Athens in Greece. A small museum collects finds made in the ongoing excavations, but you will enjoy it most by simply wandering the site at random. Be sure to walk along the sunken stone passageway (known as a *Cryptoporticus*) while

The columns and statues that line the Canopus at the Villa Adriana are copies from the Temple of Serapis near Alexandria

TIVOLI: INSIDE INFO

Getting there It is possible to take a **train** from Termini to Tivoli, but as most trains stop frequently, this is a particularly slow, albeit painless, way of getting to the town. Tivoli's station is in Viale Mazzini, approximately 400 yards south-east of the Villa Gregoriana.

• **Buses** to Tivoli leave approximately every 20 minutes from the Ponte Mammolo Metro station on Line B and take 50 minutes to get there.

Top tips Tivoli's **visitor center** lies close to the entrance to the Villa d'Este on the north side of Largo Garibaldi (tel: 0774 311 249).

• The Villa d'Este is extremely popular, so be prepared for lots of visitors: **arrive early** to see the gardens at their least crowded. Avoid the heat of the afternoon in high summer.

Hidden gem In the Villa Adriano look out for the **Teatro Marittimo**, or Maritime Theater, a small colonnaded palace built by Hadrian on an island in an artifical lagoon. It is thought that this was the emperor's private retreat, the place to which he would retire for a siesta or to indulge his love of poetry, music and art.

The fountains are one of the highlights of the gardens at Villa d'Este

exploring the Villa Adriana. Artists from the past – including Bernini – have burned their names on the ceiling with candle smoke.

The Villa Adriana is a 15-minute walk from Tivoli town. If you don't want to walk, take a taxi or catch the local No. 4 CAT bus from the bus station in Tivoli's Piazza Massimo.

✉ Via di Villa Adriana 📞 0774 530 203 🕐 Daily 9–6:30, Apr.-Sep.; 9–4, Oct.–Mar. 💲 Moderate

TAKING A BREAK

A good restaurant choice in Tivoli is the **Antica Osteria dei Carrettieri** (Via Domenico Giuliani 55; tel: 0744 330 159; closed Wed.). Out of town, on the road to the Villa Adriana, the best option is **Adriano** (Via di Villa Adriana 194; tel: 0744 382 235), where you have the option of eating outside in summer. Or you can buy food and drink from stores in Tivoli and take them to the Villa Adriana, whose grounds make an excellent place for a picnic.

Frascati

Frascati offers a cool, calm retreat from Rome's heat and hustle on hot summer days, providing a pleasant combination of good food, local wine and sweeping views of the city.

If you have little time to spare, Frascati is the place to go. Trains leave from Termini approximately hourly and the trip takes about 30 minutes. Along the way you are treated to the ever-more attractive rural scenery as the train makes its way into the Colli Albani (Alban Hills) south of Rome.

Steps from Frascati's small station lead through gardens to Piazzale (or Piazza) Marconi, the town's principal square. Above the square stands the **Villa Aldobrandini**, one of the few old buildings to survive the bombing during 1943 and 1944 that destroyed 80 percent of old Frascati.

The villa was built for Cardinal Pietro Aldobrandini between 1598 and 1603 and is still owned by the Aldobrandini family. Though the villa itself is closed to the public, part of the grounds, which are noted for the excellent views of Rome in the hazy distance, can be visited. Be sure to see the garden's Teatro dell'Acqua, a semicircular array of fountains and statues in which the central figure of Atlas is said to be a represention of Pietro Aldobrandini's uncle, Pope Clement VIII.

Vineyards in the hills above Rome produce Fascati's famous white wine

Frascati's other major public park is the less appealing **Villa Torlonia**, entered from close to the town hall building (the Municipio) near Piazzale Marconi. In the rest of the town, leave some time for the rebuilt Duomo in Piazza San Pietro and the church of the Gesù (Piazza del Gesù), known for its late 17th-century paintings by Andrea dal Pozzo.

TAKING A BREAK

Cacciani (Via Diaz 13, tel: 06 942 0378), which has an outdoor terrace for dining in summer, is the best restaurant in Frascati. For something simpler and less expensive, try **Zaraza** (Viale Regina Margherita 45, tel: 06 942 2053).

Villa Aldobrandini gardens

🕐 Mon.–Fri.: 9–1, 3–6, Mar.–Aug.; 9–1, 3–5, Sep.–Apr. 🎟 Free, though passes must be obtained from Visitor Center at Piazzale Marconi 1 (tel: 06 942 0331). Note that the visitor center is closed on Sat. afternoon and all day Sun.

Walks

1 GHETTO TO TRASTEVERE

Walk

This walk takes you to three of the city's smaller and prettier enclaves: the old Jewish Ghetto area, a lovely labyrinth of quiet streets; the Isola Tiberina, an island on the River Tiber; and the larger Trastevere district, an equally appealing but better-known collection of cobbled lanes, tiny squares and interesting stores, cafés and restaurants.

DISTANCE 2.5 miles TIME Allow 3–4 hours
START POINT Piazza del Campidoglio ✚ 199 F1
END POINT Campo dei Fiori ✚ 198 C2

1–2

Start in **Piazza del Campidoglio** (➤ 48–49) just off Piazza Venezia. With the church of Santa Maria in Aracoeli on your left, walk to the rear of the piazza and take the lane to the right of Palazzo Senatorio, the palace ahead of you. Follow the lane as it winds downhill, admiring the views of the **Roman Forum** (➤ 50–55) on your left. Turn right at the bottom on Via della Consolazione and cross Piazza della Consolazione. Bear left off the piazza down Via San Giovanni Decollato. At the end of this street on the left stands **San Giorgio in Velabro**. The church takes its name from the marshy area (the Velabro) by the Tiber where – according to legend – the shepherd Faustulus found Rome's founding twins, Romulus and Remus (➤ 7). The church's simple Romanesque interior – almost bare save for an apse fresco – is one of the city's finest. There are two ancient arches nearby: the one adjoining the church is **Arco**

The view across the Forum from the Capitoline Hill

degli Argentari, or Arch of the Moneychangers, erected in AD 204 in honor of Emperor Septimius Severus; the other, in the short Via del Velabro in front of the church, is the **Arco di Giano**, and dates from the time of Constantine (fourth century).

Trastevere's quiet streets and piazzas are wonderful places to explore

2–3

Continue down Via del Velabro and Passaggio di San Giovanni Decollato, which open into the large **Piazza della Bocca della Verità**. On the right, in an area of grass and trees, stand two almost perfectly preserved Roman temples: the circular Tempio di Vesta and rectangular Tempio di Fortuna Virilis (both second century BC). Beyond them, on the piazza's left (south) flank, stands the 12th-century church of **Santa Maria in Cosmedin**. In the portico, on the left side as

La Bocca della Verità at Santa Maria in Cosmedin

you face the church, look for the round stone relief (an old Roman drain cover) known as the Bocca della Verità, or "Mouth of Truth." Legend claims that the mouth will clamp shut on the hands of dissemblers. The church, one of the few in the city to have escaped a baroque makeover, vies with San Clemente for the title of Rome's loveliest medieval interior.

3–4

From the area in front of the church walk north-west following the line of the Tiber on Lungotevere dei Pierleoni. Continue past Piazza Monte Savello on your right until Lungotevere dei Pierleoni becomes Lungotevere dei Cenci and you see Rome's distinctive **synagogue** (Sinagoga) ahead of you on the right. Turn right, before you pass the synagogue, on Via del Portico d'Ottavia. This takes you to the **Portico d'Ottavia**, a tiny fragment of a great Roman

The Isola Tiberina and the ruined Ponte Rotto

building begun in 146 BC, now partly enmeshed in the eighth-century church of Sant'Angelo in Pescheria. Turn right (north) here on Via del Sant' Angelo in Pescheria and then left at the top of the street on Via dei Funari. This takes you to **Piazza Mattei** and the heart of Rome's old Jewish Ghetto, where Jews were segregated after 1556. The walls were torn down in 1848, but many Jewish families and businesses are still based in the area. Piazza Mattei is known for one of the city's most charming fountains, the **Fontana delle Tartarughe**, or Fountain of the Tortoises (designed 1581); it takes its name from the little bronze tortoises drinking from the fountain's upper basin.

4–5

From Piazza Mattei you should explore some of the surrounding side streets and piazzas at random for a flavor of the area. Then take Via della Reginella left (south) off the piazza, and on reaching Via Portico d'Ottavia turn right then left through Piazza delle Cinque Scole to rejoin Lungotevere dei Cenci. Turn left and then take the first right on the Ponte Fabricio which crosses the Tiber to the **Isola Tiberina (Tiber Island)**. Much of the island is given over to a hospital, continuing a tradition begun in 291 BC when a temple here was dedicated to Aesculapius, the

god of healing. Walk around the island's perimeter and look into the 10th-century church of San Bartolomeo in the square in front of the piazza before crossing the Ponte Cestio on the island's south. This brings you to the **Trastevere district** (▶ 95–98).

Like the Ghetto, this is an area you may want to explore in more depth. This walk simply takes you through Trastevere's heart, but almost any random route through the web of streets is rewarding.

La Fontana delle Tartarughe in the Piazza Mattei

5-6

Beyond the Ponte Cestio cross the main, busy Lungotevere dell'Anguillara and continue straight into Piazza in Piscinula. Turn right out of the piazza on Via della Lungaretta. Cross Piazza Sonnino-Viale di Trastevere and pick up the continuation of Via della Lungaretta and follow it to Piazza di Santa Maria in Trastevere and the church of **Santa Maria in Trastevere** (▶ 96–97). Leave the piazza to the right of the church as you face it, then bear right at the rear of the church into Piazza Sant'Egidio. From the piazza follow Via della Scala until you reach Via Garibaldi. Turn right here on Via di San Dorotea, a street that leads to Piazza Trilussa, a small square almost on the Tiber. From here cross the Tiber on the pedestrians-only Ponte Sisto, turn left, then take the right fork into **Via Giulia**, framed by a pretty vine-draped archway.

6-7

Walk down Via Giulia, one of Rome's most elegant streets, noting the stone skulls on the facade of **Santa Maria dell'Orazione e Morte** (▶ 100) on the left at the intersection with Via dei Farnesi. Via Giulia was laid out in 1508 for Pope Julius II (hence Giulia), providing what, at the time, was the city's main approach to

St. Peter's. In 1655 a major city prison was established at the present-day No. 52.

Where Via Giulia opens out into a piazza, turn right onto Vicolo della Moretta, a short street that takes you to an intersection of several streets. If you have time, turn left and walk a little way down Via dei Banchi Vecchi, which, like Via Giulia, is dotted with interesting stores. Otherwise, turn right on Via del Pellegrino and then take the first right on Via dei Cappellari.

7-8

Via dei Cappellari is one of the most distinctive streets in this part of Rome, chiefly because it is still lined with traditional artisans' workshops, most of which are given over to furniture-making and restoration. It has a long history of artisan-ship, taking its name from the *cappellari*, or hatters, who were once based here. Other streets in the vicinity are named after similar trades (Via dei Baullari – the street of the trunk-makers; Via dei Chiavari – the street of the lock-smiths; and Via dei Giubbonari – the street of the tailors). Continue down Via dei Cappellari, passing under the dark arch midway down and you emerge into **Campo dei Fiori** (▶ 80–81).

Places to Visit

Santa Maria in Cosmedin

➕ 205 D4 ✉ Piazza della Bocca della Verità
18 ☎ 06 678 1419 🕘 9–6

Santa Maria in Trastevere, noted for its facade mosaics

2 PIAZZA VENEZIA TO PIAZZA NAVONA

Walk

This walk meanders through the heart of the medieval and Renaissance city, taking you to several key sights – notably the Trevi Fountain (Fontana Trevi) – but also to a succession of lesser churches, streets and monuments that you might not otherwise discover on a tour of the area's major attractions.

1–2

Start on the northern flank of **Piazza Venezia** facing the Vittorio Emanuele Monument. Walk out of the piazza to your left (east) along Via Cesare Battisti and turn left into Piazza dei SS. Apostoli. On

The Galleria Colonna

your right in the piazza stands the 15th-century Palazzo Colonna, home to the **Galleria Colonna**, an art gallery filled with first-rate paintings by mostly Italian masters. Alongside to the left lies the church of **SS. Apostoli**. Behind a palace-like facade, the baroque interior is known for its huge altarpiece by Domenico Muratori, and Antonio Canova's 1789 *Tomb of Clement XIV*, in the north (left) aisle by the sacristy door. Continue to the end of Piazza dei SS. Apostoli.

2–3

Turn right at the intersection with Via del Vaccaro and first left on Via dell'Archetto. Cross Via dell'Umiltà and continue down Via delle Vergini. Turn right on Via delle Muratte to emerge in the square containing the **Fontana di Trevi** (▶ 124–125). Take Via dei Crociferi from the piazza's northwest corner (to the rear left as you face the fountain) and continue straight along Via dei Sabini to emerge on Via del Corso. Across the Corso to the right lies the open area of Piazza Colonna, named after the Colonna di

Marco Aurelio at its heart. The column was raised between AD 180 and 196 to celebrate the military victories of Marcus Aurelius in northern Europe. The sculpted reliefs portray episodes from the Emperor's campaigns.

3–4

Walk across Piazza Colonna and through either of the small streets off its western flank – Via della Colonna Antonina is the one on the left. Either one brings you to Piazza di Montecitorio, another large piazza, dominated by Bernini's 1650 Palazzo di Montecitorio, seat of the lower house of Italy's parliament, Camera dei Deputati. Take Via Uffici di Vicario west off the piazza, passing the historic Giolitti café on the left, then turn right up Via di Campo Marzio. Take the third left, Via dei Prefetti, and then turn right on Via della Lupa to emerge in **Piazza Borghese**, which takes its name from the Palazzo Borghese (closed to the public), the large palace across the street. This was the main city home of the Borghese, once one of

---

DISTANCE 2 miles TIME Allow 2–3 hours
START POINT Piazza Venezia ✚ 199 F2
END POINT Piazza Navona ✚ 198 C3

The Bar della Pace, one of Rome's prettiest and most popular cafés

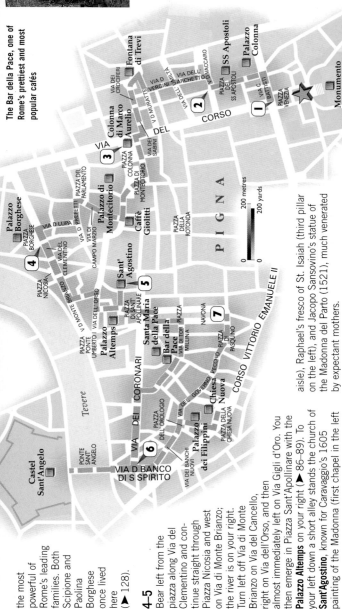

the most powerful of Rome's leading families. Both Scipione and Paolina Borghese once lived here (▶ 128).

4–5

Bear left from the piazza along Via del Clementino and continue straight through Piazza Nicosia and west on Via di Monte Brianzo; the river is on your right. Turn left off Via di Monte Brianzo on Via del Cancello, right on Via dell'Orso, and then almost immediately left on Via Gigli d'Oro. You then emerge in Piazza Sant'Apollinare with the **Palazzo Altemps** on your right (▶ 86–89). To your left down a short alley stands the church of **Sant'Agostino**, known for Caravaggio's 1605 painting of the Madonna (first chapel in the left

aisle), Raphael's fresco of St. Isaiah (third pillar on the left), and Jacopo Sansovino's statue of the Madonna del Parto (1521), much venerated by expectant mothers.

5–6

Return to Piazza Sant'Apollinare and walk south to the adjoining Piazza Cinque Lune and into **Piazza Navona** (▶ 82–85). Take Via di Sant Agnese in Agone (which becomes Via di Tor Millina) right midway down the piazza on its west side. You might pause for a drink at Bar della Pace (▶ 108) on the corner of Via della Pace. As you face the bar, a short distance away to its right stands **Santa Maria della Pace**, a charming (if rarely open) church begun in 1482. It contains frescoes of the Sibyls by Raphael and a cloister added in 1504 by Bramante, one of the architects of St. Peter's. Return to the bar and turn right down Via della Pace and then go straight down Vicolo delle Vacche and Via della Vetrina. Turn left on **Via dei Coronari**, a street renowned for its antiques shops. At the end of the street continue straight down the short Vicolo del Curato to emerge on Via del Banco di Santo Spirito. You may wish to turn right here to look at the **Ponte Sant'Angelo** and **Castel Sant'Angelo** (▶ 165).

6–7

If not, turn left and then take the first left on Via dei Banchi Nuovi. This leads eventually to **Piazza dell'Orologio**, named after the delightful clocktower, or Torre dell'Orologio, on the

building on the piazza's far right. This forms part of the **Palazzo and Oratorio dei Filippini**, a complex largely rebuilt by Francesco Borromini after 1637. For a closer look at the Oratorio's facade, turn right (south) off the piazza down Via dei Filippini. You emerge on the busy Corso Vittorio Emanuele in front of the 16th-century **Chiesa Nuova** ("new church"); the Oratorio is squeezed between the palace on the left and the church facade on the right. Look inside the Chiesa Nuova to admire Pietro da Cortona's ornate frescoes and the decoration (1664) of the vault, apse and dome, and three majestic paintings by Peter Paul Rubens (1608) in the presbytery around the high altar. Return to Piazza dell'Orologio and turn right to follow Via del Governo Vecchio – a more interesting walk than following Corso Vittorio Emanuele – to Piazza del Pasquino and back to Piazza Navona.

One of many antiques shops on Via dei Coronari

Taking a Break

Try the trendy, ever-popular **Bar della Pace** (▶ 108) or the equally hip but quieter **Bar del Fico** (▶ 112). There are plenty of other cafés from which to choose in the Piazza Navona.

Places to Visit

Galleria Colonna
⊞ 199 F3 ◻ Via della Pilotta ☎ 06 679 4362 ◷ Sat. 9–1. Closed Aug.

Sant'Agostino
⊞ 198 C4 ◻ Piazza di Sant'Agostino ☎ 06 688 1962 ◷ Daily 8–noon, 4–8

Santa Maria della Pace
⊞ 198 C4 ◻ Vicolo dell'Arco della Pace 5 ☎ 06 686 1156 ◷ Mon.–Sat. 8–noon, 4–7, Sun. 10–1

Chiesa Nuova
⊞ 198 B3 ◻ Piazza della Chiesa Nuova ☎ 06 687 5289 ◷ Daily 8–noon, 4.30–7

3 PIAZZA DI SPAGNA TO PIAZZA DEL POPOLO

Walk

DISTANCE Just under a mile **TIME** Allow 1–2 hours
START POINT Piazza di Spagna ✛ 199 F5
END POINT Piazza del Popolo ✛ 202 A4

This short walk offers memorable views of the city from above Piazza di Spagna and concludes in Piazza del Popolo, the northernmost square of the "old" Rome. It also gives you the chance to explore the Pincio Gardens (Giardino di Pincio), on the fringes of the Villa Borghese, the city's principal park. The walk can easily be extended to take in the park.

1–2

Start in Piazza di Spagna (▶ 126–127), allowing time to look at the stores here and in the surrounding grid of streets. Admire the **Fontana della Barcaccia** at the foot of the Spanish Steps, and decide if you wish to visit the **Keats-Shelley museum** to the right of the steps (▶ 135). Then climb to the top of the Spanish Steps. Turn to admire the view of the piazza below and spend a few moments inside the church of **Trinità dei Monti** at the top of the steps. It is best known for its frescoed chapels and for two faded 16th-century paintings by Daniele da Volterra. The

obelisk in front of the church was raised here in 1788, but was brought to Rome in the second or third century AD, when its hieroglyphics were carved to emulate those on a similar obelisk in Piazza del Popolo.

2–3

From the piazza in front of Trinità dei Monti turn left as you face the church. This takes you into **Viale Trinità dei Monti**, a street that hugs the side of the hill and offers fine views of the city's rooftops toward the dome of St. Peter's in the middle distance. After the street kinks slightly to the left, you pass the **Villa Medici** on your right, bought by Napoleon in 1801 and home to the French Academy since 1803. It was built in about 1540 for a Tuscan cardinal, and purchased in 1576 by Ferdinando de' Medici, a member of the famous Florentine family. Much of the family's

sculpture collection was kept here before being returned to Florence. The scientist Galileo was famous, if reluctant, occupant of the villa, having been kept here by the Inquisition between 1630 and 1633. The villa is open only rarely, but hosts occasional exhibitions. The magnificent gardens also open intermittently – currently Sunday morning – but are well worth seeing.

3–4

Viale Trinità dei Monti ends at the intersection with Viale Mickiewicz (or Viale Mickiev) and Viale Gabriele d'Annunzio. Turn right on the former to climb to the **Pincio**, a series of gardens laid out between 1809 and 1814 on the Pincian Hill. The area has a long history as an open space, having formed ancient Rome's *Collis Hortulorum*, a series of gardens belonging to the emperors and several of the city's most

The water clock in the Pincio Gardens

An ancient Egyptian obelisk dominates Piazza del Popolo

important Roman roads, the Via Cassia and Via Flaminia, entered the city at this point, following the line of the present Via del Corso to the Capitoline Hill and Roman and Imperial forums (▶ 48–49 and 50–55). Today, the square is dominated by the obelisk of Pharaoh Rameses II, brought from Egypt by Emperor Augustus in the first century and raised here in 1589. On the northern flank stands the important church of **Santa Maria del Popolo** (▶ 103–104), while on its southern edge rise the two almost identical 17th-century churches of **Santa Maria dei Miracoli** and **Santa Maria di Montesanto**. From the piazza you can return to central Rome either down Via del Corso, which is lined with clothing stores, or by the quieter Via di Ripetta route, which allows you to visit the **Ara Pacis** (▶ 103).

prominent aristocratic families. Turn left where the Viale doglegs right to become Viale Belvedere and make for Piazzale Napoleone I, the best of several good viewpoints, before exploring the garden. If you wish to push on to the Villa Borghese for a longer walk, follow Viale dell'Obelisco east from Piazza Bucarest and its obelisk. Otherwise retrace your steps and return to Viale Gabriele d'Annunzio and turn right to follow this street down to **Piazza del Popolo**.

4–5
Piazza del Popolo's present appearance dates largely to the 16th century, but it formed the old city's northern focus long before that. Two

Taking a Break
Cavona (Piazza del Popolo 16, tel: 06 361 2231), in the Piazza del Popolo, is a lively place to stop for a drink.

Map labels:
Villa Borghese
Villa Medici
Pincio
VIALE DELL' OBELISCO
PIAZZALE NAPOLEONE I
VIALE DELLA PIAZZA DI BUCAREST
V. MICHE...
3
VIALE G. D'ANNUNZIO
VIALE TRINITÀ DEI MONTI
Trinità dei Monti
Spagna
PIAZZA DI SPAGNA
Scalinata della Trinità dei Monti
2
Fontana della Barcaccia
1
Santa Maria di Montesanto
4
PIAZZA DEL POPOLO
VIA DEL CORSO
VIA DI RIPETTA
Santa Maria dei Miracoli
Santa Maria del Popolo
PIAZZALE FLAMINIO
VIA FLAMINIA
200 metres
200 yards

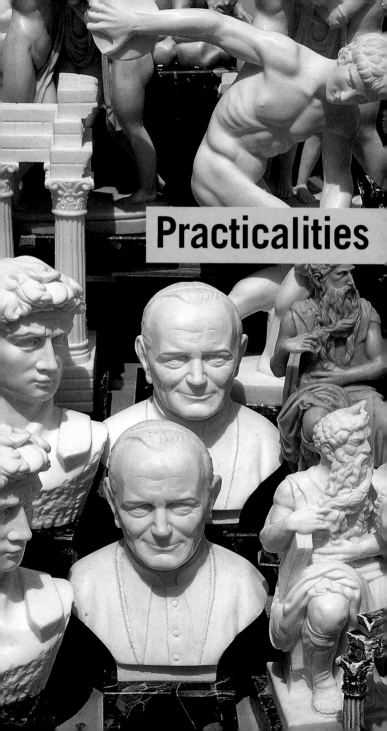

Practicalities

Websites
- Official tourism site of the City of Rome: www.informa.roma.it
- Roman and Imperial forums: www.capitolium.org

- Bus and guided tours: www.romeguide.it
- Official Vatican site for all aspects of the Holy See: www.vatican.va

In Italy
Ente Provinciale per Il Turismo di Roma (ENIT)
Via Parigi 5, Roma
☎ 06 4889 9253
   06 4889 9255

BEFORE YOU GO

WHAT YOU NEED

- ● Required
- ○ Suggested
- ▲ Not required
- △ Not applicable

	U.K.	Germany	U.S.A.	Canada	Australia	Ireland	Netherlands	Spain
Passport/National Identity Card	●	●	●	●	●	●	●	▲
Visa	▲	▲	▲	▲	▲	▲	▲	▲
Onward or Return Ticket	○	○	●	○	●	○	○	○
Health Inoculations (tetanus and polio)	▲	▲	▲	▲	▲	▲	▲	▲
Health Documentation	●	●	▲	▲	▲	●	●	▲
Travel Insurance	○	○	○	○	○	○	○	○
Driver's License (national)	●	●	●	●	●	●	●	●
Car Insurance Certificate	●	●	●	●	●	●	●	○
Car Registration Document	●	●	●	●	●	●	●	○

WHEN TO GO

Rome

███████ High season   ▭ Low season

JAN	FEB	MAR	APR	MAY	JUN	JUL	AUG	SEP	OCT	NOV	DEC
44°F	46°F	53°F	57°F	64°F	77°F	82°F	90°F	73°F	53°F	55°F	48°F

☀ Sun   ☁ Cloud   🌧 Wet   🌦 Sun/Showers

Temperatures are the **average daily maximum** for each month, although temperatures of over 95°F are likely in July and August, making the city extremely hot and uncomfortable.

Average daily minimum temperatures are approximately 42 to 50°F lower.

The best times of the year for good weather are May, June, July, August and September. Thunderstorms are possible in summer and through September and October. Winters (January and February) are short and cold, but snow is extremely rare. Spring starts in March, but March and April can be humid and sometimes very rainy. Fall weather is mixed, but often produces crisp or warm days with clear skies.

GETTING THERE

By Air Rome has two main airports: Leonardo da Vinci (better known as Fiumicino) and Ciampino. Most U.K. and other European and international carriers fly to Fiumicino. Low-cost and charter airlines usually fly to Ciampino. There are many non-stop flights to Rome from London (Heathrow, Gatwick and Stansted) as well as Birmingham and Manchester in the U.K., most major European cities and many U.S. and Canadian cities. Flights from Melbourne and Sydney make one stop, in Bangkok; from other cities in Australia and New Zealand, the best connections are in Hong Kong or Singapore.
Ticket prices tend to be highest at Easter, Christmas and in summer. Best prices are obtained the farther you book in advance, but check airlines, travel agents, newspapers and the Internet for special offers. Non-direct flights via hub airports such as Heathrow or Frankfurt may offer substantial savings. Short stays are generally expensive unless a Saturday night stay is included. City-break packages include flights and accommodations.
Airport taxes are included in ticket prices and no fee is payable at either Rome airport.
Approximate flying times to Rome: New Zealand (24 hours), east coast of Australia (21 hours), western U.S. (11 hours), eastern U.S. and Canada (8–10 hours); London (2 hours), Frankfurt (1 hour).

By Rail Ticket prices are usually the same or more than equivalent air fares. Numerous fast and overnight services operate to Rome from most European capitals, with connections from major towns. Rome has several stations, but most international services stop at Stazione Termini or Roma Tiburtina.

TIME

Rome is one hour ahead of GMT in winter, one hour ahead of BST in summer, six hours ahead of New York and nine hours ahead of Los Angeles. Clocks are advanced one hour in April and turned back one hour in October.

CURRENCY AND FOREIGN EXCHANGE

Currency Italy is one of the 12 European countries to use a single currency, the Euro (€). Euro notes and coins, issued on 1 January, 2002, replace the lira, the former unit of currency. Coins are issued in denominations of 1, 2, 5, 10, 20 and 50 Euro cents and €1 and €2. Bills are issued in denominations of €5, €10, €20, €50, €100, €200 and €500. The exchange rate is set at 1,000 lire = €0.516457.

Exchange Most major **travelers' checks** – the best way to carry money – can be changed at exchange kiosks (*cambio*) at the airports, at Termini train station and in exchange offices near major tourist sights. Many banks also have exchange desks, but lines can be long.

Credit cards Most credit cards (*carta di credito*) are accepted in larger hotels, restaurants and stores, but cash is often preferred in smaller establishments. Credit cards can also be used to obtain cash from ATM cash dispensers. Contact your card issuer before you leave home to find out which machines in Rome accept your card.

GMT 12 noon	Rome 1 p.m.	U.S.A. New York 7 a.m.	Germany 1 p.m.	Rest of Italy 1 p.m.	Australia Sydney 10 p.m.

WHEN YOU ARE THERE

CLOTHING SIZES

U.K.	Rest of Europe	U.S.A.	
36	46	36	
38	48	38	
40	50	40	
42	52	42	Suits
44	54	44	
46	56	46	
7	41	8	
7.5	42	8.5	
8.5	43	9.5	
9.5	44	10.5	Shoes
10.5	45	11.5	
11	46	12	
14.5	37	14.5	
15	38	15	
15.5	39/40	15.5	
16	41	16	Shirts
16.5	42	16.5	
17	43	17	
8	34	6	
10	36	8	
12	38	10	
14	40	12	Dresses
16	42	14	
18	44	16	
4.5	38	6	
5	38	6.5	
5.5	39	7	
6	39	7.5	Shoes
6.5	40	8	
7	41	8.5	

NATIONAL HOLIDAYS

Jan 1	New Year's Day
Jan 6	Epiphany
Mar/Apr	Easter Monday
Apr 25	Liberation Day
May 1	Labor Day
Jun 29	St. Peter and St. Paul Day
Aug 15	Assumption of the Virgin
Nov 1	All Saints' Day
Dec 8	Feast of the Immaculate Conception
Dec 25	Christmas Day
Dec 26	St. Stephen's Day

OPENING HOURS

○ Stores   ● Post Offices
● Offices   ● Museums/Monuments
● Banks   ● Pharmacies

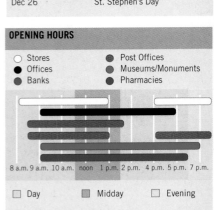

8 a.m. 9 a.m. 10 a.m. noon 1 p.m. 2 p.m. 4 p.m. 5 p.m. 7 p.m.

☐ Day   ■ Midday   ☐ Evening

Stores Hours vary. Usually Tue.–Sat. 8–1, 4–8; Mon. 4–8. Many stores now open all day (*orario continuato*).
Restaurants Usually 12:30–3, 7:30–10:30 p.m.; many close Sun. evening and Mon. lunchtime, with a statutory closing day (*riposo settimanale*)
Museums Hours vary greatly: usually Tue.–Sat. 9–7, Sun. 9–1.
Churches Usually daily 7–noon, 4:30–7 p.m., but closed during services.
Banks Major branches may also open Sat. and have longer weekday hours.
Post offices Usually Mon.–Fri. 8:15–2, Sat. 8:15–noon or 2.

EMERGENCY	113
POLICE	113 or 112
FIRE	113 or 115
AMBULANCE	113 or 118

PERSONAL SAFETY

Rome is generally safe – pickpockets are the main worry – but take precautions:

- Carry money and valuables in a belt or pouch.
- Wear your camera – never put it down.
- Leave valuables and jewelry in the hotel safe.
- Avoid gangs of street children. If approached, hang on to your possessions, raise your voice and – if necessary – use force to push them away.
- Guard against pickpockets, especially in tourist areas.
- Avoid parks and the streets around Termini at night.

Police assistance:
☎ **113** from any phone

TELEPHONES

Telecom Italia (TI) phone booths are on streets and in bars, tobacco shops and restaurants. Most take coins or a phone card (*una scheda telefonica*), bought from post offices, stores or bars. Tear the corner off the card before use. To dial numbers in Rome while there, dial the 06 code then the number. Low rate is Mon.–Sat. 10 p.m.–8 a.m. Hotels usually add a surcharge to calls from rooms. Dial 170 to make collect calls. Dial 12 for operator or information.

International Dialing Codes
Dial 00 followed by

U.K.:	44
U.S.A. / Canada:	1
Irish Republic:	353
Australia:	61
Germany:	49

MAIL

Rome's central post office (*ufficio postale*) is at Piazza San Silvestro 18–20. Stamps (*francobolli*) are bought from post offices and bars. Mail boxes are red with two slots: one for city mail (*Per La Città*) and one for all destinations (*Tutte Le Altre Destinazioni*).

ELECTRICITY

Current is 220 volts AC, 50 cycles. Plugs are two-round-pin continental types; U.K. and North American visitors will require an adaptor. North American visitors should check whether 110/120-volt AC appliances require a voltage transformer.

TIPS/GRATUITIES

Tipping is not expected for all services and rates are lower than those elsewhere. As a general guide:

Pizzerias	Nearest €0.50 or €2.50
Trattorias	Nearest €0.50 or €2.50
Upscale restaurant	10 percent or discretion
Bar service	€0.10–€0.25
Tour guides	Discretion
Taxis	Round up to nearest €0.50
Bell-hops	€0.50–€1 per bag
Chambermaids	€0.50–€1 a day

U.K.
☎ 06 482 5441

U.S.A.
☎ 06 46 741

Ireland
☎ 06 697 9121

Australia
☎ 91 579 0428

New Zealand
☎ 06 441 7171

HEALTH

Insurance It is essential to take out full travel insurance when visiting Rome. E.U. citizens can reclaim medical expenses if they travel with the E111 form, available in the U.K. from health centers, post offices and Social Security offices.

Doctors Ask at your hotel for details of English-speaking doctors.
Dental Services Travel insurance should cover dental treatment, which is expensive.

Weather Minor health worries include too much sun, dehydration or mosquito bites: drink plenty of fluids, and wear sunscreen and a hat in summer. Insect repelent may be useful if you have to sleep in rooms with windows open in summer.

Drugs Prescriptions and other medications are available from a pharmacy (*una farmacia*), indicated by a green cross. Hours are Mon.–Sat. 8:30–1 and 4–8, but a rotation system ensures there some are always open. Two 24-hour pharmacies are: Piram (Via Nazionale 228, tel: 06 488 0754); Farmacia della Stazione (Piazza dei Cinquecento-corner Via Cavour, tel: 06 488 0019).

Safe Water Tap water is safe. So, too, is water from public drinking fountains unless marked "*Acqua Non Potabile*."

CONCESSIONS

Young People/Senior Citizens Young visitors and students under 18 from European Union countries are entitled to free entrance or reduced rates to most state and other galleries. Similar concessions are available to senior citizens over 60 . A passport will be required as proof of age.

Museums/Galleries You can buy a ticket, valid for three days, that will give you admission to four of the city's most important sights: the Colosseum, Palatino, Palazzo Massimo alle Terme and Palazzo Altemps. The ticket costs around €10 and can be bought from any of these places.

TRAVELING WITH A DISABILITY

Rome is a difficult city for those with disabilities, especially if you use a wheelchair. Streets are narrow, busy, often cobbled and usually filled with badly parked cars. There are few sidewalks or dropped curbs. Transportation, museums, hotels and other public spaces are improving, but much remains to be done. For information on accessibility, contact the Consorzio Cooperative Integrate (CO.IN), Via Enrico Giglioli 54, tel: 06 2326 7504 (www.cion@inroma.roma.it) or the "COINtel" phone information service 06 2326 7695.

CHILDREN

Most hotels, bars and restaurants welcome children, but few have diaper-changing facilities. Be extremely careful with young children on Rome's busy streets

RESTROOMS

Best facilities are in hotels, but Rome has few public restrooms. Bars have facilities, but standards are poor. Ask for *il bagno* or *il gabinetto*.

LOST PROPERTY

Buses 06 581 6040 or toll free 800 431 784
Metro 06 487 4309
Railroad 06 4730 6682

SURVIVAL PHRASES

Yes/no **Sì/non**
Please **Per favore**
Thank you **Grazie**
You're welcome **Di niente/prego**
I'm sorry **Mi dispiace**
Goodbye **Arrivederci**
Good morning **Buongiorno**
Goodnight **Buona sera**
How are you? **Come sta?**
How much? **Quanto costa?**
I would like... **Vorrei...**
Open **Aperto**
Closed **Chiuso**
Today **Oggi**
Tomorrow **Domani**
Monday **lunedì**
Tuesday **martedì**
Wednesday **mercoledì**
Thursday **giovedì**
Friday **venerdì**
Saturday **sabato**
Sunday **Domenica**

DIRECTIONS

I'm lost **Mi sono perso/a**
Where is...? **Dove si trova...?**
　the station **la stazione**
　the telephone **il telefono**
　the bank **la banca**
　the restroom **il gabinetto**
Turn left **Volti a sinistra**
Turn right **Volti a destra**
Go straight **Vada dritto**
At the corner **All'angolo**
the street **la strada**
the building **il palazzo**
the traffic light **il semaforo**
the intersection **l'incrocio**
the signs for...
　le indicazione per...

IF YOU NEED HELP

Help! **Aiuto!**
Could you help me, please?
　Mi potrebbe aiutare?
Do you speak English? **Parla inglese?**
I don't understand **Non capisco**
Please could you call a doctor
quickly? **Mi chiami presto un
medico, per favore**

RESTAURANT

I'd like to reserve a table
　Vorrei prenotare un tavolo
A table for two please
　Un tavolo per due, per favore
Could we see the menu, please?
　Ci porta la lista, per favore?
What's this? **Cosa è questo?**
A bottle of/a glass of...
　Una bottiglia di/un bicchiere di...
Could I have the check?
　Ci porta il conto

ACCOMMODATIONS

Do you have a single/double room?
Ha una camera singola / doppia?
with/without bath/toilet/shower
　**Con/senza vasca/gabinetto/
　doccia**
Does that include breakfast?
　E'inclusa la prima colazione?
Does that include dinner?
　E'inclusa la cena?
Do you have room service?
　C'è il servizio in camera?
Could I see the room?
　E' possibile vedere la camera?
I'll take this room **Prendo questa**
Thanks for your hospitality
　Grazie per l'ospitalità

NUMBERS

0	zero	12	dodici	30	trenta	200	duecento
1	uno	13	tredici	40	quaranta	300	trecento
2	due	14	quattordici	50	cinquanta	400	quattrocento
3	tre	15	quindici	60	sessanta	500	cinquecento
4	quattro	16	sedici	70	settanta	600	seicento
5	cinque	17	diciassette	80	ottanta	700	settecento
6	sei	18	diciotto	90	novanta	800	ottocento
7	sette	19	diciannove	100	cento	900	novecento
8	otto	20	venti			1000	mille
9	nove			101	cento uno	2000	duemila
10	dieci	21	ventuno	110	centodieci		
11	undici	22	ventidue	120	centoventi	10,000	diecimila

MENU READER

acciuga anchovy
acqua water
affettati sliced
  cured meats
affumicato
  smoked
aglio garlic
agnello lamb
anatra duck
antipasti
  hors d'oeuvres
arista roast pork
arrosto roast
asparagi
  asparagus
birra beer
bistecca steak
bollito
  boiled meat
braciola
  minute steak
brasato braised
brodo broth
bruschetta
  toasted bread
  with garlic or
  tomato
  topping
budino pudding
burro butter
cacciagione
  game
cacciatore, alla
  rich tomato
  sauce with
  mushrooms
caffè corretto /
macchiato
  coffee with
  liqueur/spirt, or
  with a drop of
  milk
caffè freddo
  iced coffee
caffè lungo
  weak coffee
caffellatte
  milky coffee
caffè ristretto
  strong coffee
calamaro squid
cappero caper
carciofo
  artichoke
carota carrot
carne meat
carpa carp

casalingo
  home made
cassata
  Sicilian fruit
  ice cream
cavolfiore
  cauliflower
cavolo cabbage
ceci chickpeas
cervello brains
cervo venison
cetriolino
  gherkin
cetriolo
  cucumber
cicoria chicory
cinghiale boar
cioccolata
  chocolate
cipolla onion
coda di bue
  oxtail
coniglio rabbit
contorni
  vegetables
coperto
  cover charge
coscia
  leg of meat
cotoletta cutlets
cozze mussels
crema custard
crostini canapé
  with savory
  toppings or
  croutons
crudo raw
digestivo after-
  dinner liqueur
dolci cakes /
  desserts
erbe aromatiche
  herbs
fagioli beans
fagiolini
  green beans
fegato liver
faraona
  guinea fowl
facito stuffed
fegato liver
finocchio fennel
formaggio
  cheese
forno, al baked
frittata omelette
fritto fried
frizzante fizzy
frulatto whisked

frutti di mare
  seafood
frutta fruit
funghi
  mushrooms
gamberetto
  shrimp
gelato ice cream
ghiaccio ice
gnocci potato
  dumplings
granchio crab
gran(o)turco
  corn
griglia, alla
  broiled
imbottito
  stuffed
insalata salad
IVA Value
  Added Tax (VAT)
latte milk
lepre hare
lumache snails
manzo beef
merluzzo cod
miele honey
minestra soup
molluschi
  shellfish
olio oil
oliva olive
ostrica oyster
pancetta bacon
pane bread
panna cream
parmigiano
  parmesan
passata sieved
  or creamed
pastasciutta
  dried pasta
  with sauce
pasta sfoglia
  puff pastry
patate fritte
  chips
pecora mutton
pecorino
  sheep's milk
  cheese
peperoncino
  chilli
peperone red /
  green pepper
pesce fish
petto breast
piccione
  pigeon

piselli peas
pollame fowl
pollo chicken
polpetta
  meatball
porto port
  wine
prezzemolo
  parsley
primo piatto
  first course
prosciutto
  cured ham
ragù meat sauce
ripieno stuffed
riso rice
salsa sauce
salsiccia
  sausage
saltimbocca
  veal with
  prosciutto and
  sage
secco dry
secondo piatto
  main course
senape mustard
servizio compreso
  service charge
  included
sogliola sole
spuntini snacks
succa di frutta
  fruit juice
sugo sauce
tonno tuna
uova strapazzate
  scambled egg
uovo affrogato /
in carnica
  poached egg
uovo al tegamo /
fritto
  fried egg
uovo alla coque
  soft boiled egg
uovo alla sodo
  hard boiled egg
vino bianco
  white wine
vino rosso
  red wine
vino rosato
  rosé wine
verdure
  vegetables
vitello veal
zucchero sugar
zuppa soup

Picture credits

Front and back covers (t) AA Photo Library/Dario Miterdiri, (ct) AA Photo Library/Alex
Kouprianoff, (cb) AA Photo Library/Jim Holmes, (b) AA Photo Library/Clive Sawyer

The Automobile Association wishes to thank the following photographers and libraries
for their assistance with the preparation of this book.
AKG, LONDON 14b, 17l, 57t, 71; ART DIRECTORS AND TRIP PHOTO LIBRARY 12t
(C Rennie), 47b (C Rennie), 65t (C Rennie), 114t (C Rennie), 118/9 (C Rennie); AXIOM
PHOTOGRAPHIC AGENCY119 (J Morris); BRIDGEMAN ART LIBRARY, LONDON 6
The Colosseum and Alban Mount (w/c and gouache over pencil, chalk and ink) by
Samuel Palmer (1805-81) Ashmolean Museum, Oxford, UK, 13t David by Gian Lorenzo
Bernini (1598-1680) (marble) (detail) Galleria Borghese, Rome, Italy, 13b View of the
exterior facade, designed by Francesco Borromini (1599-1667) 1638-77(photo) San
Carlo alle Quattro Fontane, Rome, Italy/Joseph Martin, 21bl Ignudo from the Sistine
Ceiling (pre-restoration) by Michelangelo Buonarroti (1475-1564) Vatican Museums and
Galleries, Vatican City, Italy, 104 The Conversation of St Paul, 1601 (oil on canvas) by
Michelangelo Merisi da Caravaggio (1571-1610) Santa Maria del Popolo, Rome, Italy,
131 The Entombment, 1507 by Raphael (Raffaello Sanzio of Urbino) (1483-1520)
Galleria Borghese, Rome, Italy, 134 La Fornarina, c. 1516 (panel) by Raphael (Raffaello
Sanzio of Urbino) (1483-1520) Palazzo Barberini, Rome, Italy, 144 Sistine Chapel ceiling
and lunettes, 1508-12 (fresco) (post restoration) by Michelangelo Buonarroti (1475-
1564) Vatican Museums and Galleries, Vatican City, Italy, 146t Sistine Chapel Ceiling:
Creation of Adam, 1510 (fresco) (post restoration) by Michelangelo Buonarroti (1475-
1564) Vatican Museums and Galleries, Vatican City, Italy, 153 Sistine Chapel Ceiling,
1508-12 (fresco) (post restoration) by Michelangelo Buonarroti (1475-1564) Vatican
Museums and Galleries, Vatican City, Italy; CEPHAS 174 (Mick Rock); MARY EVANS
PICTURE LIBRARY 6-8 b/g, 8t; GETTYONE/STONE 2 (i), 2(iii), 3 (iii), 5, 20-3, 21br,
43, 45, 56, 66b, 82/3, 125, 126, 154, 156/7, 169; THE RONALD GRANT ARCHIVE 124;
ROBERT HARDING PICTURE LIBRARY 58b, 60, 90/1; JOHN HESELTINE ARCHIVE
10t, 11b, 12b, 14t, 16tr, 16c, 64/5, 65b, 87, 165, 171; IMAGES COLOUR LIBRARY 3 (ii),
3 (iv), 18/9, 20, 51b, 116b, 143, 145, 161, 175, 177; THE KOBAL COLLECTION 8b
(20th Century Fox); MARKA 81b (M Cristofori), 116t (F Garufi), 121 (F Garufi), 123
(F Garufi); POPPERFOTO 19; SCALA 2 (iv), 3 (i), 15, 17r, 47c, 61, 62, 75, 86, 88, 96,
113, 120, 122, 128, 129, 130b, 146b, 149t, 149b, 150b, 151t, 160t, 162.

The remaining photographs are held in the Association's own photo library (AA
PHOTO LIBRARY) and were taken by ALEX KOUPRIANOFF except for the following:
Jim Holmes 7, 20/1t, 20/1b, 22tr, 22br, 23b, 25t, 44, 57b, 62/3, 77t, 77b, 80b, 81t, 83t,
84, 89, 93, 97b, 106, 117t, 135, 147t, 147b, 150t, 158/9, 159, 160b, 163, 180; Dario
Miterdiri 16tl, 24/5, 48/9, 58t b/g, 69, 100, 101, 103, 117c, 127, 130t, 133, 157; Clive
Sawyer 22cb, 25b, 54/5, 76t, 76b, 85, 164, 173; Peter Wilson 55, 58c, 59, 67, 151b, 158.

Streetplan

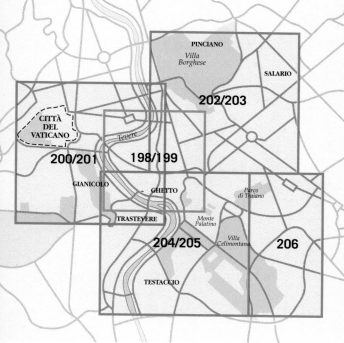

PINCIANO

Villa Borghese

SALARIO

202/203

CITTÀ DEL VATICANO

Tevere

200/201

198/199

GIANICOLO

GHETTO

Parco di Traiano

TRASTEVERE

Monte Palatino

Villa Celimontana

204/205

206

TESTACCIO

Legend

‒‒‒‒‒ Main road

‒‒‒‒‒ Other road

▦▦▦ Steps

‒‒‒‒‒ Rail line

■ Park

■ Important building

▢ Featured place of interest

● Metro station

198/199 | 0 100 200 300 400 500 metres
0 100 200 300 400 500 yards

200-206 | 0 100 200 300 400 500 metres
0 100 200 300 400 500 yards

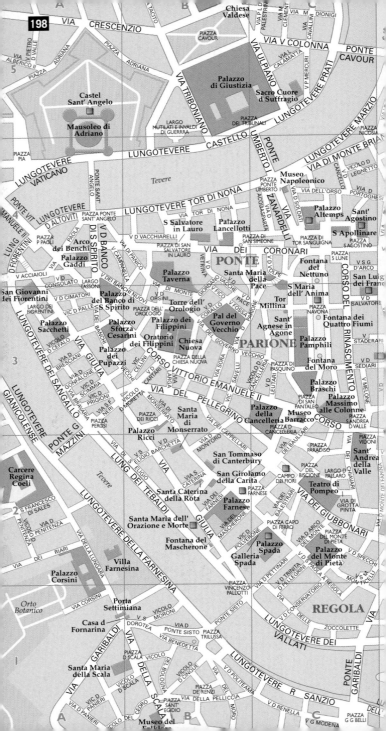

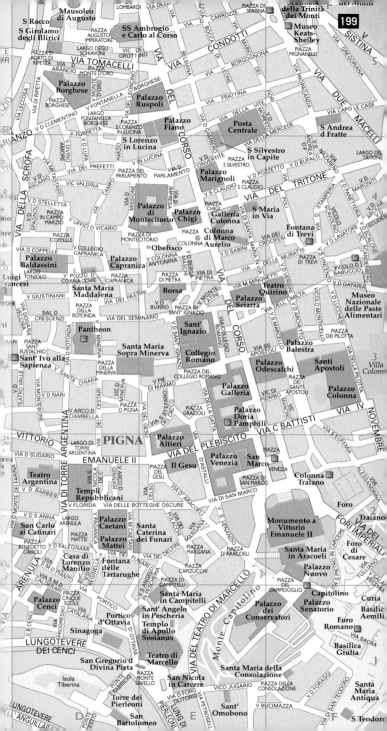

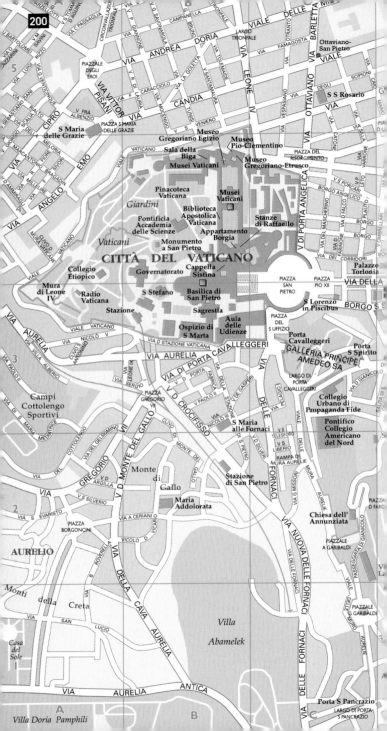

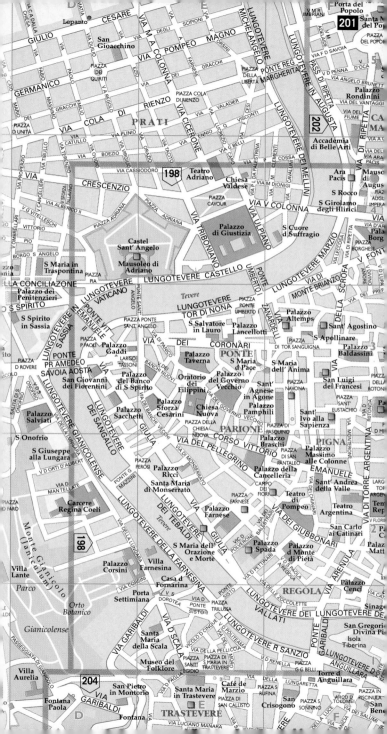

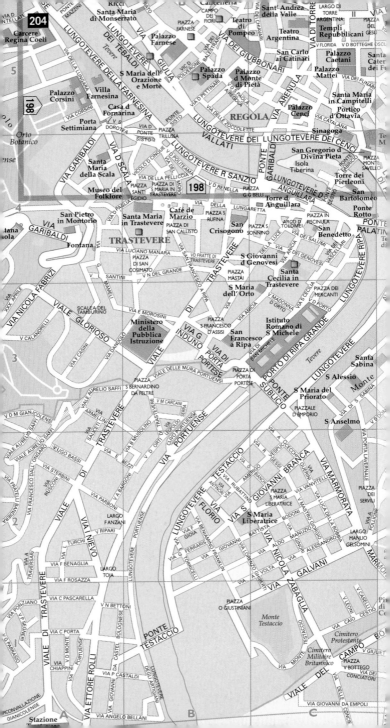

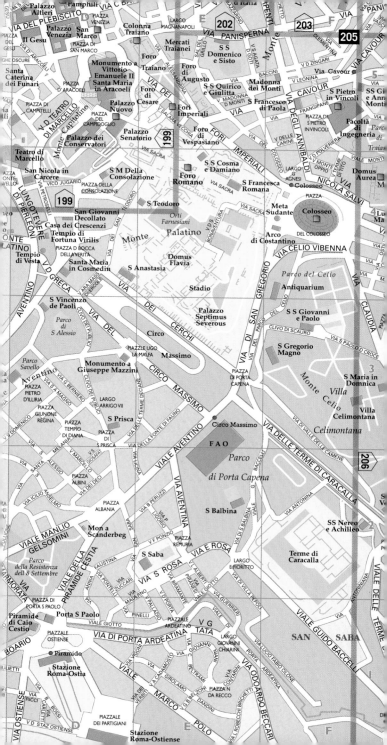

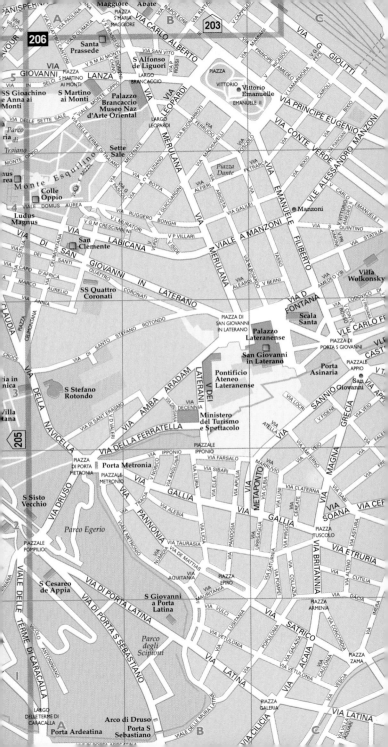

Questionnaire

Dear Traveler

Your comments, opinions and recommendations are very important to us. So please help us to improve our travel guides by taking a few minutes to complete this simple questionnaire.

Send to: Spiral Guides, MailStop 66, 1000 AAA Drive, Heathrow, FL 32746–5063

Your recommendations…

We always encourage readers' recommendations for restaurants, nightlife or shopping – if your recommendation is added to the next edition of the guide, we will send you a FREE AAA Spiral Guide of your choice. Please state below the establishment name, location and your reasons for recommending it.

_____

_____

_____

_____

_____

Please send me AAA Spiral_____
(see list of titles inside the back cover)

About this guide…

Which title did you buy?

_____ **AAA Spiral**

Where did you buy it? _____

When? m m / y y

Why did you choose a AAA Spiral Guide? _____

_____

_____

_____

Did this guide meet your expectations?

Exceeded ☐   Met all ☐   Met most ☐   Fell below ☐

Please give your reasons _____

_____

_____

_____

continued on next page…

Were there any aspects of this guide that you particularly liked?

_____

_____

_____

_____

_____

Is there anything we could have done better?

_____

_____

_____

_____

_____

About you...

Name (Mr/Mrs/Ms) _____

Address _____

_____ Zip _____

Daytime tel nos. _____

Which age group are you in?

Under 25 ☐   25–34 ☐   35–44 ☐   45–54 ☐   55–64 ☐   65+ ☐

How many trips do you make a year?

Less than one ☐   One ☐   Two ☐   Three or more ☐

Are you a AAA member? Yes ☐   No ☐

Name of AAA club _____

About your trip...

When did you book? m m / y y   When did you travel? m m / y y

How long did you stay? _____

Was it for business or leisure? _____

Did you buy any other travel guides for your trip? ☐ Yes ☐ No

If yes, which ones? _____

Thank you for taking the time to complete this questionnaire.